The Pillars of Successful Management

First published by
BBCTA Publishing
P.O. Box 666
Leamington Spa
Warwickshire
CV32 6YP

Printed in Great Britain by
Butler & Tanner Ltd
Frome and London

Contents

1	Emotional Intelligence – The lost keys to management **Elizabeth Morris**	1
2	Cash is King – The importance of cash flow **Stanley J. Smith**	17
3	Passion & Purpose – The key practices **Michael Lewis**	33
4	Performance Apraisals – A tool for better business **Jan Phillips**	54
5	How to produce a team of 'Want to' people **Ken Marshall**	72
6	How to increase sales – The Artist sales process **Richard Owers**	89
7	Increasing shareholder value **Michael Harrison**	110
8	Stress management for managers **David Mackey**	134
9	How to define priorities, set & meet deadlines **Gillian Horton**	151
10	Effective Coaching in the Workplace **Sheila Holt**	166
11	Turnover is Vanity – Profit is Sanity **Michael Ogilvie**	187
12	How to save time and money by managing organisational change effectively **Andy Gilbert**	209

1 Emotional Intelligence – The lost keys to management

How Emotionally Intelligent are you? This is a big question for you. If you are the manager of a team (large or small), a senior executive of an organisation (large or small), a business owner (new or well established), a recruitment agent or a personnel manager (in fact anyone who wants to get on in life and who deals with other people) the answer must be a resounding 'YES'.

Emotional intelligence is the concept at the forefront of the revolution steadily changing the face of 'best practice' management. We have spent many years making logic and rationality our holy grail. Systems, checklists, TQM, re-engineering, SBU's, analysis. These work well for tasks and machines – but they have not been so successful for people.

The price organisations have paid for the emotionless approach is most definitely a reduction in profits. Deeply suspicious relationships, intense internal competitiveness at the cost of co-operative success, disappearing loyalty and mounting frustrated anger that is acted out instead of worked out: all take their cut from valuable available resources. Individuals commonly say they are feeling out control and out of touch – with themselves, their colleagues and their teams.

Think of your organisation and imagine how it would be if everyone was able to unleash the powerful force of their full energy, energy that is currently locked up and wasted in repressed, thwarted emotions, anger, frustration and despair. They would stop using their energy to complain, get in each other's way, criticise the company and complain about the customers. Imagine your team using sensitivity with one another so that the emotional climate is warm, mutually supportive and so pleasant to be part of that everyone looks forward to coming in to work.

High EQ is the essential skill for a Supermanager

Success in life does not depend on IQ; it's EQ that really counts. (EQ is the popular catch phrase for emotional intelligence.) The emotional intelligence revolution began, when as part of a series of studies, one on 'superperformers' found that people who were successful in their work and home lives scored very highly on both interpersonal skills and personal mastery and not necessarily very highly on the more usually admired IQ. Researchers concluded that whilst IQ may get you a job, it's your EQ that is going to get you promoted.

So what is Emotional Intelligence?

According to Dr John Mayer of the University of New Hampshire and Dr Peter Salovey of Yale, who were the first to coin the phrase, emotional intelligence is the 'psychological capacity for making sense of and using emotional information'. According to Daniel Goleman, the first person to take this concept and apply it to the working world, it shows itself in the abilities to:

- be aware of ourselves and our own feelings and needs
- self motivate so that our internal emotional commitment to our goals powers our daily actions
- wait to enjoy a long term goal rather than going for short term satisfactions
- to be hopeful and realistic
- cope with all our own emotions – from joy to sadness, fury to contentment.
- understand and manage the whole range of other people's emotions so that they feel free to carry on with their tasks relieved and enthused for their work.
- be sensitive to other people and convey this to them through empathic responses.

The definition we work with is that it is our psychological capacity to notice, think about, make sense of and act on emotional information from ourselves and other people.

Emotional Intelligence at work

There are three particular advantages to Emotional Intelligence. Firstly you can measure the capacities it involves, so that you can isolate the different aspects of it and check out your competencies. Secondly, like IQ, it is composed of many different capacities but unlike IQ each area has measures so you get a profile of your abilities across the whole range. This is much more practical to use than just one score. And thirdly you can increase any or all of these abilities once you know the ones you want to concentrate on.

Think about the implications, at American Express a group of their sales people were trained in only one of the emotional intelligence related skills – coping – for 20 hours. They then outperformed the control group by 10%. Can you imagine what that increase did to the bottom line?

At Randolph Airbase in Texas they used EQ testing to cut down recruitment failure rates. They established a model of a 'star performer' recruit by testing previous recruits who had turned out to be very successful in the Force. After discovering that these people exhibited high levels of EQ they made a new recruiting procedure and revamped their training. This meant that they started to select candidates whose performance in their new roles was **2.6 times more successful** than the previous applicants who had not fitted the model. The head of education and training at the base now believes EQ knowledge is vital for business success in four ways.

- Selection and hiring, to save expensive recruitment mistakes.
- Building high performance teams, to boost performance on all current and future projects.
- Career development, to save time, expense and energy otherwise wasted by following the wrong path.
- Restructuring and workforce planning decisions, to save unknown potential 'star performers' (often currently hiding in low profile or wrongly allocated positions, and appreciated only by their colleagues) from being fired.

Taking the EQ test

The great edge that knowing about your emotional intelligence gives you is that you can develop it. Enough research has now been done to enable you to take an emotional intelligence test to find out what your EQ profile is in the same way that you can check your IQ score. Not only that – the tests enable you to find out the EQ profiles of new recruits and long standing employees too. Since high EQ equates with 'star performance' this measurement is something you can't afford to be without.

This chapter contains short questionnaires on the most significant areas of Emotional Intelligence which are designed to get you thinking about your EQ profile. They will certainly give you an indication of your EQ but they are not meant to be a comprehensive test.

IF YOU WANT A RELIABLE COMPREHENSIVE TEST OF YOUR EQ, OR AN EQ TEST FOR RECRUITMENT PURPOSES PLEASE CONTACT ME AT THE NUMBER GIVEN. I'LL BE PLEASED TO HEAR FROM YOU.

The background to EI

There have been great advances in the scientific understanding of the brain and intelligence. An early researcher in this field was Howard Gardner who gave us the challenging theory of Seven Multiple Intelligences. For years we had believed that intelligence is a given at birth and that there is very little we can do about it. We had also equated it with logical, mathematical and analytical abilities only. However Howard Gardner has shown us that not only do we have a number of intelligences because we need to have this range of capabilities to cope with life, but that each of them can be improved and developed.

Of the seven intelligences he identified that the last two combined, constitutes Emotional Intelligence:

Logical/rational – this is the ability to reason, calculate and work systematically; as displayed by scientists, accountants and engineers.
Musical – this is the ability to keep rhythm, remember and compose music as displayed by musicians and composers.
Spatial – this involves being able to think in three dimensions, and to picture a result as displayed by architects and artists.
Language – this is the ability to read, write, and understand language construction and to communicate with words as displayed by journalists, linguists and translators.
Kinaesthetic – the ability to use your body to as a source of information about the world or your task, as displayed by athletes or mechanics.
Intrapersonal – the capacities to manage ourselves through knowing and understanding our feelings, wishes, needs, wants and purpose, to be self motivated, capable of delaying our impulses if it will benefit us, and able to persist in tasks even if we hit a hard patch. It is difficult to think of a field in which these capacities are not a prerequisite for high performance.
Interpersonal – this intelligence means that we have the capacity to be sensitive to other peoples' emotions and psychological states, and to choose how to respond appropriately. We can 'read' the subtle currents in relationships, and are empathic and clear communicators. Examples are good sales people and managers, counsellors, teachers.

Try working out your general Multiple Intelligence profile from these outlines.

You and your EQ

There is one pre-requisite for a well developed emotional intelligence and that is the right mind-set. Your mindset is about the way you approach yourself, other people and life. The more open, accepting and emotionally tuned this is, the better equipped, you will be and the higher your EQ will be. Changing our mindset can be the most profound thing we ever do and it can open the doors to massive personal development. In all my years as an emotional coach I have no doubt that working with a person's mindset is the key to everything else. With a fixed closed mind we will judge ourselves and our friends and colleagues against really rigid criteria. These then get in the way of seeing any value in anything other than the ways you know and internally approve of. This is incredibly limiting and no manager can afford to have this problem.

The Elephant Story

Have you ever seen a picture of an elephant tethered with a piece of rope to a stake? Think about it. What stops that massively strong animal from just walking away? It probably wouldn't even notice the tug as the stake popped out. Belief is what stops that happening.

In India baby elephants are tethered by rope to a stake in the ground. At that stage they aren't strong enough to pull away and they learn to associate a rope with being restricted. Even if there is the most delicious looking branch of leaves 10 metres away they won't pull – because they believe they can't. Ten years later and many tons heavier an elephant will still wait patiently for the rope to be untied. It will never test out and find that there has been a major change in the situation – namely that its own power and strength has simply exploded. Think about what it stops itself from achieving.

This is how it is with humans too. We develop beliefs and a mindset towards things and then we just carry on having them. We're lazy. It's easier that way. Until the moment when we find out that it is stopping us getting to our 'delicious branch'. Then, unlike the elephant, we do have the choice to snap the rope and experience our true personal power. Luckily for us we do have a smart part to our brain that allows us to do this.

So check out your beliefs and mindset first to find out if you are tethering your Emotional Intelligence up with a flimsy piece of rope.

EQ Mindset Test

Do you accept yourself?
Do you look at life optimistically?
Do you consult your heart as well as your head?
Do you listen to your gut feelings?
Do you believe that you can change?
Do you believe that people are different?
Do you enjoy the differences?
Do you see situations as opportunities?
Do you believe that you are important?
Do you believe it is OK to make a mistake?
Do you believe that other people are trustworthy?
Is your first response to new people, ideas or things excitement and interest?

These particular questions highlight the basic beliefs that act like ropes around our personal power. By thinking about them and changing any that don't apply now you will be able to pull your stake out of the ground and be free. Of course if you answered 'yes' to all of them you already have a flying start at being a super-performer.

If you were less sure about some of the statements then the good news is that you too are a great candidate for EQ development. This is because you know yourself well enough to answer 'no'! People who can do this and be open to exploring their beliefs are actually already operating with a higher degree of emotional intelligence than many.

If you answered 'no' to most of them you are in danger of being a 'leopard'.

There was one trick question in the list. If you answered 'yes' to this you are off to a flying start. It was the one about change and believing that it was possible. However if you regularly say things like 'I'm too old to change my ways' or 'leopards never change their spots' you are seriously blocking yourself from having an effective emotional intelligence and you need to be very clear as soon as possible that you are not a leopard but a human being with choices!

If you aren't sure whether you can change yourself, no matter what you do to increase you EQ you will unconsciously block yourself from really moving forward, even if you consciously think this is a good thing to be doing. Don't shoot yourself in the foot! Think this through first. Check on the evidence about your past changes. Check whether you found the process easy. Check whether you found anything particularly helpful. Check whether you controlled them. Check whether there are people around you who don't believe in change. If there are limit your contact with them if possible. Even better, hang out with positive, open, dynamic people more.

Managing yourself adroitly by using your Intrapersonal Intelligence

Now that we have the all-important mindset going in the right direction we can look at your intrapersonal intelligence. In this section we'll look at the different aspects of this pivotal intelligence and show you how to get going developing it in yourself.

The Intrapersonal EQ questionnaire

1. Do you pay attention to what you're feeling?
2. Do you use your body signals to pick up your feelings?
3. Can you easily tell what you're feeling?
4. Can you work out why you feel the way you do?
5. Do you know what you need and want?

The Pillars of Successful Management 7

6 Can you 'gear up' whenever you want?
7 Do you stay hopeful in the face of setbacks?
8 Do you reward yourself for your achievements?
9 Can you use your self talk positively?
10 Can you act productively even when you are very angry?
11 Can you stay calm when you are the target of anger?
12 Can you hear criticism without getting defensive?

In this exercise the more you answered 'yes' the higher your intrapersonal EQ will be. Now look at the same issues again but with a different slant.

1 How often do you pay attention to what you're feeling?
2 How often do you use your body signals to pick up your feelings?
3 How often do you act thoughtfully on what you are feeling?
4 Do you often work out why you feel the way you do?
5 How often do you work out what you need and want when you have a stong feeling?
6 How often do you 'gear' yourself up? Do you often reward yourself for your small achievements?
7 Do you frequently use your self talk positively?
8 Do you usually act productively even when you are very angry?
9 How often do you stay calm when you are the target of anger?
10 Do you usually hear criticism without getting defensive?
11 Do you often take time to calm and relax yourself?

In managerial, leadership positions it is truly important to learn to know your emotional self. It is also truly important not just to think that that is all there is to it – you must act constructively on the knowledge you have. If you don't, nothing will change, certainly not your EQ score. If you do act – and act often – on the information you receive from your emotions you will stop making knee-jerk responses to all kinds of situations and gain far more personal control. Our emotions power our actions and decisions – the trick is getting to know ourselves well enough so that we have the opportunity to use both the information from our logic **and** our emotional preferences to make a decision.

If you look again at the questions you'll see that they cover different areas of intrapersonal intelligence. These are your capacity to notice and identify your emotions, your capacity to think about what you are feeling and your abilities to manage yourself whether you are under pressure or operating under normal conditions. Have a look again at the questions and see which ones you were stronger in.

Noticing and identifying your emotions

This is a key skill for both intrapersonal and interpersonal intelligence. If you don't know what emotion you're experiencing it is hard for you to make much sense out of it.

Ways that you can develop this capacity in yourself include:

1 Making a note at the end of each day.
    When you are doing your planning for the next day – which you do, do at the end of each day – don't you! Jot down a few notes about the feelings you noticed yourself having during the day. You may find it helpful just to make columns headed with: anger, sadness, apprehension, jealousy, disgust, surprise, calmness, happiness, excitement. Then put a checkmark by the ones that apply on each day. You'll soon build up a picture of the ones you experience most often.
2 Another way to get good at knowing what you are feeling is to pay attention to your body. Picking up these signals is easier for some people than monitoring themselves for a feeling. Your body faithfully reflects your feeling state, so if you can feel when your body is tightening, or heating up, or getting colder, or your heart beat is speeding up, or your stomach is fluttering and your head hurting, you can be certain that you are feeling something significant at that time. Try it and see.

Thinking about your feelings

After identifying the emotions you have comes making sense out of them. Psychologist, Peter Salovey, calls this the **metamood skill.** Your mood management skills mean that you can reflect on what you are feeling, connect it to its trigger and recognise what you need. This sort of analysis is often helped by thinking about your past experiences, actions and feelings. People who *believe* that it is possible to observe and monitor their own feelings are far less likely to take time off work through sickness. And people who regularly *do* these things tend not to be ill very often, so they don't even need to take time off. Think about that when you are next looking at your team's sick leave records!

Developing your metamood skills can give you enormous personal advantages.

There are two ways in which you can use your metamood skills. One is in managing yourself when the pressure is on. The other is in managing your personal emotional 'hijackings'.

Managing yourself in situations where you are being blamed, or attacked, or put on the spot and pressurised by too many demands for too few resources is a challenge for most of us. Imagine yourself walking into your office. You've got an important deadline coming up in forty eight hours and you're eager to get on with the day and get everything in place to meet it. The moment you walk in you discover that your team supervisor isn't coming in until 11am because her child is ill again. You then hear that the paper stock that was supposed to have been ordered for the job two weeks ago wasn't, but 'should be here any minute'. Next you learn that the computer has crashed again and work that should have been saved has been partially lost or corrupted. The next person into your office tells you that the reason they are unable to complete their task is because you delayed signing the purchase orders for several days and by-the-way can they leave early tonight for a dentist's appointment?

What's most likely to happen next?

1   You say 'No, not a chance'.
2   Ask why and then make a decision.
3   Let rip a tirade on staff, their irresponsibility, stupidity, and lack of commitment, and say that everybody is basically just a waste of space.
4   Say yes but fume inwardly thinking that they were insensitive to ask for time off then.
5   Say 'I don't know yet: ask me again in a few hours time.'

If you answered yes to 5 you were displaying the most emotional intelligence. This option gives you the chance to consult your own feelings about the situation and to get more information to enable you to do what's best. It also treats the other person with respect by giving them information and not nastily blaming them or setting up the situation where you'll act resentfully later.

However your job isn't done yet! Now answer the following:
Once you have answered your assistant what are you most likely to do next?

1   Be unperturbed and carry on expecting that it'll all work out in the end.
2   Take a time-out break to calm down.
3   Have another cigarette and start hassling other people.
4   Sit down, find out what your emotions are telling you, work out what you want in the situation and make a new plan.
    Be honest!

Answering yes to statement 4 is the one that shows the most emotional intelligence as it allows you the opportunity to take control and be in charge of yourself and the situation. It is called problem-focused coping, as opposed to emotion-focused coping, and is a skill that can be developed easily.

A low EQ answer would be 3; going into agitated action isn't going to help you take charge of the situation at all. People tend to do this because they don't know how to notice and think about their feelings. In the end they just do these things automatically and the bad habits get set in stone. If this applies to you, experiment for a day with making a point of saying 'let me think that over' before you give your first reaction to anything.

Now for the big question that will really sort the out the big EQ scorers from the rest. After you have resolved the situation and got the project completed,

1. Will you reflect on all of this later and decide what you can do differently in the future?
2. Will you reflect on it later and notice what you were feeling at the different points of the morning?
3. Will you remember how your body felt when you were experiencing all of that?
4. Will you never give it another thought?
5. Will you moan about your team to your partner or boss?

Doing 1, 2 and 3 show that you are really operating with emotional intelligence and developing your metamood skills very productively. You should be finding that you are able to accomplish your goals effectively and economically. If you would do 5 there is a chance that you could use this opportunity to think through your feelings and learn something new, which would be an emotionally intelligent thing to do.

Now for those 'emotional hijacks'

These are the situations where you feel as if you've got no control, you are just reacting. Your actions are entirely dictated by your feelings, your feelings are out of all proportion to the situation, and the behaviour they dictate is unhelpful.

Think about the last time you flew off the handle at somebody. Or the time you froze when you were the target of your partner,s anger. Or the time you got into a panic because you knew you were going to miss the deadline you'd promised your biggest customer and you just couldn't think straight to sort it out. These situations are what Daniel Goleman calls 'emotional hi-jacks'.

Scientists have now established that there is a very good reason for these happening. There is a neural pathway leading directly from the part of the brain where we perceive a situation to the amygdala. The amygdala is one of the parts of the brain where our emotions are triggered and it sends signals straight into the body to prepare itself for the worst. Until now scientists had thought that everything was relayed first through the neo-cortex, where there would be an opportunity for the new situation to be run past all sorts of databanks and made sense of. This is not the case. Some situations seem to dial 999 internally and go straight to the emergency centre. This is why we just flood with emotion. We are temporarily taken over by our nervous and endocrine systems.

However with good metamood skills and some time to analyse what has happened you now have a chance to change that and get some control back. Try the following exercise and make notes as you go through the prompts or talk it through with someone you trust, like a mentor. Think about the last time you were swamped with a strong feeling. What happened? Did you freeze? Bluff it out? Try to pretend it wasn't happening? What was it? Was it familiar? What did your body feel like? What sort of thoughts were you having? Is there a particular situation or person who acts as a trigger for this feeling in you? Can you remember any time when you didn't feel as strongly about these things? What changed? How do you think someone you admire would cope with that situation? What mood do you think they would be in during it? At the end of it? Try rehearsing managing the situation differently by using your imagination. This will not mean your hijackings are at an end – but it will show you that you can make yourself less vulnerable to those situations. By doing this thinking about your emotions and actions you will begin to open up a new pathway to your cortex which will help next time a situation triggers you off.

The secret of self motivation

Being able to self motivate is such an important and difficult thing for most people that it needs a place here in intrapersonal intelligence. Self motivation and its cousin, willpower, mean that you can accomplish things once you set your mind to it, you can stop or change ineffective habits, you can bounce back after a set back and you can focus on problem solving. All these things rest on two abilities: to know what it is you want or need to take care of your feelings, and to manage your energy levels on a consistent basis. The more tired, tense and generally fatigued you are the harder it is to feel motivated. The best you can do is to drag up some sort of automatic pilot and 'do your duty'.

Self motivation is like having an internal engine purring away, powering your actions. This engine needs fuel and attention. Your can give it this by regularly noticing the small things you want and need, then going about getting them for yourself fairly soon after you noticed. If you do this, you will find that your energy will increase and you will feel less tense. This affects your fatigue level and so your motivation.

Knowing what you want doesn't sound like a hard thing to do but amazingly many people find it quite a surprise to begin thinking this way. Here is a simple exercise to help you sort out what it is you want.

Think of a recent work situation that you were unhappy about. Now instead of thinking about how you want the other person to be different – the usual way managers go about sorting their 'situations' out – try remembering what you were feeling at the time. Then think about what you wanted to help you with this feeling. Say you felt really angry with another person, perhaps what you wanted to do was shake them, or run away or yell in frustration. Now let yourself imagine doing these things. Your imagination is a secret ally, these fantasies don't hurt anyone or ruin a working relationship – but to your body and the 'primitive' in you they seem real. Real enough to let it calm down and return to a balanced position anyway. This is a sophisticated use of your metamood skills.

If you find it hard to work out what you want try the following steps.

- Try thinking what you would need if you were 8 years old.
- Try listing all the things you don't want.
- Imagine what you might want and need if you were someone else in this situation.

Managing other people adroitly with your interpersonal intelligence

If you remember back to the elements of emotional intelligence that we outlined at the beginning this involves:

- understanding and managing other people's emotions in a way that frees them to carry out their tasks, relieved and enthused for work.
- being sensitive to other people and conveying this to them through empathic responses.

Here is a short test that will give you an indication of your interpersonal abilities.
The Interpersonal Intelligence relationship questionnaire.

1   Can you identify what another person is feeling by observing them?
2   Do you put yourself in the other person's shoes?
3   Can you convey your empathy?
4   Do you listen without intruding with your own opinions and feelings?
5   Can you read between the lines in a conversation?
6   Do you think about your feelings about your conversations and interactions with other people?
7   Do you give constructive feedback and appreciation frequently?
8   Can you feel compassion for someone and still hold firm about what you want?
9   Do you communicate your feelings and opinions clearly and respectfully?
10 Do you know the impact of your behaviour on other people?
11 Do you think of how you can tackle your interactions with different people in different ways?

Well, how did you do? If you answered 'yes' to all these questions you are a natural 'superformer' in this area of intelligence. What usually happens is that people are good at parts of this and not so strong on others, or they are good at all of it with certain types of people and not with others. To check this out try answering the questions again and apply them to your boss, your partner (personal or business), your colleagues, your team members. For example here's a selection:

1   Can you communicate your feelings effectively to your boss?
2   Do you know the impact of your behaviour on your boss?
3   Can you put yourself in your partner's shoes?
4   Can you read between the lines in a conversation with your colleague?
5   Do you think about your interactions with your assistant?
6   Do you change your approach, once you've thought it through, when you deal with your friend?
7   Do you give constructive feedback and appreciation frequently to your partner?

How was that? Did you notice that you find some relationships easier to manage than others? Or that you were good at giving positive feedback to everyone but not good at knowing the impact of your behaviour? Once you have this information you are ready to being doing something about it – that all important aspect of emotional intelligence.

These questions were divided up to demonstrate the main areas of ability in interpersonal relationship management: noticing and identifying other people's feelings, thinking about the interactions between you, doing something different if necessary, and the ability to communicate clearly and empathetically.

Noticing and identifying other people's feelings

How tuned are you to other people's emotions? Are you an inveterate people-watcher at airports or are you more interested in the planes? How good are you at picking out their emotions from their faces and body language? Obviously you have to be paying attention to this level of their communication in order to pick anything up. The more attuned to it you are the more people-smart you are going to be. Some research on this has shown that we convey 57% of a message through our body language and 36% of it through our voice inflections! It is the language of our emotions that comes out in these unconscious ways and the ability to read it accurately is a must for interpersonal intelligence.

Ways to increase your ability

Make it a game in your house. Watch a TV programme with the sound turned off and everybody has to guess what is going on and how each person is feeling. After a minute turn the sound up and check it out. Another way to develop this is to work with a colleague and have an arrangement where you identify what you think they are feeling and then check it out with them. If you do it this way you will not be forcing your interpretation on another person – a very unpleasant thing to be on the wrong end of – or acting on assumptions that are quite wrong!

Interpersonal metamood skills

You can use your metamood skills by turning them onto the conversations and interactions you have with other people. Do you tend to think about what has happened between you and another person? Many people do. They go over it and over it, replaying it, saying something different in their minds, imagining the other person reacting differently – but all this energy is usually wasted. This is because they are doing it to try to make their point or score hits that will hurt. The likelihood of them actually doing anything different next time is really slim. Please don't let this be you.

You have a choice. You can put that energy to use in working out how to tackle the situation differently next time. For example, going to your secretary later and saying: "I've been thinking about what you said and I imagine you've been finding it hard to tell me about your home difficulties. I'm sorry I haven't had more time for you. Are you free to talk some more at four this afternoon?", can repair a fruitless earlier conversation where you snapped and rushed on to the next task, impatient that you'd been kept waiting again and apprehensive that this was going to be an emotional conversation.

Here is a way you can help yourself improve this aspect of your emotional intelligence.

This is called a Game Plan and will help you structure your thinking and planning.

What keeps happening to you over and over again and leaves you feeling bad?-
How does it start?
What happens next? And then?
How does each person feel when it ends?
How could you make it different?
What could you have done differently at any stage?

Conveying empathy and understanding

This is the ability to 'walk a mile in another man's moccasins' as the American Indians are supposed to have described it. If you are able to imagine yourself into your colleague's mindset, understand the problem from their point of view and then show them that this is what you've been able to do it makes a profound difference to your relationship.

Empathy is one of the key capacities for developing trust and deepening a relationship into a true working alliance rather than a 'director – directed' relationship. Imagine, or remember, how you have felt when your boss or a colleague has been able to really listen to you without getting defensive and interrupting with their own agenda and then helped you work out solutions. Didn't you feel good then? The more you do this with your team or customers the better they are going to feel too – and the more loyal they'll be.

Understanding the power of empathy

Many problems just shrink or even disappear when they are met with empathy. People truly want to be understood. It makes us feel less alone, less unusual, more accepted, relieved . . . It may seem hard to believe, but if you try it you will be amazed at the response. Just let someone know that you heard and that you understood how it is to be them and that will be enough for them. If it isn't they will at least have begun to let go of whatever it is they are upset about and be ready to begin sorting it out with you.

Interactive listening skills and clear communication

Interactive listening involves being attentive to the other person and then letting them know you have heard them by saying back to them the things they have been saying, including their feelings about it, by summarising, paraphrasing or repeating their words. It doesn't sound like much of a skill – but it most definitely is! Try doing it with the next person you meet: don't interrupt them with your own opinions, don't jump to judging what they are saying as to whether it is stupid or wise, don't blame them for whatever it is they are talking about, just listen and repeat back their words and feelings. 'Sounds like you're really fed up about Stores. You want them to get up to date with all the requisitioning immediately.' Now notice the response you get. The way to get good at this skill is to practice, and to experience being listened to yourself like this as much as possible. It is a skill easier to take in by example and experience than going over it in a book.

Putting yourself through a programme of communication skills training is invaluable for improving your interpersonal emotional intelligence. These skills are the oil that makes relationship management run smoothly. Basic skills such as interactive listening and assertiveness, and advanced skills like negotiation, mediation and feedback are skills that will pay off everyday, with everyone you know. They are a lifetime investment in good relationships. If you manage your tasks by managing your people, then you need to be able to get the most out of each relationship.

Emotional coaching – developing other people

One of the most exciting aspects to emotional intelligence is that it can be developed and that its development makes peoples' performance more and more effective. As you develop your emotional intelligence you are in a very powerful position to act as an emotional coach to your team members (also your boss and board if that applies!). The more the you are able to do that, the more your organisation or team will stand out as models of exemplary good practice, not to mention their steadily rising productivity. The more you and your team are good models, the faster other people and teams will follow you, and before long you can be operating in an emotionally intelligent organisation where the culture is co-operative open and positively solution focused. Organisations who operate without this kind of culture are like cars which are being driven with one foot on the accelerator and one the brake. All the power goes surging through to the engine, all systems are go but the resistance of the brakes hold everything back. Emotional coaching programmes takes the feet off the brakes.

Emotional coaching skills self test

1. Can you facilitate other people to find their own ways forward?
2. Can you recognise when you have your own agenda?
3. Can you give accurate and clear feedback?
4. Do you practice what you preach – are you a good model?
5. Can you coach, mentor and counsel?
6. Can you listen?
7. Are you able to be open and non-defensive?
8. Do you have a problem-solving attitude?
9. Can you sense and understand the feelings between people?
10. Can you help other people sort these out sort these out?

If you answered 'yes' to these questions you are a natural born emotional coach and an invaluable asset to your organisation and I advise you to start a coaching programme straight way! If you are not, then begin to develop a programme of emotional education for yourself. One of the best ways to do this is to have your own emotional intelligence coach. The skills of facilitation, for example, are more easily picked up by experiencing them being used with you rather than reading about them in course notes.

You have now got a firm understanding of this very important topic – a topic you will be hearing about more and more over the next few years. You are in on it now before most people are aware that it will be the next organisational revolution. Use this time to get ahead, skill up and make yourself into the superperformer who leads by example – the most powerful kind of leader there is.

- High Emotional Intelligence makes you a supermanager.
- You can measure and develop your EQ – and other people's.
- A winning mindset is open, accepting and tuned to emotions.
- Intrapersonal intelligence means managing yourself better with metamood skills.
- Intrapersonal intelligence gives you self motivation and energy.
- Interpersonal intelligence means you manage other people adroitly.
- Noticing, identifying and acting on others' emotions makes you friends and influences people.
- Being a clear communicator makes a difference to every minute, everyday with everybody.
- Emotional coaching takes the feet off the brakes of any organisation.

2 Cash is King – The importance of cash flow, its meaning and potential consequences

What is the number one concern facing British Business today?

You read about it every day in the national press and it's not competition or taxation. It is cash flow and for small to medium sized companies which account for 90 per cent of the UK's businesses, money is always tight.

Caught between slow paying companies who owe them money and creditors to whom they owe, most are caught in a debt trap and frequently, through no fault of their own.

But who can a company turn to when it runs into a problem debt or a cash flow difficulty. Creditors have collection agencies and solicitors to act on their behalf, generally for the vast majority of debtors; there is no one to represent their interests.

There are thousands of businesses everywhere that are having difficulty paying their debts on time. These are mainly small to medium sized companies, run by dedicated owners and managers, who are harassed and overworked just trying to survive in today's difficult economic climate.

It is not strictly true that the debtor has no one to represent their interests, as there are some highly experienced companies and consultants specialising in assisting companies with debt and cash flow difficulties. However since such people are little known and difficult to locate, as they are less well publicised due to the confidential nature of their work, the intention of this chapter is to assist you in avoiding the need for such a service.

Before we progress, perhaps I should explain, my emphasis on cash and it's importance is based on my own personal experience. Starting a business from scratch, with little or no money, building three companies, each of which went through the various stages of growth and development with all the inherent difficulties, obstacles, trials and tribulations that no doubt you may have already, or, are going to encounter.

In my opinion all the difficulties and challenges that we ever faced during what was an exciting twelve year period, pale to insignificance compared to the challenges posed by a **shortage of cash.**

We operated in what was then a booming economy, the eighties, and whilst we are now over the subsequent recession and business is again booming, perhaps I could be forgiven for saying that it really is no different today. All the same situations are there and happening all around us each and every day, therefor my intention is very clear, to impact the importance of cash flow vigilance, as **cash is the lifeblood of any business.**

The principle objective of any business is first and foremost to make a profit, however, this simply has no meaning if cash is not available to pay the business owner or to pay dividends to shareholders. It is also important to understand that cash flow and profitability are not generally related, no matter how profitable a company is, or how healthy its balance sheet, **it is insolvent,** if it is unable to pay its debts as they fall due.

Regardless of how the economic climate is at any given time, it is vital that you remain ever mindful of potential factors that may be beyond your control. Take the current economic environment, whilst I would never dampen enthusiasm and optimism, which I believe to be vital ingredients of success, in any field of human achievement and endeavour. You can not ignore the facts, there are always, many underlying economic and other factors that even if slightly affected, could tip the balance the wrong way and once underway momentum is very difficult to slow down and reverse.

At the time of writing we have had no less than seven interest rate rises in a twelve month period, whilst some were possibly expected at least half were unexpected particularly the most recent. How will these impact businesses? If mortgage interest rates follow, as they surely must, how will the housing market be affected? Always a powerful economic barometer.

Press releases reporting adverse data about the economy or specific media coverage can cause complete market trend reversals sometimes with devastating effect on an entire industry and the secondary repercussions can be just as devastating.

No matter how well you run your business, you can sometimes, due to circumstances beyond your control, and through no fault of your own, find your cash flow seriously affected.

In such difficulties and situations whether individual company or general to the economy, **"Cash Is King"** with a healthy positive cash flow surplus, and a sound financial structure you will always ensure that there is sufficient time to review your position and strategy without pressure, which can be vital to your future, ensuring the right corrective action is taken. With cash in hand you can take the longer-term view, that would not be possible under the pressures that are compounded by cash flow problems. The majority of cash starved businesses are only ever in fire fighting mode, managing and going from one crisis to another with little or no hope of ever being in a situation to develop and grow the business.

Know what you want from your business?

First and foremost, and absolutely of paramount importance is to know why you are in business and what you want from your business. "If you don't know why, then quite simply you don't need to know how".

This, in my experience, is at the very route of many of the problems facing the majority of small to medium sized businesses. They do not have a plan because they don't know where they are going, how can they know if they don't know what they are trying to achieve.

If yours is such a business? Or you feel that perhaps you're not sure, **then stop reading, put down the book, take pen to paper and start setting out your reasons why.**

Now whatever your reasons might be, you also need to know your ultimate objective for your business, are you in it just to make a good living? are you building it to sell out? these factors can be critically important as to the manner in which your business needs to be structured.

However, whichever course you choose, our old friend cash strongly comes into the equation, if it's a good living, then you will want be able to draw sufficient cash whilst still maintaining sufficient working capital. And if its to sell, you will require an even stronger cash flow to maintain a suitable standard of living whilst showing good results on the profit and loss account and building a strong balance sheet.

You could be forgiven for thinking that perhaps this is all a bit basic, well of course your absolutely correct, as I am firmly committed through my experience that all success is built on getting the basics right. No amount of sophistication can do anything to add to this philosophy, and modern technology only serves to enhance and make them far easier to apply, it is then your application that determines your ultimate success.

Cash flow and credit background . . .

The passage of cash is a two-way flow, cash inflow generated from sales receipts and Vat and out flow for payment of goods and services, wages dividends, Vat etc.

Generally businesses have to grant credit to their customers, both in order to gain custom in the first place, and certainly to prosper and grow. This is simply an understood and accepted facet of business life. However, in order two make the books balance, the majority of businesses have to seek credit from their suppliers, to make up any shortfalls in their own cash funds. And when there is an overall shortfall, further sources of funding are required, such as a bank overdraft or loan, new capital investment into the business, etc.

This all creates what is essentially a huge credit merry–go–round, and on the basis that most business are to some degree involuntarily but inextricably wrapped up in this, they expose themselves to the slings and arrows of outrageous business fortune.

Following is a recent survey of 86,621 businesses of all sizes, illustrating the payment performance of trade debt in relation to agreed credit terms . . .

Payment Performance Against Agreed Credit Terms			
Region	Good Payers On time	Poor Payers 1-29 days late	Late Payers over 30 days late
England			
South West	21.45%	71.23%	7.32%
South East	19.96%	71.50%	8.55%
East Anglia	19.45%	73.08%	7.48%
West Mids.	16.58%	74.78%	8.64%
East Mids.	18.30%	73.28%	8.42%
North West	18.35%	73.91%	7.74%
North	19.45%	73.52%	7.03%
Yorks & Humb.	17.71%	75.03%	7.26%
Wales	17.72%	73.78%	8.50%
Scotland	19.83%	72.59%	7.57%
Average	18.88%	73.27%	7.85%

In terms of the actual size of this entire "credit pond", it is believed that the total sum involved is in the region of **£230 Billion**, whereas the amount attributed to overdue payments is approximately **£70 Billion**. It is without question from the proof of the market generally and from the history of business that undeniably, where credit is granted, there will always be risk, however large or small.

And it should always be remembered that in any business, its customers and suppliers alike that are equally involved in the credit merry-go-round, as customers can be suppliers and suppliers can be customers, and so on.

So, it can be seen that every business which grants credit to its customers, and buys goods or services from its suppliers, can become the victim of not only direct trading risks, but also this often underestimated notion of third party risks, **the unseen danger.**

The following table shows corporate and non-corporate business failures

The Pillars of Successful Management

during 1997 demonstrating the extent of the problem of insolvencies. Whilst the trend has been reducing for all categories during the six years shown, the current figures are non the less, staggering.

Corporate & Non-Corporate Insolvencies							
Company Liquidations		Receiverships	Bankruptcies		Voluntary Arrangements		
Compulsory	Creditors Voluntary		Self Empld.	Personal	CVA	IVA
1992	9,734	14,691	9,319	19,525	12,581	76	4,686
1993	8,244	12,464	5,362	18,561	12,455	134	5,679
1994	6,597	10,131	3,877	15,114	10,520	264	5,103
1995	5,519	9,017	3,226	13,282	8,651	372	4,384
1996	5,080	8,381	2,701	12,667	9,136	459	4,466
1997	4,735	7,875	1,837	11,668	8,224	629	4,545
	24,575	37,286	18,558	53,200	35,556	474	15,468

Good cash flow, How to achieve it . . .

It is critical to plan your cash forecast in line with your business budget and plan. In general I have found that regardless of the degree of sophistication or size of business this is best done by first establishing a simple formula for a monthly cash flow/budget statement of income and expenditure.

This is a basic starting point for any small to medium size business and can be used for any business by applying the principle to Departmental or Divisional Managers in the case of larger businesses.

This principle is applied to period, quarterly and annual cash flow projections, which show the fluctuating, cash balances, which result from variations in actual cash, receipts. These should be set up on a spreadsheet and updated on a regular basis. The examples show simple layouts that are easy to operate, regular systematic monitoring will enable you to forecast and update future cash trends and availability of funds.

Cash is King – The importance of cash flow

(Example Company / 1.)

Average Monthly Income & Expenditure/Cash Flow

AS / /   For The Year Ending   /

Income (exc. Vat)		£
Sales Income (Normal Business Activity)	Gross - Per Annum 145,000	
Total Monthly Income		12,083

Average Monthly Expenditure (Exc. Vat)

Accountancy/Bookkeeping, Etc.	146
Advertising	542
For Sale/Sold Boards	208
Cleaning/Tea/Coffee	83
Computers/I.T.	208
Insurance's (office)	63
Maintenance	208
Motor Cars	500
Petrol/Tax/Servicing/Insurance's	417
Photography	167
Postage	292
Printing/Copying	208
Promotional	167
Proprietor-Gross Drawings	3,042
Rent	750
Stationery	417
Subscriptions	18
Telephone	625
Utilities	208
Wages PAYE, etc.	2,513
Total Monthly Expenditure	**10,881**

Monthly Income	12,083	
Monthly Expenditure	10,881	
Anticipated Surplus	£1,203	

PROJECTED CASH FLOW, BASED ON TURNOVER — SAMPLE COMPANY 2.

	MTH 1	MTH 2	MTH 3	MTH 4	MTH 5	MTH 6	MTH 7	MTH 8	MTH 9	MTH 10	MTH 11	MTH 12	YEAR TO / / TOTALS
INCOME -													
Gross Sales & Accounts Receivables	150,000	200,000	225,000	150,000	0	0	0	0	0	0	0	0	725,000
Other Income	0	0	0	50,000	0	0	0	0	0	0	0	0	50,000
TOTAL INCOME	150,000	200,000	225,000	200,000	0	0	0	0	0	0	0	0	£ 775,000
PURCHASES -	98,298	131,064	147,447	98,298	0	0	0	0	0	0	0	0	£ 475,107
VAT Payments	0	0	0	34,683	0	0	0	0	0	0	0	0	34,683
Gross Profit	51,702	68,936	77,553	67,019	0	0	0	0	0	0	0	0	£ 265,210
EXPENDITURE -													
Accountancy	0	0	0	0	0	0	0	0	0	0	0	0	0
Advertising	2,500	0	0	0	0	0	0	0	0	0	0	0	2,500
Bank Charges & Interest	0	0	2,000	0	0	0	0	0	0	0	0	0	2,000
Directors Remuneration	12,000	12,000	12,000	12,000	0	0	0	0	0	0	0	0	48,000
Heat & Light	1,500	1,500	1,500	1,500	0	0	0	0	0	0	0	0	6,000
Hire Purchase/Leasing	2,000	2,000	2,000	2,000	0	0	0	0	0	0	0	0	8,000
Insurance	5,000	0	0	5,000	0	0	0	0	0	0	0	0	10,000
Maintenance	0	0	0	1,500	0	0	0	0	0	0	0	0	1,500
Miscellaneous	0	0	0	0	0	0	0	0	0	0	0	0	0
Mortgage Repayments	10,000	10,000	10,000	10,000	0	0	0	0	0	0	0	0	40,000
Motor Expenses	800	800	800	800	0	0	0	0	0	0	0	0	3,200
Office Sundries	0	0	0	0	0	0	0	0	0	0	0	0	0
Other	1,000	1,000	1,000	1,000	0	0	0	0	0	0	0	0	4,000
Rates	2,000	2,000	2,000	2,000	0	0	0	0	0	0	0	0	8,000
Rent	0	0	0	0	0	0	0	0	0	0	0	0	0
Telephone/Fax	1,000	1,000	1,000	1,000	0	0	0	0	0	0	0	0	4,000
Wages, Inc. National Insurance	18,000	18,000	18,000	18,000	0	0	0	0	0	0	0	0	72,000
TOTAL EXPENDITURE	55,800	48,300	50,300	54,800	0	0	0	0	0	0	0	0	£ 209,200
MONTHLY SURPLUS (DEFICIT)	(4,098)	20,636	27,253	12,219	0	0	0	0	0	0	0	0	£ 56,010
CASHFLOW - B/Fwd	0	(4,098)	16,538	43,791	56,010	0	0	0	0	0	0	0	
Balance	(4,098)	16,538	43,791	56,010	0	0	0	0	0	0	0	0	

At this point you could be forgiven for thinking that this is all well and good, but I have to get my debtors to pay. So how do we achieve this?

By now you will have no doubts left that my firm beliefs are keep it simple and stick to basics, well the same is true when getting your debtors to pay on time. There are no rare skills, or sophisticated methods required, just an understanding of your own terms of trading and why debtors don't pay. Then you can structure your credit control system and procedures accordingly.

The following is a summary of main actual reasons why your debtors don't pay on time or don't pay at all.

1   The debtor doesn't know or if he knows, he doesn't understand your terms of trading. Strange as it may seem, it really can be that simple.
2   Whilst he runs and knows his business well operationally, its an administrative nightmare, and though his intentions may be honourable, he just can't put his hands on the Appropriate due or overdue invoices.
3   His intentions are not so honourable, you are not that important to him, and he is only ever concerned about his own business and does not care at whose expense his business succeeds.
4   He is short of funds and struggling, although perhaps not about to go under he is using creditor funds to see him through cash flow difficulties.
5   He has not got the cash and is unable to pay and may be or is about to go into liquidation.

There are an abundance of routine, and in some cases more creative reasons given for not paying i.e. your cheques in the post, (but it never seems to arrive) your invoices have not been checked or they have not been received, we are waiting for a (spurious) credit note, the cheques are in for signature, the boss is away or in hospital (obviously not suffering from writers cramp) the computers gone down in the middle of the cheque run, etc. etc. etc. Although the list is endless, these reasons along with all those not mentioned are, without exception, covered in or are part of the five real reasons listed above.

The following (listed in order) are some suggestions and pointers to countering and avoiding the above, prevention is always better than cure.

1   **Does not understand terms . . .** The most fundamental of all, ensure at the outset that your Terms of Trading are clearly understood and agreed. Your basic stationery and invoices should also have your Terms and Conditions clearly shown. The minimum that this should cover, should include retention of title until paid for (known as a Romalpa clause) or general retention of goods (lien) for service providers such as hauliers, shipping etc.

    Your system for invoicing system should be regularly reviewed to ensure that it is error proof, and that resulting invoices are correct and beyond dispute.
2   **The administrative nightmare . . .** The first time your invoices are put in doubt you will have an indicator that the debtor's administration is not as it

should be. It has been my experience, that any poorly administered business will eventually go the same way as the business that is not operating and or trading profitably. Proceed with caution and ensure your business relationship allows for good communication.

3   **Not interested and unethical . . .** If you are running a tightly controlled business, providing a first class product or Service that is strictly according to previously agreed terms, and your debtor just gives you the run around, you should cease to do business and replace them. If this is not possible because perhaps they are too important, then you should seriously consider your strategy as such situations have inevitable consequences.

4   **Short of cash and using your funds . . .** Communication as always is critical, establish as quickly as possible what the seriousness of the problem is, as it may be temporary and with help can be overcome. It may be possible to come to an arrangement for adjusted terms, which can be preferable to constant badgering, argument and uncertainty that such situations create.

There are many points to be considered before making such an arrangement, i.e. is he a long established customer, what has he's value been to date, has he previously paid to terms or has he always needed chasing. What is your exposure and how will this effect your own cash flow. How many other creditors is he stringing out. Is he basically sound, if so why the present cash shortage. There are many more points; however, the example is to demonstrate that you need to establish cause and effect, before you can see if a solution is available.

5   **Out of funds and cannot pay . . .** If you are of the opinion that your debtor is in such difficulties that he is about to go out of business or into liquidation, you should first Recover, any unpaid for goods, (if applicable) as covered by your Romalpa clause, and occasionally it can be possible to negotiate part payment, in full and final settlement of your debt. A bird in the hand can be worth two in the bush, as such situations are universally bad news for unsecured creditors.

Good Cash Flow – How to Operate and Protect It . . .

A credit policy is essential to all businesses no matter what size. You should ensure that you have in place clear-cut no nonsense action plans that are systematic and impactful. Your debtors should be aware of your terms and credit control policy as previously covered. There are many **myths** when it comes to being paid, such as companies with no bad debts are not trying hard enough, they simply do not want to take risks, or chasing payment and spending too much time on credit control is too costly and can be bad for business.

As previously stated these are only ever **myths**. You should always, no matter how aggressively you market simply ensure your customers know your terms and you should never be afraid to request payment when it is due, for goods and services that have been provided on credit.

Suggested outline of points to cover and be included in your system . . .

Having made sure that your terms of trading have been clearly agreed, before commencing with your business relationship, it is essential that you take up references.

This can be by way of a credit application form, which should be clearly laid-out, requesting all relevant information. Such as, Full trading name of business, entity, i.e. Limited Company, sole trader or partnership. How long established or date of incorporation, Bankers and existing trade references. And always clarify the address to which invoices should be sent as this can often vary from the trading address. You should add anything that might be applicable to your particular situation. And finally a point which is often overlooked, request the full name and title of the person responsible for payments i.e. Financial Director. Also take up the references, as there is no point in going through the process of gaining the information and then not using it.

1. If you have not been paid by the due date, make an enquiring phone call, (chasing on the phone is generally more effective than writing alone) always be polite and courteous whilst asking if the payment has been made.
2. If you have still not been paid after seven days then send a letter; follow up the letter by phoning to enquire if your letter has been received and when the cheque is to be sent. If the letter has not been received, it is a good idea to fax a copy during the conversation.
3. At fourteen days overdue, a second letter should be sent, requesting payment within seven days, the letter should clearly state that in line with your terms, if payment is still not received, the matter will be automatically passed to your Solicitors. Receipt of this letter should also be confirmed with a follow up telephone call.

It is very important that you take action when you have said you will, otherwise your policy lacks credibility and will soon become a meaningless waste of time.

You should consult a solicitor and agree a cost for the procedure that is to be followed, most firms will have set costs and will be happy to supply an explanatory action flow chart of the procedure and time that each stage should take. They should also advise as to the alternatives should the matter reach the courts.

The legal proceeding stage will generally produce a result as the majority of genuine businesses and business people would wish to avoid the resultant actions affecting their ability to obtain future credit.

However, if they are unable to pay, and had previously traded to your terms, generally your basic credit control system would not have enabled you to know if they had been having such difficulties with other creditors. It is therefore fundamental to your credit control system, to have a constant update, on any adverse data that could be affecting your customers' potential future viability. It can be as equally important to have such data on suppliers that are vital to your business, as you would need to be planning alternatives if they were in difficulties, as sudden key supplier failure can put your business in difficulty just as easily as customer bad debt.

There are a number of specialised service providers offering business update information, but generally such data can be difficult to understand and interpret with varying degrees of ease of information accessibility and comprehensiveness.

I have studied and used the majority over a period of time and without question have found that "Risk Alert" is the most comprehensive and easy to use. It is specifically designed to give immediate notice to its subscribers on a daily basis of the critical changes in financial and general status.

The following is a summary guide to meaning & potential consequences of the data, which is provided in the report, and you may also find it of use when taking up references.

Account Arrears

The number of days over the period which a company, by Law, has to file its Audited Accounts. Financial penalties are incurred if a company fails to comply.

Delays in filing are often innocent mistakes, however it could mean that the company is attempting to hide, for as long as possible, either very favourable results from its competitors, or poor results from the market place in general. Usually the latter! How might this affect your business?

Filing History

Companies have the ability to change their names, addresses as well as their directors. All such changes must be registered. Again, such registrations (filings) may be perfectly innocent however you should ask yourself: Why the change? Am I already aware of it from the company direct? Are the directors "deserting the sinking ship?" Is there an intention to hide something or mislead the outside world? How might the real reason for the change affect your business?

Court Actions

Court Actions of any type will be of concern to you, as at best the action has resulted from poor administration (reflecting a poorly managed business), whilst at worst, an inability to pay a Debt which is both due and outstanding!

County Court Judgements (CCJs), are registered via the County Court, follow-

RISK ALERT SAMPLE REPORT

Subject Name: Sample Company

Status: LIMITED Company No:01234567 **RAS No.** R000660854 **Accnt:** No N/A

Date of Incorporation: 1.10.89 **Last Filed Accounts:** 31.03.96
Accounting Ref. Date: 31/03 **Accounts Arrears :** 0 Days

SUMMARY FLAGS

Filing History	Y/N	Date	New	Value
Name	Y	26.11.93		
Registered Office	N			
Directors	Y	6.08.07		

Court Actions – most recent				
County Court Judgements	CCJ	1.10.97		1060
	CCJ	12.09.97		770
High Court Writs	CM	15.09.97		
	HCGS	13.08.97		1
	HCGS	4.08.97		1
	HCGS	2.07.97		1
	HCGS	30.06.97		1
Winding Up Petitions	Y	31.10.97		
Dissolved Warning	N			
Dissolved	N			

Financial			
Mortgage or Charge	Y	24.05.96	
Analysed Accounts	Y	31.03.96	
Annual Return	Y	22.08.96	

Insolvency			
Administration	N		
Receivership	N		
Vol. Arrangement	N		
Liquidation	Y	31.10.97	

Financial Summary

Nominal Capital	Issued Capital	Employees
1000	50000	
Date 31.03.94	31.03.95	31.03.96
Turnover		
Net Assets 114000	71000	113000

ing the issue of a Summons, and reflect debts, which have been adjudged as outstanding in the eyes of the Law. This is often the first step to other debt recovery actions (such as Liquidation). Whilst a single judgement may not mean that the business is in imminent danger of demise, you need to be very vigilant and give close attention to your future relationship with such businesses.

High Court Writs, are usually debts or claims, so significant in amount that the Creditor, or claimant is prepared to pay the additional costs incurred in the High Court, compared to those in the County Court. Whilst a single Writ may not bring about the immediate demise of a business, the issue of the Writ should be of major concern to you. Establish the facts as soon as possible, being exceedingly mindful of any current and future trading relationship.

The only possible exception to this are Writs issued against major businesses. But remember even major businesses go Bust!!

The following Codes are used in this category, which imply that some form of Court application has been made, or some hearing has taken place, in respect of the category shown

HCGS	–	High Court, Goods & Services, meaning normal trade transactions involving Money/credit, rather than litigation for (non) performance of a contract, etc
VOL	–	Voluntary Arrangement
CM	–	Creditors Meeting, suggesting the onset of Insolvency Proceedings.
WP	–	Winding Up Petition.
WO	–	Winding Up Order.

Winding Up Petitions, In all likelihood the Company will shortly cease to be! Recover any money owed to you if possible!

Dissolved Warning, again can be innocent (e.g. issued for failure to file Accounts), however unless rectified immediately will result in the company being dissolved! Recover any money owed to you if possible.

Dissolved, the ultimate step if the company does not react to the notice. You may be too late to get your money back!

Financial

The latter two topics relate to the filing of audited figures. The figures themselves are available for scrutiny, but remember they relate to period of trade, which ended often several months ago! Delays in the filing of figures are discussed above under "Accounts Arrears".

The registration of a Mortgage or Charge usually relates to Lending Institutions (such as a Bank) taking security for a loan. Again, this may be totally innocent but could also be an indicator of "stormy waters ahead". Consider this information alongside any other information received in respect of the company, and balance your thoughts in respect of any potential impact on your business.

Insolvency

Means here that a formal Insolvency Procedure is in place. Universally bad news – it may already be too late to recover any outstanding money, with the exception of Receiverships where there could be a small return to creditors.

In general, The Risk Alert Report provides you with a "Snapshot" of the target businesses Record's status, as at the time of issue. Over time, if more than one Report is triggered a valuable "picture" will build up as more reports are issued, so giving you as complete a view as possible as to the nature of increasing trading risk.

The indicators shown in the Summary Flags section could well suggest that it might be already too late for any effective recovery action to be implemented. Most adverse/declining situations are preceded by a build up of initial Court Proceedings, such as the issue of Summons' and Writs, which lead to Judgements. Unfortunately, only County Court Judgements are reportable, whereas the details of High Court Judgements are kept totally confidential by the Court system.

By having as much and varied information as is possible, this knowledge base will enable you to take effective, often preventative action at a time when other creditors/customers are unaware of the deteriorating situation. And therefore would inevitably suffer a far worse outcome than you would have suffered, because you had been able to take earlier corrective action.

There is course credit insurance, however since the basic principles outlined in this chapter are, according to my own practical experience of consultancy and business, I am not generally in favour of credit insurance.

However you should check this option out carefully before deciding, as there is a powerful fundamental principle to consider. You need to insure your business premises, factory, warehouse or offices, stock, fixtures and fittings etc. public liability motor vehicles etc. etc. All of which are accepted as normal risks that require insurance, why then should you not insure, what to many businesses is their most valuable and sometimes most tangible asset, your debtors.

I am of the opinion that you can build satisfactory safeguards into your business through the methods outlined and in addition you should include in your overheads the cost of credit insurance to at least equal the cost you would be paying if you were insured.

The cost should be written off your weekly or monthly management accounts as a contingency liability. The fund that you will accumulate (assuming no bad debts) will not be allowable as a cost for tax relief, as would the insurance, and will need to be written back at the year end. I am sure there is not a business or business person anywhere who would be at a loss as to how to use surplus funds created by becoming your own credit insurer, take your accountants advice.

What you can do if you should run into cash flow difficulties or debt problems . . .

By the very nature of business, you can sometimes get into difficulties that no degree of control and due diligence could have avoided. However if you have followed the guide lines to good cash management, and have a priority awareness of cash and its importance, you will at least have known that you were getting into trouble and taking corrective action should become your number one priority.

Knowing that you have such difficulties and that they will not just disappear on their own, recognising that something needs to be done, and making a decision to take corrective action is more than half the battle won. All to often in my experience people just somehow seem to bury their head in the sand and try to ignore the situation, hoping and wishing, that something will eventually turn up, and everything will be ok. This may sound like a crazy exaggeration, but you may be assured it is very true, as a consequence they are then seeking help when it is often to late, or they go out of business without even realising they were so close to brink.

However, although your priority is to resolve your cash flow or pending debt difficulties, due to the day to day pressures of running your business, you may not have the time to give the situation the attention it requires. It is also generally the case in such situations that you are too close to look objectively at the solutions, even if you are aware of what they might be.

The options open to you are various, and with time you can and will no doubt find a solution yourself, but if time for what ever reason, is not on your side, then you should seek help. Your accountant may be able to assist, but generally his advice is not tuned to the commercial aspects of the problem, unless you are fortunate enough to have what I term as a commercial accountant. It has always been my experience that you are best helped when in any difficulty by someone that has experienced and resolved similar difficulties themselves.

There are companies and consultants that specialise in assisting companies and businesses solve cash flow difficulties and reduce debt by negotiation and mediation, with very successful outcomes. These are informal arrangements and have an unquestionably high success rate, whilst maintaining a good working relationship which has future benefits for both parties.

There are other options such as A Company Voluntary Arrangement (CVA). A voluntary arrangement for a Company is a procedure whereby a plan of reorganisation or composition in satisfaction of its debts, is put forward to creditors and shareholders. There is limited involvement by the court and the scheme is under the control of a supervisor, who must be a licensed insolvency practitioner (IP).

These are alternatives, that very often save businesses from sliding into the area of no return, and require the involvement specialist help, which, is at hand if you know where to look for it. When seeking help it is very important that you clarify the person is qualified to assist you. This is best achieved by requesting testimonials or referrals, from people that they have previously helped.

The intention of this chapter has been to increase your awareness of the importance of good cash flow, and give an indication of the size of the total credit swill and some of the problems that exist within it. Outline some pointers to control, monitoring and prevention, which I trust will assist you to avoid the need for the actions that have been briefly covered in the closing few paragraphs.

Summary

Maintain a constant awareness of the need for good cash flow, its meaning and potential consequences.

Be mindful of potential situations that are beyond your control and their possible effect on your business.

Know what you want from your business, your reason why determines your direction, and focuses your awareness.

Never forget that you are just a tiny drop in a giant credit pond, and that you need to maintain a tight credit policy.

Have a good information provider, that builds a picture of any current or potential risks, and include your key suppliers.

If you do have difficulties, recognise that you have them and take corrective action, seeking help if and when you need it.

Cash is King . . .

If you would like more information regarding Risk Alert or information on alternative service providers, copy draft letters for credit references and overdue payments, please contact me direct. I will be happy to provide these, **(FREE of charge)**. Meanwhile I sincerely wish you every success in building your cash-mountain.

3   Passion & Purpose – The key practices

'A structured approach to identify and enhance value requirements for organisations and individuals.'

by Michael Lewis

To: identify key issues facing your organisation. How to conduct an internal and external analysis and establish the needs, wants and values of key stakeholders. Identify solutions and develop an action plan for your organisation success and monitor your plan via a value matrix.

It is a truism that everything in life changes and that such change is an on-going process where nothing stands still. This chapter examines how you can enhance and develop the value of your organisation in a turbulent, constantly changing environment, and increasingly global marketplace by adopting a more structured approach to identify value requirements.

Furthermore it is equally true that there is no single right way to achieve absolute success – no panacea to guarantee organisational success or solve human resources issues. What works for one organisation may be completely inappropriate for another, *but*, there are two issues that will remain constant:-

1. Strategic business goals should never be considered without linking them with your human resources, and,
2. Whatever your business, if you have got the right people with you in the right place with the right values, then your chances of real success are significantly enhanced.

Sadly within too many organisations people still remain a costly, yet wasted resource. This anomaly, coupled to the rapid pace of change prevents too many organisations from enhancing their real value. Change is as far reaching as it is rapid, cutting across all sectors of the economy. During the last decade in the UK and the USA:-

- nearly half of all organisations were re-engineered,
- nearly 100,000 firms were acquired or merged,
- several 100,000's of companies were downsized, and
- nearly 750,000 organisations went bust!

Many other organisations simply expanded too rapidly, revamped their products and services, extended into new untested markets, overhauled their internal systems and policies, relocated, introduced new or different technologies, introduced new management teams, rationalised core activities, changed their organisational culture, were de-regulated, etc, etc. During the last decade, most Western organisations have been clearing debris. Downsizing, delayering, decentralisation, consolidation, productivity gains, and focus on quality – all have redirected attention towards doing more with less, becoming more efficient, improving processes and cutting costs to become more profitable. The pace of such change is exhausting – but you saw all this didn't you? You and your organisation have probably lived through all of this and have been watching the pace of change accelerate over the last decade. Furthermore my crystal ball suggests that change won't go away or relax its pace within the foreseeable future. Indeed your organisation will probably be challenged still further by sharper economic swings, new competitive pressures, further globalisation of the marketplace, new and more sophisticated technologies, and regulatory changes – it's a daunting prospect isn't it? A primary difference between future winners and losers will not be the pace of change, but the ability to respond to the pace of change. Winners will not be surprised at the unanticipated changes they face; they will have developed the ability to adapt, learn and respond. Losers will spend time trying to control and master change rather than responding to it.

Sadly evidence still suggests that too few organisations are really prepared to see change as much a real business opportunity as a source of concern. The necessary range of an organisations responses to change must expand as the pace of change outside the firm increases. Three general response types can be identified: initiatives, processes and cultural adaptations. Initiative changes focus on implementing new programs, projects or procedures. Through strategic planning, specific initiatives are identified as necessary and are implemented as part of an evolving management improvement process. Process changes focus on the ways in which work gets done. Organisations first identify core processes and then try to improve them via work simplification, value-added assessments and other reengineering efforts. Cultural changes occur within an organisation when the fundamental ways of doing business are reconceptualised. The options are to adjust (change) or die! What's necessary is for you and your company to accept change and make it work for you. Invent the future for your organisation instead of trying to re-design the past. By all means accept the past and maintain that which works – but increasingly focus on the future and anticipate what's coming; what needs to happen; and most importantly how you can rise to the occasion. Easier said than done?

Action Point One:

1. No-one likes being reminded of their past mistakes – what's past is past, so help colleagues to re-visit their current practice, encourage them to review their current processes, and get them to move forward and assume ownership for their (and your) future success.
2. Focus colleagues on key objectives for the future – don't dwell on the past or even current problems!
3. Link all activity and objectives clearly to your organisational aims and ignore everything else – if in doubt, stick to your core business!
4. Create and encourage environments within your organisation that will encourage creativity and use these to brainstorm new ideas.

The purpose of developing a structured approach is to help you to determine the current performance of your organisation; to understand the needs of the business, directors and other relevant stakeholders; and, to establish the key issues facing your business in the forseeable future. These will then help you to place your company in a more competitive position in your marketplace.

The corporate mission is the over-riding *raison d'être* for your business. Ackoff (1986) suggests that the primary objective of a mission statement should not address what an organisation must do in order to survive, but what it has chosen to do in order to thrive. It should be positive, visionary and motivating. Ackoff suggests that a good mission statement should have five characteristics-

1. It will contain a formulation of objectives that enables progress towards them to be measured.
2. It differentiates the company from its competitors.
3. It defines the business(es) that the company wants to be in, not necessarily is in.
4. It is relevant to all the stakeholders in the firm, not just the shareholders and managers.
5. It is exciting and inspiring.

In a recent survey 34 middle managers from different organisations were asked to repeat their organisations mission statement. All confirmed they had one, but only 17 could remember bits of it. Only 11 thought the statement was something with which they could identify, and rather worryingly only five believed that their organisations were actually working towards meeting the mission statement? One of the great values of the UK governments initiative, *'Investors in People'* (IIP) is that *all* stakeholders must understand what their organisations mission statement is, as a key element in a cycle for continuous improvement. To be of any value to the organisation you must ensure your mission statement reflects your corporate values and that you and all your other staff pro-actively support and pursue it. Campbell (1989) argues that there are four key issues involved in developing a useful mission:

Purpose – Hanson plc, led by Lord Hanson stated that the central tenet of his faith is that the shareholder is king. His aim was to advance the shareholders interest by increasing earnings per share.
Strategy – describes the business and its activities, and clarifies the position it wants to achieve in its chosen field.
Values – how does the company intend to treat its employees, customers and suppliers, for example?
Behaviour standards – it is important that the organisation behaves in the way that it promises it will, as this will inspire trust in employees and others who significantly influence the organisation.

Good examples of mission statements are:
Sainsburys: '.....contribution to the public good and the quality of life.'
Body Shop: '.....To continually enhance our ability, to trade creatively, ethically, and profitably.'
Sock Shop: '.....our merchandise continues to be not merely 'lifestyle' – we provide everyday necessities in a fashionable manner.'
Coca Cola: '.....to put a Coke within arm's reach of every consumer in the world.'
Canon: '.....Beat Xerox!'
Nasa: '.....Put a man on the moon by the end of the decade.'

But remember the creation of your mission statement is more important than the possession of it, since it should be a process to align your management and your staff behind a common purpose which defines the strategic purpose of the business.

Companies also have to think about social responsibility for themselves. Witnessing this new 'society of organisations' – a world where business is just one of many organisations, each with its own specialist function, and with attitudes and actions that help to create other operating environments – is the commercialisation of social purpose and the socialisation of commerce. Companies need to promote passion and a true sense of purpose amongst its staff. Employee motivation is no longer just about money or simply working harder – it needs to be increasingly about the sheer joy of research, innovation and creativity coupled to the belief that staff are contributing something to humanity – passion is what makes them tick – profit is there to feed the passion. As companies seek to globalise their markets, to respond to ever-changing situations and to create networks of knowledge and ideas, so it becomes increasingly important that your staff stand at the centre of any business strategy to create sustainable competitive advantage. This is a radical shift for many organisations to accept, from a time when money or better technology created the means by which they were able to outmanoeuvre their competitors. With capital and technology more widely available, more organisations are competing on a more-even playing field. The shift from financial capital to human capital is becoming ever more profound.

Action Point 2:

In addition to developing a mission statement to clarify the organisations aims, a review of the financial performance is also required to establish the key issues. A way forward is to:

1. Identify all trading activities of your organisation, including subsidiaries, etc. Summarise the profitability for the past four years, the current year and the years for which you have future projections, in a line-graph showing turnover, gross profit, profit before tax, and profit after tax. Review what is represented. What are the trends? What is the gross profit in percentage terms in comparison with other years? What are your options to improve the position – sell assets? reduce overheads? boost revenues by increasing cost of goods/ services? *(NB: Most small organisations wrongly underprice themselves through fear of not generating sufficient income. If you're delivering a quality product or service – stick to your price!)* or, reduce borrowing by further injection of shareholders capital?

2. Look carefully at costs in all operating areas, especially central office. By allocating direct/fixed costs to each area, what gross profit (%) change is seen? Also analyse all current liabilities (– bank loans and overdraft, trade creditors, taxation and social security, etc,) and all creditors due after more than one year (– bank loans and overdraft, directors/shareholders loans, etc.) Is the organisation over-geared? Can you re-negotiate interest rates with your bankers, or agree a capital/ interest holiday period? What other financial commitments does your organisation have? Can they be re-structured? Are there any impending cash-flow problems – as any future spending plans may have to be carefully researched and any investments into opportunities outside the core business may need to be self-financing in order for a period of consolidation to build-up funds in the structure of the core business itself? (PS: A word of warning – don't kill the goose that lays the golden egg – or, in other words, don't sacrifice a successful core business activity for the sake of a speculative venture that appeals to your entrepreneurial spirit without very careful research!)

3. Share key information with staff to better enable them to understand the strategies and visions you have determined. Have the confidence to confide

in your staff so that they can play their full part in securing the organisations, and thereby their own, future success.

Having undertaken this soul-searching exercise how do you know whether or how your efforts compare with your competitors? Initially employed by the Xerox Corporation to meet the Japanese competitive challenge of the 1970's, *benchmarking* is an external focus on internal activities, functions or operations in order to achieve continuous improvement. David T Kearns, CEO of Xerox Corporation, states that benchmarking is:

'the continuous process of measuring product, services and practices against the toughest competitors, or those companies recognised as industry leaders.'

This definition suggests a movement away from a concern with simple cost reduction and debate over the size of budgets, to a much better understanding of what activities customers really value and what level of performance they expect. An increasing number of companies world-wide are realising that future success will require more than gutfeel and intuition, and more than just doing what they've always done just a little bit better. Success in the next decade requires fact – not fiction; and analysis – not guesstimates, with a clear, ongoing focus on meeting and exceeding customer expectations. The continuous pursuit of excellence is the underlying and ever-present goal of benchmarking. The starting point in achieving excellence is the customer. Whether external or internal to your organisation, your customer sets the expectations for performance and is the ultimate judge of your organisations quality. A customer is anyone who has a stake or interest in the on-going operations of your company. Richard Schonberger, in his 1990 book *'Building a Chain of Customer's'* notes that:

. . . 'The wide-awake now see the final customer as just the end point in a chain of customers. Everybody has a customer – at the next process (where your work goes next). Making the connections along the chain is our common task.'

Beating the competition and adding value to your own organisation requires looking increasingly outside your own company by using benchmarking and related techniques to peel away the layers of 'difference'; make valid comparisons against other similar organisations; and, to learn from them. This process of continuous improvement, or *Kaizen*, means gradual, un-ending improvement; doing little things better incrementally, and setting – and achieving – ever-higher standards. The essence of Kaizen is simple – Kaizen means improvement – on-going improvement involving everyone in the organisation. Benchmarking is an excellent vehicle for developing a Kaizen culture in your company. It is a continuous process of evaluating current performance, setting goals for the future, and identifying areas for improvement and change. It is a dynamic, on-going effort by both management and workforce alike. It sows the seeds of organisational and cultural change that must occur if survival, let alone competitive advantage, is to be achieved. The ambition therefore, is to put benchmarking to work to help you and your company achieve world-class competitive capabilities.

Action Point Three:

1. In order for you to assess your company's performance, compare key financial performance statistics (i.e.: turnover, pre-tax profit, return on capital, total debt/net worth) to such information from your competitors. If you can't get access to this information use your own industry sectors figures using the Standard Industry Classification (SIC) codes. Bar charts should then be produced showing percentile figures for your organisations sector which will benchmark comparative statistics. This exercise will help you to identify key issues, such as, a possible high debt ratio which may need to be addressed by selling some of your assets, or adopting more radical actions to seriously reduce the level of borrowing.
2. You may have to consider an alternative approach and examine selling an equity share to new stakeholders – one benefit of which would be to reduce debts, and the second benefit would be to provide greater incentive for these new stakeholders to ensure future organisational success. (PS: Don't fall into the benchmarking trap – make sure you benchmark like with like, as best practice should not be assessed in isolation from other organisational issues. Ensure your organisation uses benchmarking to find out what others do, not so you can do it the same way, but so you can do it *better*!)

By benchmarking your organisational performance externally, this should provide your organisation with greater market orientation, i.e: what business are we really in? This will provide a better strategic framework and awareness of, and for your company. How good is your information? How well are you doing and why? Where are you going? Where are your opportunities and threats? How can you capitalise on your strengths and reduce your weaknesses as well as helping you to accept strategic change? Where do you want to go? What alternatives have you got? How do you choose? What is realistic? What can(not) you do? How do you make the strategy work? How do you manage the changes?

According to the UK's Institute of Management, good management exists when :

- the organisation has defined its purpose
- in order to achieve its purpose, objectives have been determined for the organisation and all its constituent parts
- strategy and policies are determined and formulated for meeting these objectives
- plans and targets are set for the achievement of these objectives

- responsibilities and accountability are clearly defined
- progress is monitored, and action taken as necessary, to ensure achievement within defined timescales and allocated resources.

The need for managers to think strategically has already been proven. There are three aspects to strategic management: firstly the strategy itself, which is concerned with the establishment of a clear direction for the organisation and a means of getting there, which requires the creation of strong competitive positions: secondly, excellence in the implementation of strategies in order to yield effective performance; thirdly, innovation to ensure that the organisation is responsive to pressures for change and that strategies are continually improved and renewed.

Business strategy is all about competitive advantage. Without competitors there would be no need for strategy, for the sole purpose of strategic management is to enable your company to gain as effectively as is possible a sustainable edge over your competitors. A good strategy is one by which your company can gain significant ground on its competitors at an acceptable cost to itself. Kenichi Ohmae in his best selling book *The Mind of the Strategist* (1982) suggests there are four ways:

- Identify the key success factors for your industry/business sector, and concentrate resources in a particular area where your company sees an opportunity to gain the most significant strategic advantage over its competitors.
- Exploit any area where your company enjoys relative superiority, i.e.: better technology or larger sales network, for other products or services.
- Aggressively attempt to change the key success factors by challenging the accepted assumptions concerning the ways business is conducted in your industry or business sector.
- Innovate – open up new markets or develop new products or services.

The principal objective is to avoid doing the same thing in the same business sector as your competition. The aim is to attain a competitive situation in which your company can (a) gain a relative advantage through measures your competitors will find hard to follow, and (b) extend that advantage further and further!

To claim that your organisation is being managed effectively from a strategic point of view, you need to demonstrate firstly,

- that your management appreciates fully the dynamics, opportunities and threats present in their external competitive environment, and.
- that they are paying due regard to wider societal issues (Political/Economic/Social/Technological – **PEST** analysis), and,
- that the organisations resources (inputs) are being managed strategically, taking onto account its strengths and weaknesses, and,
- that your organisation is taking full advantage of its opportunities (Strengths/Weaknesses/Opportunities/Threats – **SWOT** analysis).

The development of any organisation will result from maximising its strengths whilst minimising its weaknesses, taking advantage of opportunities whilst realigning itself to minimise the affect of threats. Key success factors and core competencies would be matched. This utopian situation will not just happen – it has to be managed. Moreover potential new opportunities need to be constantly sought and resources developed. It is important therefore, that the values of your organisation match the needs of the environment and the key success factors, for it is the values and culture which determine whether the environment and resources are currently matched, and whether they remain congruent in changing circumstances. Values are traditionally subsumed as a resource in a SWOT analysis, although recent thinking has proposed further identification using E-V-R (environment-values-resources) congruence – where the greater the congruence the greater the likelihood that the organisation is managing its resources effectively to match the key success factors dictated by the environment – and strategic excellence positions (SEPs) – which describes capabilities which enable the organisation to produce better-than-average results over the longer term compared with its competitors for each product and service.

Action Point Four:

1   Undertake an appraisal of your current internal and external situation and current strategy (PEST/SWOT analysis), and if necessary produce a comprehensive (new?) business plan. Categorise your strengths and weaknesses as 'A' being most critical and 'C' being least critical. Opportunities and threats should also be categorised dependent firstly on the probability of the event happening, and secondly the likely impact of the event, both categories being rated as High (A), Medium (B) or Low (C). This assessment is necessary to determine the extent to which your organisation could introduce dramatic changes.
2   Determine desirable changes to your organisations objectives and/or strategies, i.e.: do you have a clearly defined management/organisational structure with appropriate objectives and accountabilities for all key players?
3   Search for – and consider choice of – suitable courses of action, i.e. what are the real opportunities for adding value – marketing (increased segmentation); operations (technology = cost reduction and better quality and service); finance (better use of assets); information (exploiting the potential of information technology); people (exploiting expertise, encouraging innovation); acquisition and re-structuring strategies; co-operation strategies; opportunities from changes in industry regulation; cost-cutting and concentration on core activities; synergy (greater return from assets); organisational changes (re-structuring, new processes)?
4   Implement any changes. Monitor your progress and establish an on-going appraisal process.

Marketing should not be viewed as a specialised activity as it encompasses the entire business as seen from the point of view of the customer. Marketing links selling organisations with buyers. Selling is concerned with converting finished products and services into cash: marketing involves decisions about what the product should be, how it should be promoted, and where and how it should be made available. The marketing mix includes the four P's of marketing – product, price, promotion and place, although there are other P's becoming increasingly well-known such as people and process. Marketeers should be those colleagues closest to your market, and they need to be most aware of your customers needs, opportunities, threats and changing preferences. Marketing must relate closely to innovation, and the strategy for each product and service must be linked to objectives and to other functional strategies that together comprise your organisations competitive strategy. This should address three things:

- how to meet customer needs more effectively than your competitors;
- how to compete with other manufacturers/producers;
- what use to make of the various marketing mix elements (i.e.-product, price, promotion, place, people, process).

In considering these areas, marketing managers should be aware of:

1. What might be realistically expected from a particular market in terms of revenue and profit, i.e.: market growth opportunities.
2. How might the market be segmented to facilitate niche marketing.
3. What opportunities exist for differentiating the product, adding value and establishing competitive advantage.
4. How best to 'position' the product/service in relation to the customer and the competition.
5. What strategic opportunities exist for advantageous pricing, promotion and distribution in relation to the competition?

Reis and Trout (1986) suggest four alternative marketing strategies to 'outwit, outflank and outfight competitors': **Defensive marketing** – a strategy for a market leader who continuously introduces new products and services which make existing ones obsolete, thereby making it very difficult for competitors ever to catch up, i.e.: Gillette who constantly introduce yet another new razor. **Offensive marketing** – for companies who are strong but not market leaders who attack a perceived weakness in the market leaders strategy, i.e.: Hertz vs Avis with Avis proclaiming 'We may be Number 2 – but we try harder'. **Flanking marketing** – the aim here is to find a new market position ahead of the competition, i.e.: Timex selling their watches through a far wider range of retailing outlets than the traditional jewellery store, and Swatch selling watches as fashion accessories rather than just timepieces. **Guerrilla marketing** – where companies focus on just one segment of the market.

Competitive and functional marketing strategies for a product or service vary according to the stage that it is at in its life cycle where sales follow a pattern – they grow slowly, then more quickly, peak and are either extended by product development, etc, or decline.

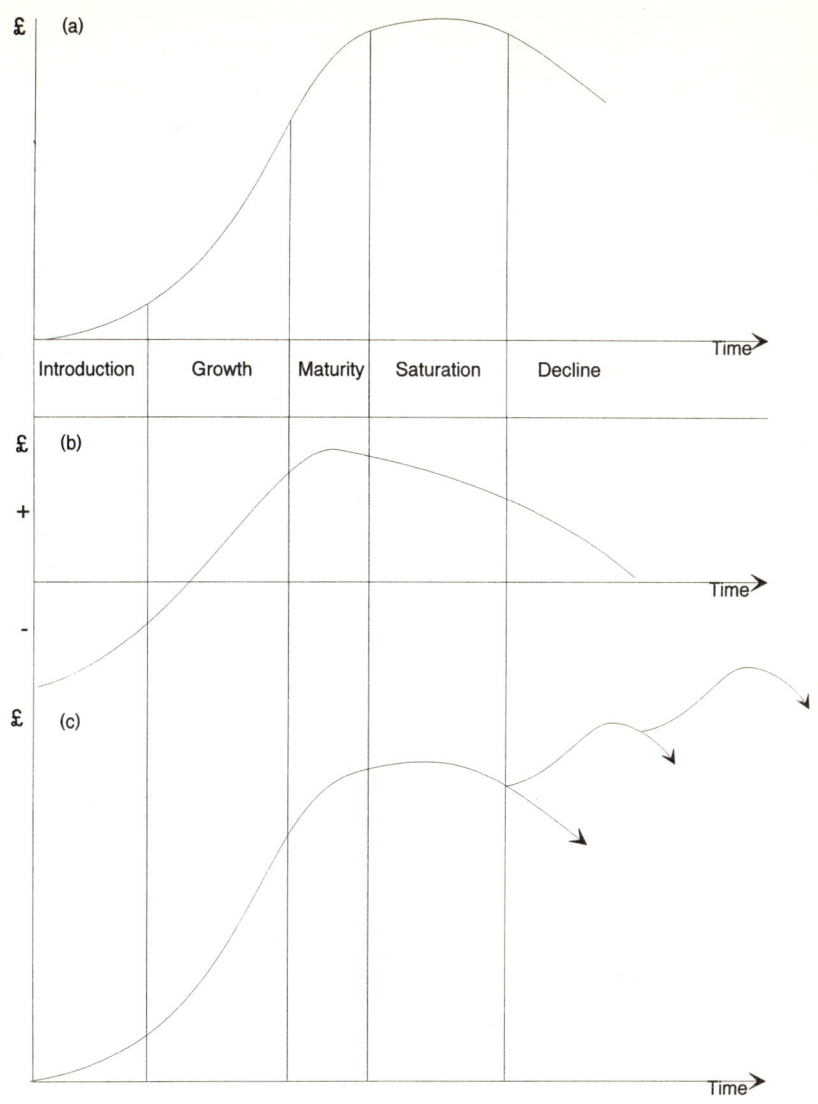

The product life cycle (a) Sales volume/revenue, (b) Profitability and (c) Extending the life cycle

Another tool for strategic planning is the Boston Matrix (BCG) which can be used to evaluate the significance of each individual product or service produced by an organisation in relation to all the others in order to establish future priorities and needs, as well as to evaluate the current position and future potential opportunities for products and services within a market sector in order to establish the appropriate marketing strategy.

44 Passion & Purpose – The key practices

(a)

Cash use
Market growth rate

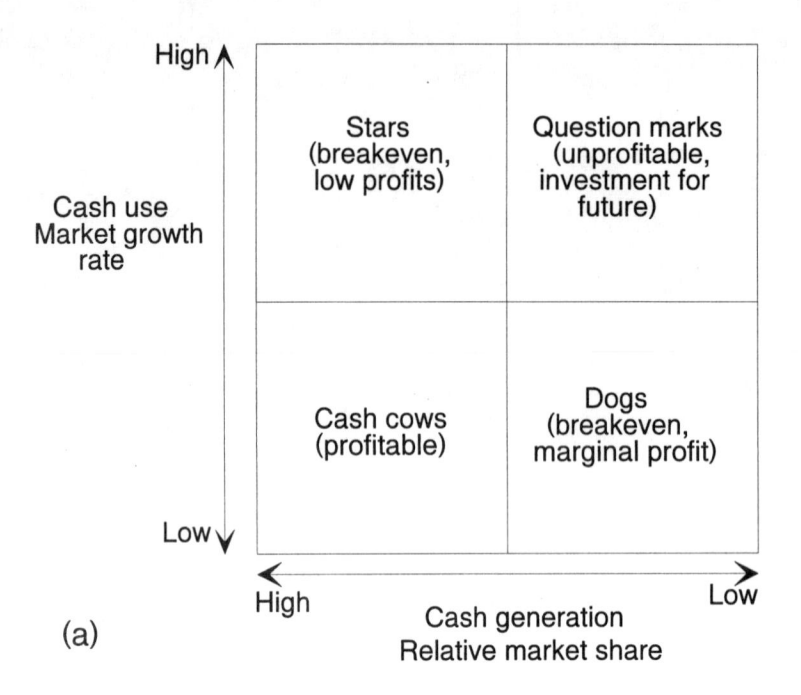

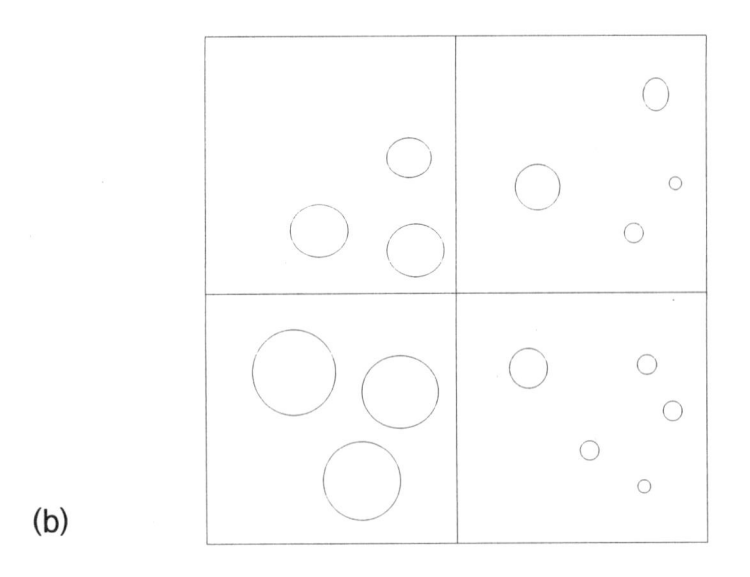

High ↑ — Low ↓

	High Cash generation / Relative market share	Low
High	Stars (breakeven, low profits)	Question marks (unprofitable, investment for future)
Low	Cash cows (profitable)	Dogs (breakeven, marginal profit)

(b)

The Boston Consulting Group growth share matrix.

The matrix is thus divided into four cells each representing a particular type of business – **Question marks** – are product or services which compete in high growth markets but where market share is relatively low – ie: a new product launched into a high growth market, with an existing market leader would normally constitute a question mark. Successful question marks become rising **Stars** – market leaders in growth markets that still need investment to maintain the rate of growth. Stars are only marginally profitable. **Cash cows** are mature market leaders. As market growth slows there is less need for high investment, hence they are the most profitable products in the portfolio, boosted by the economies of scale resulting from the position of market leadership. Cash cows fund the businesses in the other three cells. **Dead Dogs** describe businesses which are slowly losing market share and should be withdrawn when they become loss makers if not before.

Action Point Five:

1. Review your organisations marketing by examining your products/services life- cycle and consider how appropriate your marketing is between the different stages in the cycle.
2. Construct a Boston Matrix for your organisation and assess how balanced your portfolio of activities seems? Where are the strengths and weaknesses? Develop an action plan?

Human resources – people – are an essential strategic resource. They are essential to help you implement any strategies devised and to this end they must understand and share the corporate vision, objectives and values you've identified. People ultimately determine whether or not competitive advantage is created, and more importantly sustained. They can be an opportunity and a source of great competitive advantage, or they can act as a constraint to you and the whole organisation. You should seek to develop people with appropriate and cross functional skills who can work together effectively and have synergy. Ideally your staff should be:

- committed (though not literally!!) – commitment can always be improved.
- competent – competence's can be developed, and can bring significant improvements in product/service quality and productivity.
- cost-effective – ideally staff costs should be relatively low and performance/output relatively high, although this should not be interpreted as low rewards for success.
- sympathetic with the aims of your organisation.

These points do not imply that all staff should be good at everything, but that the appropriate skills for the position held are present in large part. Sir Bob Reid,

Chairman, British Railways Board said: ... 'There is a simple rule for success in business: get the right people you need in the right place and in the right numbers with the right skills and competencies to do the job and let them get on with it.' In reviewing your organisation, where there are weaknesses, development and training should be swiftly introduced. Cadbury Schweppes appraise their executives in terms of 50 skills and competence's broken down into six main groups – strategy (the ability to think critically and challenge conventional wisdom whilst being aware of the business environment), drive (self-motivation), influence (communication skills, networking and team-building), analysis (information gathering and reasoned analysis), implementation (understanding the impact of decisions taken on and in other parts of the organisation), and personal factors (i.e.: ambition). To help you ensure you have the right people in the right place doing the right thing for you the Belbin Model is a useful framework to use, as is the Thomas International Profile system. Prof. Meredith Belbin argues that a good team of people will have compensating strengths and weaknesses, and that as a group they will be able to perform tasks such as : create useful ideas, analyse problems effectively, get things done, communicate effectively, have useful leadership qualities, evaluate problems and options logically, control their work and report effectively. If people are to be truly committed to your organisation they *must* be involved. If they become more involved and are encouraged to contribute their ideas for improvement, the results can be innovation and/or quality improvement. Whilst money and position in your organisation can motivate, there are other essential factors such as those mentioned earlier in this chapter.

Action Point Six:

1   To add real value, ensure that your employee's jobs are:- interesting, challenging and demanding; that they know exactly what is expected of them and when they are meeting your expectations; and ensure rewards and sanctions are clearly linked to the effort they make and the results they achieve for your organisation. Appraise their current contribution regularly and if necessary agree new personal objectives.

Operations management is concerned with having the right product or service ready at the right time produced to the right quality, but also to the right cost to ensure that profits are earned. Thus operations management can deliver competitive advantage to your organisation in a number of ways: product design, production to exact specification, and production and delivery on time and to the appropriate levels of quality. Therefore your customer is provided with what he or she wants profitably to the benefit of both parties. There is an important link between marketing and operations. Consumer and customer satisfaction are measures of effectiveness, and cost-effective production is a measure of efficiency. In our fast moving economy, operations management has become a central aspect of strategic thinking for all organisations and should no longer be regarded an essentially supportive function. Total quality management (TQM) is a key feature within operations and was recognised by the Japanese in the 1960's. It happened when certain organisations realised that their policies to deliver improved product quality, were also resulting in lower unit costs and they looked for further ways of improving the quality of service they offered their customers. American companies responded in the 1970's after a number of their key markets (i.e.: computers and cars) had been eroded by Japanese competitors. It is only in the 1980's and early 1990's that Britain and the rest of Europe have regarded TQM as a strategic issue. Companies who have pursued total quality have been able to benefit in a number of ways, specifically they have:

- improved the company image
- improved productivity
- reduced costs
- created greater certainty within their operations management
- improved the morale of staff
- and perhaps most importantly, have committed customers.

The most important transaction with the customer is through the product/service itself. The degree to which it satisfies customer expectations will be the most powerful and lasting communication regarding your organisation and its business, of all. It is widely accepted that there are numerous characteristics of quality, any of which might be crucial in particular circumstances:

1. Primary performance – in the case of cars performance, primary objective measures would include speed, acceleration, noise levels, etc.
2. Secondary features – i.e.; free drinks on aeroplanes, clever remote controls for a hi-fi set.
3. Reliability – refers to the probability of a product such as a consumer durable breaking down whilst in use.
4. Conformance – for example dimensions of a product within agreed tolerances.
5. Durability – refers to the expected product life of, say a washing machine.
6. Serviceability – refers to the speed, ease, competence and courtesy with which a service is provided.
7. Aesthetics – the look, feel, sound, taste, smell of a product is clearly a subjective measure.
8. Perceived quality – refers to consumers perception of quality which may or may not be the same as reality.
9. Factor X – does it please the customer? Is there an extra attribute of peculiar interest to one customer which may not be of interest to another customer? Price is also an important ingredient in this mix.

Operations also entails reviewing exactly how your organisation appears to all stakeholders, and how it might be improved. Check your organisations premises? decor? location? Does it have a degree of corporate uniformity? Are the internal layout and furnishings attractive? Is it a conducive and stimulating environment for you and your staff to work in? Are you properly resourced in, say IT? Do your customers really feel welcome when they visit?

Action Point Seven:

1. Emphasise to all your staff that total quality management is a key organisational value which can contribute significantly towards the achievement of customer satisfaction and lower costs.
2. Meet with all staff and discuss the importance of getting things right first time. Brainstorm ideas and suggestions. Encourage their involvement by initiating a reward system for the adoption of any of their proposals.

The Action Points given above are not exhaustive, but provide some structure by which added value can be generated to your organisation. From the above points some of the key issues affecting your business could be identified thus:

Key Issues:

Issue	Reason for addressing issue
Strategy and Organisation	
No Strategic Plan	Identifies objectives, establishes long-term vision provides action plan.
No benchmarking	Provides key criteria performance evaluation.
Marketing	
No pro-activity	Too passive and dependent on customers wants.
No marketing plan	Need to create a focused strategy.
Pricing policy	Need to review market position.
Sales	
Too-general sales policy	Produces a too-wide variety of customers who will require differing levels of service and product.
Human Resources	
Lack of delegation	Results in a dilution of expertise.
Operations	
Poor premises	Limited capacity, difficult layout, poor decor.

Finance and Administration

Borrowing too high	Inability to invest. Constraint on new business development.

Embracing these concepts may be akin to a paradigm shift for you and your organisation. Competition is stronger than ever before. Over half the jobs created in the last five years have *not* been full-time, permanent positions. Unemployment is no respecter of class, intellect, sex or race. Organisations are outsourcing both core and peripheral activities more and more. As Sir Michael Heron, former Chairman of The Post Office recently stated, ...*'It's a sobering thought that over 99% of all computer scientists are still alive today'*. Yet despite these huge changes, our attitudes towards work are still entrenched in the economic and social models of the past. We cling to the traditional paradigm of the job because it helps us to define who we are, what our function is and gives our life some structure and purpose. As the traditional job begins to break down and portfolio working takes over, it is hardly surprising we risk social upheaval.

To significantly enhance the value-added for your organisation you will need to create a strong, innovative culture, and establish common values amongst all stakeholders. I see a growing interest in values as a concept and as a legitimate area of management interest and activity. However whilst managers talk about the necessity of creating strong cultures and common values in their organisations, it is also clear that organisations will need transformational leadership that can implement the sort of values that will increase competitiveness in the marketplace. As indicated earlier in this chapter, research suggests that there is a clear, steady, but slow, shift from high estimations of material safety to post-materialism freedom values amongst staff. This implies an increased value is being accorded to the individual's autonomy, well-being and personal development (their needs, motivations and aspirations).

The motive behind the concept of leading by values and creating common values for your organisation is the ambition to increase personal 'well-being' for you and your staff just as much as the ambition to increase efficiency and economic growth for your organisation. Emphasising values such as involvement and commitment should be seen as important because they all support human growth and closer partnerships. But to strive for common values is really important for your organisation because it reflects both human and economic needs = win:win.

However interest in values should not be a one-sided focus on the vision of top management, but an interest in the common values that grow from within and from below the organisation. This implies that the methods used to create common values must also reflect an innovative and process-orientated way of working which allows as many staff as possible to become actively involved. To lead such a far-reaching and profound operation requires leaders who can liberate powers of learning and change in a pro-active way. Richard Branson attributes

Virgin's success to: ... 'good ideas, motivated staff and a real understanding of consumer needs.'

Creativity starts with the unrestricted flow of thoughts into reality. To ensure that all stakeholders are engaged in this paradigm shift provides both extensive opportunities and extensive risks. Talk about values is often well-meaning, embracing lots of words and concepts which people think have positive connotations. But a note of warning – if the talk does not correspond to the factual behaviour within your organisation then it may instead generate a great deal of disappointment and frustration. Empty rhetoric may result in your losing credibility; staff beginning to resent and manipulate in their turn against management; and, the organisations human energy taking a totally different direction from that which you originally intended or hoped. But if you get it right, the output in both creative ideas and productivity can result in $-1+1=3$!! Human resource management can either be planned or emergent – regardless you must link business strategy to human performance!

Action Point Eight:

1. To establish a high performance workplace YOU must formulate and implement the correct values and establish the correct organisational 'culture'. Remember to 'walk the talk'.
2. Create the resources (time and space) for mutual reflection and increased organisational consciousness so that all stakeholders from the bottom-up can identify with the common values of your company.
3. Inspire groups and liberate individuals to reflect, possibly via brain-storming, on creating conditions for common values and common visions to grow from within the organisation. Use the Thomas International Personal Profile Analysis to provide an insight as to your key staffs needs, motivations and aspirations. (Such a strategy for change is, however, a long term task – not a quick fix!)

Any debate within your organisation about power, influence and control should shift to a debate about value creation. Value creation begins not with what happens inside a group, but with what the group's users or customers receives from it. Value should be defined by the receiver not by the giver of services. You as a manager must learn to create value not as you perceive it, but much more importantly as your colleagues and other stakeholders perceive it. The key question must be: What value can my work create for this business to add value for our customers in economic terms? Starting with this question shifts the focus from what is done to what is delivered. By sharing power and delegating some control, management expresses implicit trust in their employees ability to do a job well as well as providing them with the motivation to achieve personal, and thereby corporate, success. As long as employees understand and are committed to your organisations goals decision regarding the means of adding value, your goals can be shared and the organisation will benefit from real value-added. Business activity should always be reducible to a fundamental business proposition based on creating value for customers in economically viable ways. Managers must create a value proposition aligning business practices to commercial realities – serving customers, meeting deadlines, making profits, leveraging technology, and satisfying investors. This is not a new call to arms – this message has been stated in many forms for the last thirty years. But it is time for you as a manager to stop talking and make it happen.

Management investment in the future must focus increasingly on value creation and on developing a value equation for your organisations services and products.

The *following matrix* identifies the issues and needs of AnyCo Ltd on the vertical axis and the business needs or solutions to these issues and needs along the horizontal axis. An indication has been given as to the direct benefit and cost of implementing these solutions. The figures indicated should be treated as a guide only and would need to be agreed as part of a detailed terms of reference with the person(s) responsible for their implementation

Issues/Needs \ Business Needs	Strategic planning	Benchmarking	Recruit new CEO	Customer survey	Management Information	Corporate finance	Investment in premises	Training	Teambuilding	Marketing plan	Financial forecasting
No strategic plan	✓										
No benchmarking		✓									
Lack of delegation	✓		✓					✓	✓		
Inconsistent marketing		✓		✓	✓					✓	
Limited scope for growth	✓	✓	✓	✓			✓			✓	✓
Sole income source	✓		✓	✓			✓			✓	✓
Lack of skills in management			✓					✓	✓		
Poor utilisation of resources	✓				✓		✓	✓		✓	
Low customer numbers	✓	✓		✓			✓			✓	
Uncertainty about use of assets	✓			✓		✓				✓	
High level of borrowing	✓					✓					✓
Layout/decor of premises	✓			✓			✓				
Resistance to change			✓					✓	✓		
Under investment	✓				✓	✓	✓				✓

Entreprise Value Enhancement	£486,000 *										
Annual costs £'s	5,000		50,000		2,000	500	45,000	10,000		5,000	
One-off cost £'s		1,500	5,000	2,000		1,000			2,000		

* The organisational value enhancement figure is arrived at by multiplying the estimated sustainable profit that these actions will generate by a price earnings multiple applicable to the size and type of business (i.e.: say 4 times for a small group).

Summary

Key factors for success in making change happen and adding real value:

1   Leading change (*who* is responsible) – are you a leader who owns and champions the change?: who publicly commits to making it happen?: who will garner the resources necessary to sustain it?: who will put in the personal time and attention necessary to follow it through?
2   Creating a shared need (*why* do it) – do your staff see the reason for change?: understand why change is important?: see how it will help them and your business in the short -and long term?: how it will add real value to their input and the organisations success?
3   Shaping the vision (*what* will it look like in the future) – can your staff appreciate and accept the outcomes?: get excited about the results of accomplishing the change?: understand how the changes will benefit all stakeholders?
4   Mobilise commitment (*who else* needs to be involved) – as sponsor of this value added change, do you know how to build a coalition of support?:have the ability to enlist the support of key staff?: have the ability to build a responsibility matrix to make the change happen?
5   Modify systems and structures (*how* will it be institutionalised) – do you recognise the systems implications of the change?
6   Monitoring progress (*how* will it be measured) – have you a means of measuring the success of the change?: plan to benchmark progress as suggested on both the results of the change and the process of implementing the change?
7   Making it last (*how* will it get started and last) – do you now recognise the first steps in getting started?: have short- and long-term plan to keep attention focused on the change and value being added?: have a plan to adapting to further change in the future?

References:

Ackoff. R L (1986) *Management in Small Doses*. Wiley
Campbell. A (1989) *Research findings discussed in Skapinger (1989) Mission accomplished or ignored?* F.T. January 11th
Cane. S (1996) *Kaizen Strategies*. Pitman
Mitchell. A (1997) *Passion Brands*. Marketing Business October '97
Pearson. G (1995) *Integrity in Organisations*. Pearson
Reis. A and Trout. J (1986) *Marketing Warfare*. McGraw Hill
Trollestad. C (1998) *In Search of the existential leader*. MBA April 1998
Thompson. J (1993) *Strategic Management*. Chapman and Hall
Ulrich. D (1997) *Human Resource Champions*. HBS

4 Performance Appraisals – A tool for a better business

The Case for Performance Appraisal?

Nearly all of the Companies I work with claim to have an appraisal system already. On closer inspection however, you find that they have succeeded only in creating a bureaucratic process, which once a year obliges managers to interrupt their daily work to complete lengthy forms for the Personnel Department. The tiresome task complete, they return to their real work, and the forms are filed away until next year's appraisal meetings. If this description rings a bell with you, then it is certain that you are not getting the best from your appraisal process.

If you are prepared to rethink your ideas about appraisal, you will discover that this is a fantastic way of providing you with essential management information on staff performance, allowing you to track company progress against planned strategic milestones. It is also the springboard for improving on current business performance, getting more from staff and establishing a culture of positive achievement. What more could you want?

I prefer to talk about '*performance* appraisal' rather than just 'appraisal'. This small change in title is significant in that it immediately focuses the mind on what is being appraised. One senior manager in a client company recently commented that he had only thought of appraisals as 'a form you filled in for Personnel, to justify giving your staff a pay increase . . . or not'. He went on to say that the discussion we had that day about *performance* appraisal had started him thinking about the possibilities for using the process in a very different way.

In fact, of all the companies I have worked with now, there are three characteristics of those that are most successful in getting the best from their staff.

> **People Perform Best When...**
> 1 Managers are positive about staff performance and actively encourage staff to exceed their current standards, providing guidance, support and training as necessary
> 2 The company has an atmosphere of achievement, through systematically recognising good performance and positive reinforcement of successful behaviours
> 3 Managers operate an effective performance appraisals process, using it as a mechanism for linking business goals with staff targets and as a framework for regular feedback on progress

I am often asked 'What do we need a performance appraisal system for?'

Before I answer the question, I sometimes reply, 'Do you have a financial management system in your company? Do you have financial plans and set budgets? Do you track and regularly produce reports on your financial performance – by cost centre, department and overall for the company? What do you think would happen if you set out at the beginning of the year without any plans or budgets; you didn't check your bank statements as they came in; you didn't track sales or expenditure and only looked at how the company performed at the end of the financial year?'

Naturally, they are shocked at the prospect. They laugh off the suggestion as reckless and say of course that could never happen – no business could work that way and hope to survive.

I then ask them to compare the size of their salaries and wages bill with other overheads in the business. For many businesses, this can be the largest overhead by a long way and yet it is all too often neglected in terms of management. Where are the plans and budgets? How often is performance against target tracked, reported and acted upon? Is an annual appraisal, carried out in an inconsistent and lukewarm way the best way to assess staff performance?

Smart, energetic and committed managers do not always see the need for having plans, targets and regular monitoring of performance of the company's most expensive investment – staff. Even in companies where they are working on very small margins and every element of cost has to be monitored carefully, I have been surprised by the lack of attention paid to improving the return on investment made on the greatest cost item in the production process – the people.

Why is this? Well, unfortunately most people's experience of appraisal systems is not altogether positive and the reasons for that are many and varied.

- **There is often a lack of commitment from Senior Management**

As a Solicitor from a high profile firm remarked to me recently, 'We are supposed to have regular, annual appraisal meetings. The Personnel Department do their best to make sure everyone has an appraisal meeting, but some of the Partners are not very switched on about it. Some people don't have their meetings at all.'

- **It can be hard work**

When I talked to her about it all, the legal firm's beleaguered Personnel Manager replied, 'It is hard to get folk to understand that there is quite a lot of work involved in putting together a decent (..Performance Appraisal..) system. It isn't just about putting together a questionnaire and ticking boxes every year. You have to think what you want to get out of it and you have to keep it going – keep working at it.'

- **It is often seen as extra work for over-loaded managers**

Lack of time is most often given as the reason why managers don't instigate regular reviews of staff performance. They see it as separate from their daily operational responsibilities. If they don't see the value of it, carrying out appraisals takes a very low position on the list of priorities.

- **Lack of training, both for Appraisers and Appraisees can undermine the process**

The good news in fact, is that much of the discomfort and disappointment that people feel with appraisals can be overcome with some relevant training, support and practice in how to use Performance Appraisals to the advantage of everyone concerned.

- **Managers can be very sceptical about the value of appraisals**

'After the annual appraisal meeting, you forget what you've said and there's never any follow through. You are given your aims, but you don't look at them until the next year! At my meeting with my Manager, we took out the forms with the aims on, shrugged our shoulders at each other and laughed!' This was one reaction when I asked a group of team leaders at a Workshop, how important appraisals were to them in managing their teams.

Yet despite all this reticence, the performance of staff is the most consistent source of irritation and anxiety amongst the managers with whom I have worked. When I asked the same group of team leaders how they would characterise the performance of their staff, they said 'well, it's a bit sporadic – you know, up and down; they don't use their initiative; they don't think about the consequences of their actions; they aren't as committed as they should be; they work hard, but not smart'; and so on.

It was clear to me that knowing more about effective Performance Appraisal could provide a framework for tackling the frustrations of managing their staff and for getting more out of the situation.

What can Performance Appraisal do for you?

Performance Appraisal is a business management process, which allows you to:

- be clear about where you want your business to be in the next 3, 5, or 10 years and to describe what that will mean in terms that are meaningful to you – market share, brand position, financial performance, profile in your industry, etc.
- decide which are the critical activities that you must achieve in order to reach your goal and prioritise these for action by your staff
- set yourself some specific milestones, interim goals and targets in order to 'pace out' your progress towards the longer term aim
- give clear and specific direction to your staff about what needs to be achieved in the short, medium and long-term, in order to maintain a steady, incremental progress towards the business goals
- discuss these goals, priorities and activities with staff and agree what their contribution to delivering the necessary progress
- monitor individual and team progress regularly against agreed milestones and revise your overall, strategic course of action, based on good quality management information
- provide appropriate support, guidance and training to enable staff to deliver the required results and to improve on their performance

---

The basic concept is that the cumulative performance of each of your employees adds up to your overall business performance. In other words, what employees work on each day either contributes to, or detracts from progress towards your corporate goals. Anything which improves the individual's ability to deliver will have a positive impact on the business.

Integrating your Performance Appraisal system, which is integrated with your business objectives, is the approach which is most likely to result in an improvement in the bottom line for the company.

```
                Business Plan  <-->  Company HR Plan
                     |                      |
                     v                      v
              Strategic Goals      Manpower Requirements
                     |                      |
                     v                      v
          Departmental Objectives    Competency Framework
                      \                    /
                       \                  /
                        > Individual Performance Plan <
                          Operational Targets
                          Developmental Actions
                              - professional
                              - personal

              Improve                       Monitor
                  ^     (Performance Appraisal)    |
                  |                                v
                         Feedback  <---  Review
```

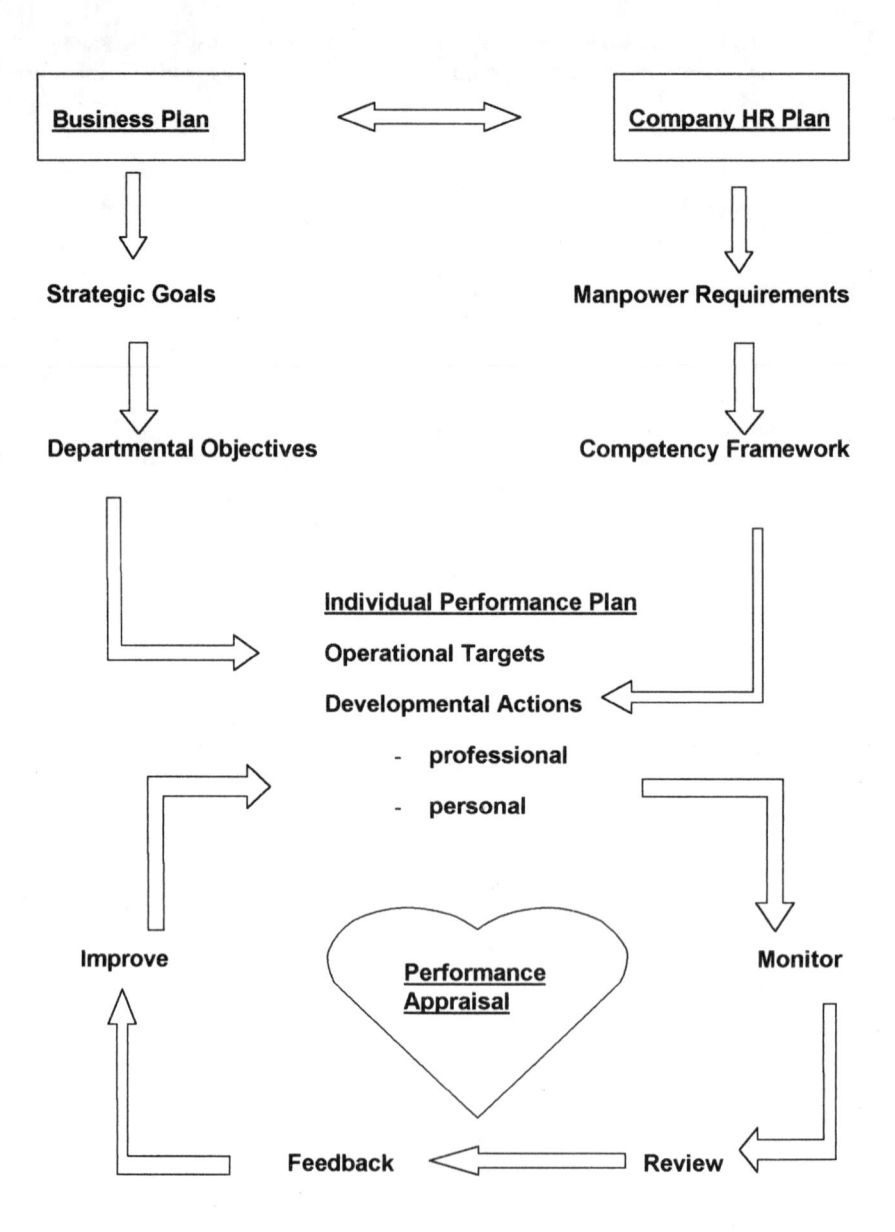

Figure 1: The Performance Appraisal Cascade
This illustrates how the relationship between the business goals and individual performance acts a vehicle for converting strategic plans into action by your staff.

Elements of Successful Performance Appraisals, A Case Study

This situation illustrates a number of important lessons when it comes to really embedding the performance appraisal process and making it work for you.

> 📖 **Case Study**
>
> Recently, I received a phone call from the Chief Executive of a local company I had worked with a number of years ago advising on a restructuring of his operational teams, facilitating team development workshops and reviewing his HR strategy in the light of his new 3-year Business Plan. I had also designed a new performance management system, to support implementation of the strategic plans made by the Management Team.
>
> He wanted to talk to me about the round of staff appraisals that were due to be held over the next two months.
>
> Following my initial work with them, the process had worked really well. Everyone was 'up to speed' and the quality of management information was much better. However, in the last two to three years, there had been a number of changes amongst the Managers, both in the Senior Management Team and at Area Manager level. A couple of people had left the company, with replacements being recruited from outside, and there had been some internal promotions.
>
> Some of the new Managers did not have as firm a focus on the benefits of the performance appraisal process and this was starting to cause some concern. Staff who reported to these managers were experiencing a fall-off in the number of informal conversations about their performance. They were used to these chats, finding them helpful. The quality of discussion at Management Team meetings, about progress being made, felt increasingly 'woolly' and generalised. Excuses for delays in meeting agreed deadlines were becoming more frequent.
>
> One of the Managers had come from a company where the attitude to appraisals was pretty haphazard and he had been heard making a few cynical remarks about the process. The worry was that this would start to have an adverse effect upon his team and that this attitude might undermine the commitment of the other Managers.
>
> All in all, the CEO felt that it was time to revisit the system and hold some training Workshops for the Managers. The objective is to give everyone the same understanding of the process – how it works and the benefits it can bring. We will also plan out the timetable for the appraisal meetings with staff. A 'Wash-Up Workshop' will follow, when the Managers will discuss the outputs of the meetings with team members and analyse the consequences for the Business Plan Review and for next year's Training Programme.

Elements of Successful Performance Appraisals: Lessons to be Learned

Reflecting on this situation, several clear messages emerge. In order to acheive and maintain a successful performance appraisal system you must ensure that the following elements are in place.

- **Strong, overt support for the system from top management**

You really do need 'buy-in' from the top. If the CEO and the Senior Management team understand and actively support the process, this sends the right messages to the rest of the company. They have to 'Walk the Talk' – be seen to value the system and to use the information it yields.

- **Active participation and involvement of staff being appraised**

In my experience, staff find a well-run appraisal process really motivating. They understand the direction the business is taking and their role in getting there. The opportunity to discuss current priorities and work progress within a generally accepted structure provides a very important focus.

- **Appropriate training and support for everyone involved**

Certain skills ensure that the process works effectively. Training in these skills – listening, questioning, coaching, facilitating, etc – should be provided at the outset, if a new performance appraisal process is being introduced. Top-up training is a good idea for renewing commitment and sustaining the quality of the process.

- **High level of commitment from line managers**

The line managers in an organisation are key people in initiating and sustaining change. They are the people who convert strategic aims into day-to-day priorities and action. They are the drivers in ensuring that operations stay on course. Line managers feed information about problems, progress and successes back to senior management. They can 'make or break' a process.

- **A corporate culture that recognises of good performance**

Where dialogue about performance is part and parcel of the daily management practices in a company, this promotes a general awareness amongst staff of the importance of consistently good performance. A sense of working towards common goals can be reinforced by regular reference to goals, targets and progress.

• Positive, constructive action to remedy unsatisfactory performance

It takes time to develop and integrate skills effectively into working practices. Managers need to understand the nature of the learning curve. Coaching, relevant training and other developmental actions are tools at the disposal of managers to improve an individual's performance. Whatever the solution, feedback needs to be immediate and remedial action swift to be effective.

• Decisive follow through on outcomes from performance appraisal meetings

Don't 'let the side down' by a sloppy approach to following up after performance appraisal meetings. Move quickly and positively to take action as agreed. Taken all together, the information produced at these meetings adds up to business performance. Arrange to discuss the implications of aggregated performance so that outcomes are quickly translated into training plans and Business Plan input.

Benefits of Using Good Performance Appraisal

The figures in a study called 'Performance Management in the UK', undertaken for the Institute of Personnel Management in 1992, the experiences of a variety of companies using performance appraisal were documented. In that report, the reasons the companies gave for using it were:

Purpose	*% of Companies*
☑ Improve organisational efficiency	85
☑ Motivate employees	57
☑ Improve training and development	54
☑ Change culture	54
☑ Link pay to productivity	50
☑ Attract and retain specialists	45
☑ Support TQM	36
☑ Link pay to skills development	16
☑ Manage wage bill	14

Source: IPM Study, 'Performance Management in the UK', 1992

The results of the study are heartening. Increasingly, businesses are using performance management systems to communicate strategic goals and reinforce key messages about company values. A greater degree of integration between the strategic direction of the business and the 'stuff' of day to day operations is producing more focused business activity in the short-term, and greater corporate efficiency in the long-term.

It is also interesting to note the use of performance management as a motivational tool. Evidence is very strong that employees respond positively, given clear and consistent messages about what the company expects of them, in terms of job responsibilities, operational goals and recognised standards of performance. This is particularly true when employees have been directly involved in developing job descriptions, agreeing their goals and designing competency standards.

As someone once said, 'I know that half of my advertising budget is wasted, the trouble is I don't know which half'; the same can be true of training budgets. Access to training is regarded by many as a perk of the job. Furthermore, training opportunities are often provided as a menu, from which the employee selects a course which sounds appealing. So, in these circumstances, it is highly probable that inappropriate training activity takes place, without reference to an identified skills gap which impacts on job performance. This lack of focus is potentially further exacerbated in the workplace, where newly acquired skills are not put to immediate use and so are lost.

The quality of information about jobs and the skills required for effective performance produced through sound performance management has a positive effect on other 'people-related' issues such as induction, recruitment & selection, training & development and succession planning.

The Facts

The experiences of people who are working in a 'live' way with these processes always provides compelling evidence. So, I decided to ask some employees in client companies what *they* thought were the benefits of having a performance appraisal system. Some of them are managers with responsibility for appraising others' performance; some are employees who are appraised.

Here's what they had to say..

- "My staff show a high level of commitment. They have a strong belief in delivering a high quality service to our clients. They are really keen to develop their professional skills.

    The performance appraisal system gives staff a chance to sit down on a one-to-one basis with their manager and discuss their individual needs. We use the system to regularly review the company's progress against three levels of plan – the individual's plan, the team plan and the annual company training plan. We also now have a Learning Resource Library to support the development of individuals learning needs throughout the company.

If you ask me to summarise, I would say – Appraisals are essential to managing staff properly".

- "Overall, I think our appraisal system is a good thing. It gives an opportunity to say certain things in a 2-way process – give feedback on things that would otherwise not be addressed.

    I think more consciously now about giving feedback and motivating staff, which I didn't always do before. I always think about the Sandwich Technique for giving feedback – say something positive about the person, then talk about the thing you are concerned about, finishing up with a positive at the end, like a new approach or training. And something encouraging to motivate them. I use this all the time and it definitely works.

    Another thing – I never talk about 'I' now. I always use 'We'. It felt a bit funny at first, but you get used to it and people respond better because it doesn't feel so 'Us' and 'Them'."

- "This is going to sound more negative than I mean it to, but having an appraisal system is better than nothing in managing performance. It does force you to sit down and think about things you wouldn't normally bother about too often, like personal development – skills such as my marketing or financial management. I think it does give the Partners information in a reasonably formal way about how you think you're doing. It makes you focus on certain aspects of your job and gives a chance for views to be aired."

- "We are supposed to have interim meetings where we keep tabs on things and this year, we did it for the first time. We made the date there and then at the appraisal meeting for 3 months later, so it was in our diaries. Actually it was quite good, if only to remind me that I hadn't been following up, but I still had time to do some things I'd agreed to do. I do think it should be more than just an annual opportunity to talk about development, and things you agree to do should happen and be tracked more often."

- "What do I get out of it? Well for me personally, I get to know how my boss thinks I'm getting on. I mean, you could toddle along all year, thinking everything is hunky-dory and not knowing that the firm doesn't really think you're developing. Also you get feedback on what's expected of you and you get to ask what progress should I be making? The company can find out what my aspirations are and I can flag up where I would want more challenging work. From the company's point of view, there is no point in putting the entire onus on the individual for development. The appraisal system is part of meeting their responsibility in supporting their staff's performance."

Assessing Individual Performance

Assessing a person's performance is sometimes regarded a something of a 'black art'. The question of pinning down what constitutes 'effective performance' is complex – there are no simple forms that can be filled in to give a complete picture.

Pieces of the jigsaw that make up 'performance impact' include:

- technical knowledge which is relevant for the job
- personal attributes which enables the individual to satisfy the job requirements
- interaction with colleagues in the same team and other departments
- relationship with clients, both internal and external
- relationship with suppliers
- perception of subordinates and peers, as well as managers

Sources of Information

It is true to say that the majority of companies tend to rely heavily, if not exclusively, on the perceptions of direct line managers in assessing staff performance. The difficulty with this approach is that a person's performance assessment is entirely in the hands of one person, who may lack the necessary skills and experience to do justice to the process.

Compiling a composite picture of an individual's performance means eliciting information, in as structured a way as possible. You may want to consider using some of the following sources for gathering data about staff performance:

- Client Feedback Sheets
- Customer Survey
- Telephone Follow-up
- 360° Feedback (Manager, Peers, Subordinates, 'Customers')
- Peer Assessment
- Manager Review
- Self-Assessment
- Assessment tools (ability tests, personality questionnaires)
- Assessment and Development Centres

Some large companies have designed models for assessing performance combining most, or all of these techniques. The model can be as sophisticated and systematised, as you like. For many smaller companies, the need is for simplicity and clarity in a system that produces useful information.

Training for everyone involved

For employees whose job performance will be appraised, explain their role in achieving a productive performance appraisal include:
- the performance appraisal process, forms used, etc
- the appraisee's role and responsibilities
- the preparation work prior to the Performance Review Meeting
- identify the skills for use in the Performance Review Meeting

Short Workshops for groups of staff members are useful vehicles for this.

For Managers who will be responsible for carrying out performance reviews, it is essential that they are given relevant training before taking on the task. Essential skills such as listening, questioning, giving feedback, coaching, and so on take time and practice to hone. Initial training should include plenty of opportunities to rehearse the skills of performance review, with support and feedback from a more experienced manager, or trained consultant.

Performance Appraisal Meeting

The Performance Appraisal Meeting remains the most popular mechanism for reviewing staff performance in a formal way.

The quality of feedback that is shared in the Performance Appraisal is vital to its success. It is worth your while to invest in developing the skill of all those involved, whether they will be appraising others, or being appraised themselves.

If you follow these Golden Rules for Successful Performance Review Meetings, you will feel more in control of the process and that staff will respond in a positive way.

Golden Rules for Successful Performance Review Meetings
- ★ Prepare Carefully
- ★ Plan For A Productive Meeting
- ★ Be Specific About Successes And Failures
- ★ Concentrate on Performance, not Personality
- ★ Aim for Dialogue
- ★ Listen and Ask Questions
- ★ Be Constructive
- ★ Talk about the future as well as the past
- ★ Follow through

Golden Rules for Successful Performance Review Meetings

1 **Prepare Carefully**
   - Be very familiar with the individual's targets
   - Gather the evidence and information upon which you are basing your assessment of the person's performance
   - Thoroughly review all elements of the person's performance and make your notes in advance of the meeting

2 **Plan For A Productive Meeting**
   - Allow adequate time for the meeting, which could be 1–1½ hours. If it turns out that this is not enough, arrange a second meeting, rather than rush through the process.
   - Ensure that your meeting will be free from interruptions. Divert calls and ask not to be disturbed.
   - Think about the physical layout of the room and aim for a semi-formal seating arrangement – not 'coffee table' relaxed, but not sitting facing each other over a table, either. Perhaps side by side at a table or at an angle to each other at one end of a table.

3 **Be Specific About Successes And Failures**
   - Give examples of events which demonstrate the person's achievements or which illustrate areas of concern
   - Avoid using meaningless generalisations which do not add to the person's understanding of what they did that was effective, or what they need to change for the future
   - Aim for an appropriate balance of praise and criticism. It is easy to find yourself dwelling on things that have not gone well, when in fact the person has performed well overall.

4 **Concentrate on Performance, not Personality**
   - In discussion of areas of concern, base your comments on the outcome or results of the person's performance, using specific examples to illustrate or substantiate your views.
   - Confine your assessment to the person's approach or results, rather than making personal remarks.
   - Avoid being drawn into emotive exchanges about performance. Choose your words carefully in order to make your point clearly, but without being offensive or accusing in your tone.

5 **Aim for Dialogue**
   - Try to explore the individual's perspective on issues affecting their performance, suspending your judgement until you feel you understand their point of view

The Pillars of Successful Management

- Aim for a greater level of shared understanding about goals and development needs, by asking lots of probing questions and reflecting back your understanding
- The review meeting should be conducted as a 2-way dialogue. In fact the appraiser should aim to speak for less than 50% of the time.

6   **Listen and Ask Questions**
- Pay close attention to what the individual says about their own performance. Keep your body language 'quiet' and maintain steady eye contact. Encourage the person to speak with occasional nods and verbal prompts, 'uh-huh, yes, I see', etc.
- Don't be too quick to offer your opinion. Instead ask questions to encourage the individual to reflect on their own performance. This is much more powerful in developing their understanding.
- Ask the individual what they think would help improve their performance and in what way.

7   **Be Constructive**
- Remember the 'Good – Bad – Good Sandwich'. Begin with a positive comment, then introduce your area of concern, and then finish by agreeing on a positive course of action, to remedy the situation.
- Be certain that your intentions are focussed on ensuring that the person leaves the meeting with a clear understanding of how they have performed and what they are expected to do following the meeting.
- If there are areas for improvement, make sure the person knows specifically what they need to do to improve, by when. Involve them in deciding on appropriate action.

8   **Talk about the future as well as the past**
- Use the Performance Appraisal Meeting as an opportunity to reconnect the individual with the bigger picture. Remind them of where their contribution fits in with company goals and speak enthusiastically about what can be achieved by continuous improvement in everyone's performance.
- Explore the individual's aspirations for their professional career progression and for their own personal development.
- Agree challenging opportunities for them to stretch their skills, with coaching and support

9   **Follow through**
- Plan the dates for your next performance review meeting, before you leave.
- Keep a written record of points of agreement and action. Honour any promises you make during the performance review meeting
- Commit to ongoing, informal feedback between formal performance review meetings

Structure of the Performance Appraisal Meeting

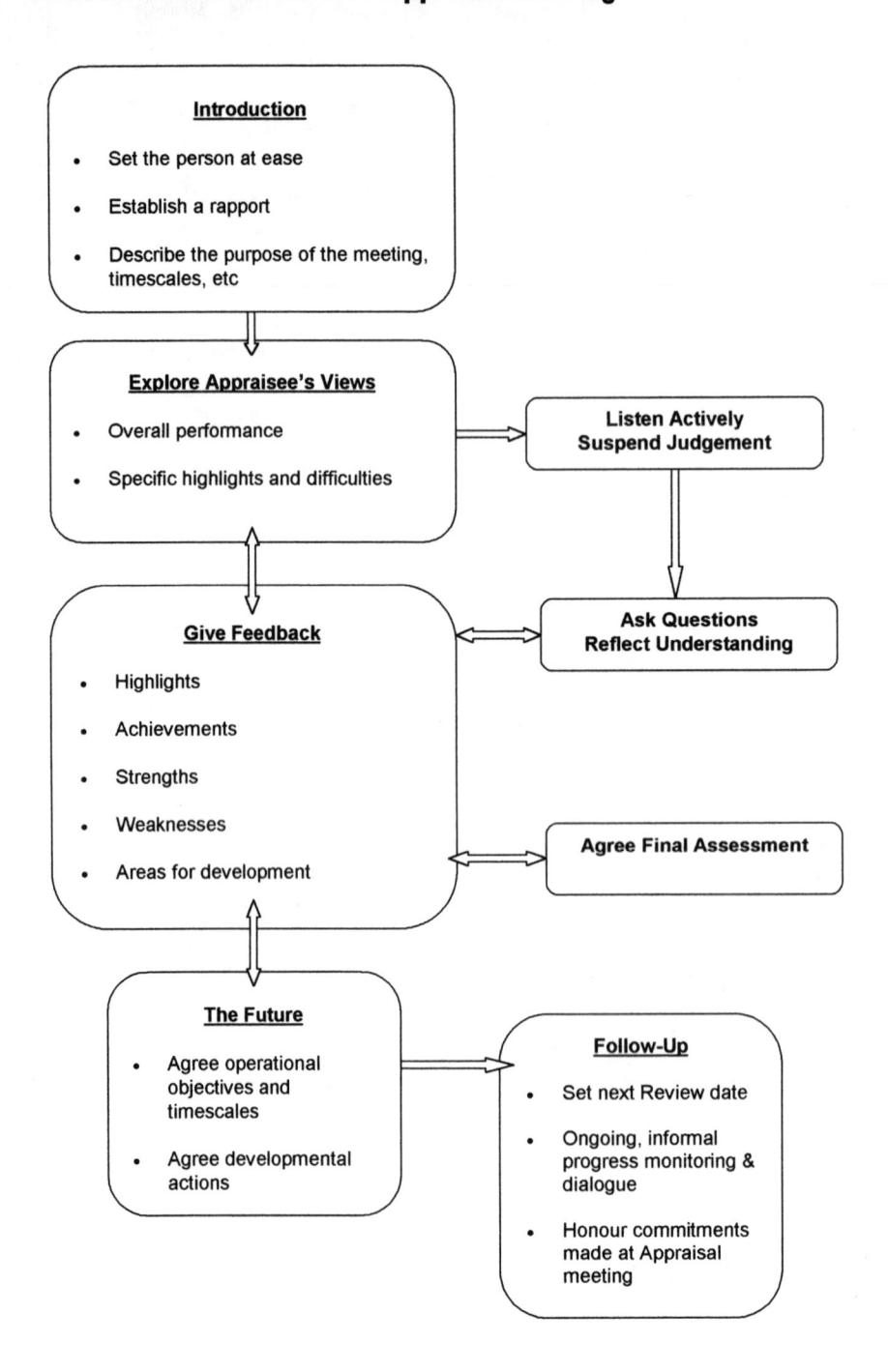

Introduction
- Set the person at ease
- Establish a rapport
- Describe the purpose of the meeting, timescales, etc

Explore Appraisee's Views
- Overall performance
- Specific highlights and difficulties

Listen Actively / Suspend Judgement

Ask Questions / Reflect Understanding

Give Feedback
- Highlights
- Achievements
- Strengths
- Weaknesses
- Areas for development

Agree Final Assessment

The Future
- Agree operational objectives and timescales
- Agree developmental actions

Follow-Up
- Set next Review date
- Ongoing, informal progress monitoring & dialogue
- Honour commitments made at Appraisal meeting

20 Essential Questions for the Performance Appraisal Meeting

1. How do you feel you've performed overall this year?
2. Are you satisfied with your performance in this area? Specifically in terms of output/ quality/ cost/ timescales/ relationship management.?
3. What went particularly well during that project?
4. What was the most difficult part? What problems did you encounter? Can you give me an example?
5. Tell me about this issue/ situation...
6. Describe what happened...
7. Describe your feelings/ reaction when that happened.
8. How did you handle the situation? Did that work? Why/ Why not?
9. What did you learn from that experience? What will you do from now on to make sure it happens that way every time/ it doesn't happen that way again?
10. What part of your job do you most/ least enjoy? Why?
11. What have you achieved that you are most proud of? What have you found most/ least challenging, interesting, rewarding? Can you give me an example?
12. Has there been anything you feel you didn't handle so well? What happened? What was your part in all of that? Looking back, what would you do differently? Is there anything you could have done to change the outcome?
13. If you were giving advice to someone in the same situation, what would it be?
14. How would a better system of (e.g. follow-up) impact on your effectiveness in this area?
15. What improvements could you make to the way you prepare for meetings/ follow-up on sales leads/ manage your daily priorities?
16. What skills development/ training/ information would help you to do this better?
17. What factors have helped/ hindered your performance in this area?
18. Would it be fair/ accurate to summarise the situation in this way? Do you have anything to add to that before we move on?
19. Can we agree on the following actions that you will take and that I will take? Let's put a deadline on that now.
20. When shall we meet again to review your progress with everything we have agreed today?

12 Keys to Performance Apraisals

If you have decided to set up your own system, I would recommend the following actions. These are based on my experience and also on comments made by managers in other companies, who want to pass on their advice to you:

- Have clear-cut objectives for the system. Decide why you want an Appraisal system and what it is you want to get out of it. Make sure it will add value to what you already do. This is critical – if you don't know what you want from the process, how will you know if you have it?
- The foundation for effective performance appraisal lies in having clear business objectives and linking these to individual targets.
- Look at what you already have by way of 'feedback'. You may already have a process or system that you can base your appraisal system on. For example, you may already use Client Evaluation Forms, which are a useful source of feedback on performance. Include the comments on these in the overall appraisal of someone's performance.
- Don't reinvent the wheel. Go out and visit or speak to other companies who have appraisal systems and see how they do it. Learn from their experiences.
- Involve your staff in designing the system and in deciding how it will be taken forward and used. That way they are more likely to understand it, why it's important and they will use it properly. Ownership breeds commitment.
- Train Appraisers in the skills needed to make the system work well. Explain how it works and why they need to apply it in a certain way. In particular make sure that the Appraisers are all reviewing staff performance in a consistent way.
- Include Performance Appraisal as a target or key result area for all Managers. This way, you will reinforce the significance of the system, as well as lay the foundation for consistent application throughout the company. Make sure you appraise your Managers on their ability to use the system and help improve *their* performance.
- Hold a series of 'Familiarisation Workshops' for staff at the outset. Let staff see you are being 'up front' with them about the process and that you want them to benefit as much as the company will.
- Review performance regularly throughout the year. Don't let it become a 'drudge task' that happens once a year.
- Timetable a strategic review session at the end of the formal round of performance review meetings. Discuss and analyse the implications of the results of the meetings for future priorities and business direction. Build this into your Business Plan, Operating Plan and Company HR Plan.

- It is important to remember that appraisals are only one component of overall performance management. Consider developing the range of sources of data you use to assess performance in the future
- Finally, remember that, if you're not managing your people's performance, and helping them to improve the way they deliver results for you, what is it you are managing at the end of the day?

5 How to produce a team of "Want to" people

Setting The Scene

Do you have people working for you?

Would you rather have people working **with** you? Displaying the same enthusiasm and commitment to the job as you do? Ha! You may be thinking, if only, but it's not possible.

By the end of this chapter, you will have learnt the essential strategies that will allow you to begin the process of creating a team of 'want to' people. People who work with real purpose. People who consistently work to their personal best. People who work conscientiously. People who actually feel a part of and proud of being a member of your team.

I intend to take you through this chapter as though you were attending one of my high impact training and coaching events. And what I am about to share with you is tried and tested. I can honestly vouch for every one of these techniques, strategies and attitudes because I used them with great success when I managed teams in Blue-chip companies myself. And for the last 12 years I have been training all management levels throughout industry the same skills. My feedback research also tells me just how successful they are.

Oddly enough, whenever I do my follow-up visits my delegates often remark that the technique that I taught them and coached them in actually worked. They are genuinely and happily surprised that something so simple and easy is so effective and powerful. I remind them of my opening statement at all of my training events.

"I will never teach you anything that is purely theory only. I will always show you, give you the 'how to' because that is what really counts. Knowing it is only half the job done, using what you know completes the process. And as I will be visiting you after this training event it is in my interests to ensure that what I teach you can be used successfully where it really matters, back in the workplace."

Through this chapter, you will learn the core principle of the whole process of creating a 'want to' team. Earning respect. Respect, as we know, is the trigger that motivates people to co-operate with one another, to support one another, to go that extra mile for one another.

Unfortunately, respect is intangible and misunderstood. I've come across countless Team Leaders, Supervisors and Managers of all levels of seniority who believe that they can either command respect or that it is an automatic right issued with the management position.

As you will also learn, your beliefs are your reality, so when the anticipated respect fails to materialise, you often go into blame mode. Your internal dialogue tells you that the team you've been given to manage obviously need some respect *managed* into them. And it is from this point that the job of managing people becomes the stressful and often thankless task that so many currently experience.

Your daily working life becomes littered with conflict, confrontation, other people's problems and a constant battle to get the job done on time and within budget. So, open your mind for the next few pages and allow me to guide and coach you to a better, more successful and rewarding management experience. Follow my tactics and I promise that you will not be disappointed.

Let's go

The Learning Agenda

Over the following pages, I will take you through five areas, which I have found to be critical in creating and maintaining a team of 'want to' people. Those five essential areas will be:

1   Understand You People
2   How To Turn Motivation Theory Into Practice
3   Establishing A Climate For Team Success
4   Practising The Characteristics Of Effective Teams
5   Creating A 'Want To' Team Strategy

At the end of the this chapter you may well have some points of your own you would like to make, perhaps you would like some clarification or other questions answered. You will have the opportunity to do this by calling me and I will endeavour to help and assist you as best I can.

Starting With The Basics ~ Understanding People

Every team consists of a number of human beings, and each one of these human beings is unique. They have needs and wants that they look to have satisfied. If we can tap into these needs and wants then we can plug into a stream of positive energy. After all, it is focused human energy you need in order to complete the objectives you have been set.

For most people though, this sadly does not happen. Their needs and wants remain undiscovered and ignored They come into work day after day purely because they have to. They need the money to live. Your department just happens to be where they currently receive their financial income. With 'have to' people their loyalty extends no further than this. And because we human beings are primarily reactionary creatures, we will react to this type of attitude and its associated behaviours. And by so doing, worsen the situation.

So, how do we break this vicious circle of negativity?

I'll be honest with you; it's no overnight job. However, it is not impossible and talking from personal experience and the experience of many managers that I have coached in this area, it is not as hard it may at first appear. We do, however, need to do a little preparation and knowledge building.

It is a proven fact, that in order to successfully manage others we need to be able to manage ourselves. But, even before we get to this stage, we need to understand the basics of human behaviours. Why do people do the things they do?

When people do the things they do, whether good working practices or bad, they always do them for a reason. People do not do things in a vacuum or isolation to anything else that is happening around them and to them. For instance, a team member starts working less conscientiously and with less enthusiasm and commitment. We notice this and with a frown, we wonder why this should be.

Usually nothing is done about it for a time. Or, we react as we feel a manager or supervisor should, you come down hard and attempt to nip it in the bud. Whichever route you take the problem remains and usually gets worse.

If we take a look at the first choice; by ignoring the changed behaviour, we are in effect condoning it. After all most people in the workplace work to the premise that if whatever they are doing is wrong then they will get told, or shouted at soon enough. This is basic one-way workplace communication. Foul-up and you sure know it, do the job well and you're left alone.

Looking at the second choice; if you choose not to ignore it, but instead you react to the changed behaviour, then in most cases our reaction will be inappropriate. Why? Simply because you react to the symptoms not the cause. What symptoms? Well, remembering that none of us behave in a vacuum, something has happened to create the behaviour change. The annoying behaviour change is the *symptom*; the something that has triggered the behaviour change is the *cause*.

So, reacting to your employees behaviour change actually worsens the problem, because they now have something else that will ensure they remain demotivated – YOU.

Okay, you say, so I shouldn't ignore the behaviour change and I shouldn't react to it. So what do I do? You respond.

Sounds easy. And like many things in life, it is easier to say than do. However, I can assure you, no, I can promise you that the effort you will need to learn how to respond to people and situations will prove to be the best investment that you will ever make.

Of course the reason why responding isn't as easy as it sounds is because we are all reactionary creatures. In fact, we are all reactionary emotional creatures. You may be one of the most logical thinkers on the planet, but most of your decisions will be based on emotion. You think you're a fair and even-handed boss. Why do some workers get more positive attention from you than others? Because you like them. An emotional reaction.

I bet you think you bought your last car based on logical decisions ~ but I bet you wouldn't have bought it if it only came in luscious pink. Colour choice is based on emotion.

The biggest purchase of the life will be your house. The location's right, it's near all the essential amenities, the school is close, it has access to all the major road networks, and it's £5,000 less than you budgeted for. So, what stops you from buying it? It just doesn't feel right. So, you keep on looking until you find one that does. Feelings are emotion.

You see, once all the logical thinking is done, that final make or break decision is always the emotional one, we just can't help reacting. It's in the genes and keeps us alive. It's called survival of the species.

However, not all situations are do or die. After all we at the top of the animal chain, we have the ability to think things through and assess the situation that faces us. And when you're trying to get the best from your team members perhaps responding to the facts as you see them would be more appropriate.

So, what should you be assessing? Let us move to the next stage and take this subject of understanding people a step further to see how you can learn to respond.

How To Turn Motivation Theory Into Practice

Let us have a look at Maslow's hierarchy of needs. Just to remind us here is a copy of that famous triangle.

Most people trained in motivation can understand the theory that Abraham Maslow presented. Few, though, actually do anything with it. And this is because they were never taught how to make the connection between the theory and real life practice.

A simple example that we can all relate to is one I often find myself in. I work from a home office and I love the work I do, sometimes to the extent that when engrossed in an interesting project, usually on the computer, I forget to eat. My motivation to complete the work and achieve the great sense of satisfaction that I know awaits me keeps me hooked. Until the hunger pangs get too much. My motivation then is to search out for food. My physiological need for sustenance becomes so great that I hurry to the kitchen raiding the fridge or cupboards for the easiest and quickest thing to satisfy my hunger. This doesn't make for a great diet by the way.

My esteem and self-actualisation needs that are driving me to complete my project are overridden by my most basic need of all, physical survival through food and drink intake. And not until I have satisfied these needs can I return to my work. If I were to try to continue working, maybe because I couldn't find anything to eat, then my concentration would be very low, and the quality of my work would suffer.

If a person in your team is not behaving how you would wish them to, then without exception you can trace the cause back to Maslow's five human needs. Understanding these theories and how they relate and connect them with real people in the real world allows us to develop strategies, which will help us to develop a 'want to' team.

Let us have a look for the moment the key aspects of the 'have to' person. The person who works for you because they need a job and therefore come to work with that attitude stuck firmly at the front of their mind.

The first thing you will notice about the 'have to' person is their lack of commitment. The only attitude you get from the 'have to' people is one of compliance. Compliance and commitment might be close in the dictionary but there is a massive chasm between them when it comes to an individual's behaviour and quality of work output.

You will discover that one of the key benefits of creating a team of 'want to' people who work with you, is that they begin to bring commitment to their daily tasks. They begin to work with you and the rest of the team.

Using Maslow's hierarchy of needs, you can check each of your team member's current behaviours and attitudes. The biggest obstacle to this is the misguided belief that people's key motivator is money. This is one of those 'suspend judgement' areas. I know that if you were to ask the people that worked for you right this minute, what they came to work for, they would most probably tell you, money.

However, learning how to change people, including ourselves, for the better, is all about asking the right question. You see, asking people why they come to work, is not the right question, is it? And usually when this question is asked, the people who are being asked have been working in a climate where team spirit, support and co-operation, has been lacking.

Let us explore this for a while and discover what the real question is.

If you want to find out what really motivates the people who work for you then you need to be very clear on what the current working climate is. Your current team climate will affect how your team actually performs day to day.

Let us have a look at the question again:

Question: "Why do you come to work?"

Answer: "Money."

Maslow's Hierachy Of Needs

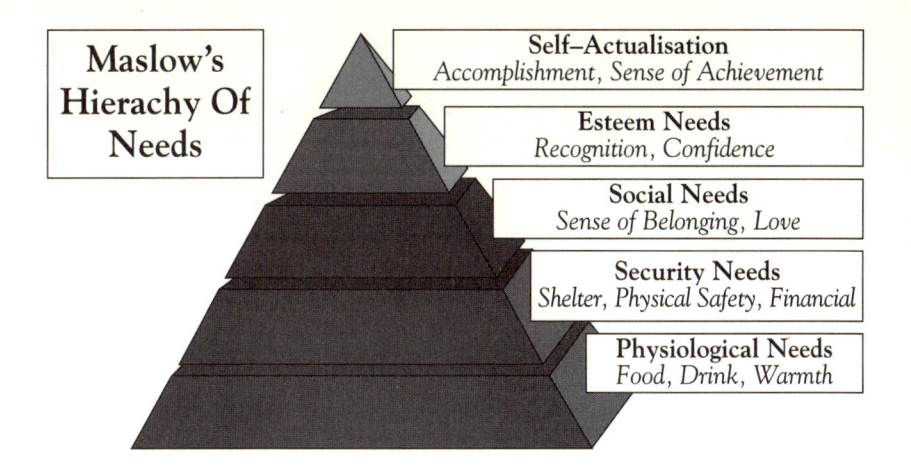

- **Self–Actualisation** — Accomplishment, Sense of Achievement
- **Esteem Needs** — Recognition, Confidence
- **Social Needs** — Sense of Belonging, Love
- **Security Needs** — Shelter, Physical Safety, Financial
- **Physiological Needs** — Food, Drink, Warmth

Depending on how poor the climate is, and remember this is the climate as perceived from your team member's point of view, not yours, then besides answering "money" they have been known to add, "you don't think I'd keep coming here every day if it wasn't for the money, do you?"

However, the real question is "What motivates you, currently?"

The real answer is: "My family and I need to eat and keep a roof over our heads." This translates to Maslow's first two needs in the hierarchy. And in order to satisfy these people need money.

Now, let us make the connection with Maslow's hierarchy of needs and real life, i.e. your current team climate. When people are totally focused on just the first two of Maslow's needs, they will only comply with instructions and requests while attending the workplace. It is the means to achieve the end, which in this case is wages. In other words, as there is no other motivational need being worked on by you, they will tolerate their position and do what you want them to do, and no more. This is compliance and not the commitment you need for a truly effective team.

Another point on money and motivation is that research shows us that when people change jobs they rarely do it for money. It is usually for better terms and conditions, better prospects, a better working climate, better treatment. If you can create those things that they go off in search for, how much more effective will that make you as a manager? To what extent will this improve your bottom line?

It's a proven fact that 'want to' people are between 8 to 10 times more productive than the 'have to's'. So how do you shift your people from the 'have to' sector of human effort to the 'want to' sector. It is actually much easier than you think. What it isn't though is instantaneous. And this is due to that good old human trait of cynicism.

The cynic is a person who knows the price of everything, but the value of nothing, as the observation goes. So cynics beware, you are not enjoyable to work for.

Okay, so what makes people want to work with you, rather than being someone who will have to work for you? The answers are in Maslow's third and fourth needs in his hierarchy. Social needs and self-esteem needs.

Everybody wants to belong, to be liked and to be wanted. This is basic human nature. And it does not shut off as soon as we walk through the work gates and clock on. People operate far more effectively when working in a climate that is both co-operative and supportive. And along with that comes that other human need, recognition.

Again, many people who have been taught the theory of Maslow's needs miss the point and look far too deeply into it. We all seek recognition in any shape or form. We often think of it though, in terms of some kind of major achievement. Such as commendations, promotion or financial rewards. And yes, these count to. However, we mustn't overlook the more obvious and easier to achieve types of recognition.

What I really like about Maslow's hierarchy of needs is the way that it so naturally fits in with human behaviours. Recognition in its simplest form is through acknowledgement. You carry out a task for me, and I say thank you. I acknowledge your effort and you feel appreciated. And we all know when this happens we are more likely to repeat the behaviour. Here's an every day example that I have experienced many times over the years, and most probably you too.

You're driving along a narrow road. There are cars parked along either side. Another vehicle is travelling towards you. You can see that one of you will have to give way when you reach a parked car. As the next parked car is on your side of the road, you stop and beckon the other driver through. At this point, you are probably feeling quite co-operative.

He travels through without giving you any eye contact or gesturing a thank you. Sound familiar? How did that incident leave you feeling? An emotional reaction is about to take place. From my own experience it left me feeling unappreciated, taken for granted, ignored and unimportant. And it left me thinking things like: "Huh! Not even a nod. The ignorant swine. What would it have cost him to wave a thank you? If I'd known he wouldn't show any appreciation I wouldn't have let him through."

Silly childish stuff I know, but very human, and all because I didn't receive any recognition for doing something that the law says I should do because the parked car was on my side of the road. Now if that is how an impersonal incident like the one above left you feeling, how does it feel when someone you work with or for treats you like that?

This happens because of the very basic human instinct of behaviour breeding behaviour. The negative experience above is a prime example. A positive experience would be the pleasant feeling of someone kindly letting us out from a side street in to the busy flow of rush-hour traffic. Most people reciprocate this by letting some one else out at the next side road. Let us relate the negative incident to the workplace.

"Thank my staff for doing a job well, but that's what they're paid to do."

Can you see that because it's expected it doesn't mean your people will continue to do it willingly if they feel that what they do is not appreciated. Taking my car experience, because of the truth of behaviour breeding behaviour, I suddenly become a 'have to' type of driver. The next time I will try to get through first and force the other driver to give way. If I don't quite make it in time, I will only be letting the other driver through because I have to, which is compliance with the rules of the road. But boy, if it'd been down to me, I would make him wait.

Sadly, this is all too common in work teams. Managers and supervisors fail to recognise their staff doing good things. Here's another simple but very true example.

When my daughters were young toddlers and just discovering the fun of drawing with crayons, they would bring me pictures. Being a proud dad I would accept their pictures and heap loads of praise and encouragement on them. How did they react? By quickly going off and producing another, equally superb drawing. And again, on receipt of this picture I would ask questions about it and tell them how good it was and how clever they were. This set off a cycle of drawings from them inspired by an appreciation from dad. And with each picture their enthusiasm and energy for the task in hand grew. Was it because they loved drawing? Not really. The drawing was the means to the end. What they craved was the recognition and acknowledgement of their talents.

No one ever really loses that need for sincere recognition. To draw a parallel with the work place, your team is no exception. Feed that very human need for recognition, which also creates the spin off into the social need of belonging and you have the beginnings of a 'want to' team.

However, it is early days yet and you have a few more strategies to learn before you can launch your own 'want to' offensive. The next step is to look at the climate of team success. Just before we move on here is a cautionary tale, which will indicate just how you will need to begin applying this simple but very powerful material.

The incident I am about to relay to you actually took place on a three-day workshop I was running a few years back. We were just ending the morning's sessions. We had been looking at the theory side of creating 'want to' people and had just covered some essential material very similar to what you have just read through. We were going to get stuck into some hands-on practical activities in order to bring the theory to life, so I was summing up the key points. When a voice from the back broke through.

"That's rubbish, that is." This came from the quietest delegate out of the twelve I had on the programme. It stopped me in mid flow and intrigued me.

"Sorry. What's rubbish?" I asked.

"All that recognition stuff. It's rubbish." He folded his arms and sat back stiffly in his seat.

Scanning the rest of the group, I could see all eyes were on me to see how I would deal with this non-believer. I remained calm and genuinely interested in his perception of the subject. "Can you expand on that a little, to give us an idea of why you think so."

"I was sent on one of these courses a couple of years back, because my manager said I needed some people skills or something. They went through all this stuff and told us how recognition works and all that. It's rubbish. When I got back to work I tried it and it didn't work."

"So," I said, "just out of interest how long did you try it for?"

"Half hour." Some sniggers came from the rest of the group. I honestly thought that perhaps I had misheard, or that he was taking the rise out of the training. I decided to get him to clarify his answer.

"No, seriously, how long did you try it for?"

"Half hour." He seemed a little annoyed that I should question this. If this was what I thought it was then Maslow's needs were about to be proven right yet again. I decided to test my understanding of his story with what I believed had taken place on his return to the workplace after his course.

"Let me see if I have got this right." A look around the room while I gathered my thoughts showed me that everyone was eager to see how this would end. "Prior to your course two years ago, you didn't give much recognition to your staff."

"No."

"You then came back from the course and launched into an onslaught of recognition as you walked around the shop floor?"

"Yes. And it didn't work."

"Tell me, did they take the mickey out of you and say things like; "What are you after?""

"Yeah, they did."

This incident allowed the group to explore the dangers of changing your management style too abruptly. This guy had a reputation of motivating by fear. He was one of the do it or else brigade. This is the classic cause of 'have to' working habits. In just thirty minutes of attempting to change his style, and most probably without much conviction or sincerity, the pain of seeing his Maslow need of esteem attacked by people who should recognise that he is the boss, was too much to bear.

He very quickly reverted to his old way of doing things, his staff stopped ribbing him and he carried on in his old ineffective and stressful ways. His people all remained 'have to' people.

So, while this stuff really does work, it will take a little longer than thirty minutes. And you will also need to change your style gradually, which I will take through over the rest of the chapter.

Let us move on now to explore the key elements of a successful team climate and see how it will help you create a team of 'want to' people.

Establishing A Climate For Team Success

There is a simple diagram that explains this process very well, which I use on my teamworking and teambuilding courses. Let's take a quick look at it.

Climate and the successful team:

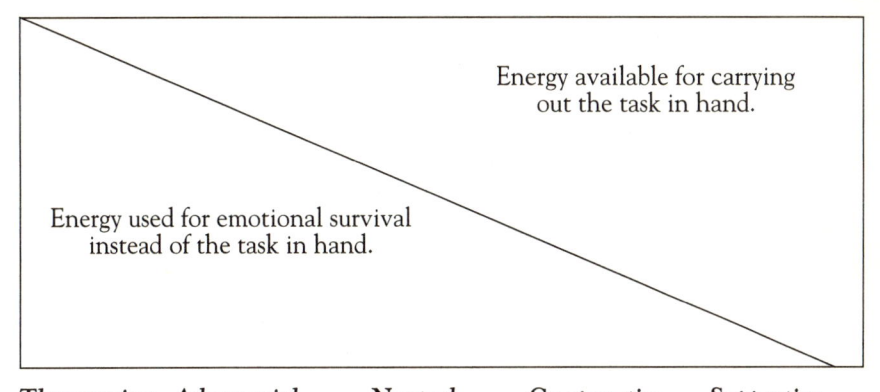

```
|                                    Energy available for carrying
|                                    out the task in hand.
|
|      Energy used for emotional survival
|         instead of the task in hand.
|
|_____
 Threatening  Adversarial   Neutral   Co-operative  Supportive
```

As you see by the diagram, there is a direct correlation to how your team performs and the climate in which they work. Again, we can all relate to times in our working life when this has been the case.

At the threatening end of the scale, for instance, we can associate with company mergers and restructuring and the subsequent downsizing, right sizing, or whatever the latest buzz term is for redundancy. I can recall first hand, how this greatly affected people's focus and energy for their job, when job losses loomed. People huddled in corridors and offices debating and speculating about the possible outcomes of the dreaded changes. Very little work got done. This meant that over the next financial quarter, when speculation outstripped production, it became even easier to justify the reduction in head count.

Take a serious look at the climate that your team currently works in. With total honesty, where on the climate scale does your team operate? Even with a neutral climate, a great deal of energy is being misdirected.

You need to channel as much energy as you can into every task and from every single team member. Everyone is and should be accountable for the team's success.

Individuals can best do this if the climate that they have to spend the best part of their waking hours is of the right quality. Can you work at your best, consistently, in a less than supportive or co-operative environment?

So, how do you create a team climate that remains at the co-operative, supportive end of the scale?

Well, part of the answer lies in the previous segment, with the identification of

Maslow's hierarchy of needs and addressing the appropriate motivational areas. Remember that every body appreciates recognition. It really is the most cost-effective way of oiling the team's wheels.

And what different forms does recognition come in? Well besides the obvious ones of money and other tangible rewards, you can behave towards your team members in a way that tells them that they are valued.

Making sure that your communication style is on an adult to adult level. Getting your people involved in the whole process from objectives, the decision-making processes, problem solving and ideas. Trusting your people and encouraging co-operation between team members. Giving people support when they need it. Making sure your people are assigned to the right roles within the team – no round pegs in square holes.

This would be a good point to move on to the six characteristics of effective teams which will further enhance your development of creating the 'want to' team.

Practising The Characteristics of Effective Teams of Want To People

When you look at the market leaders, those companies that have the competitive edge, they all have one thing in common. Effective teamwork.

You can learn a great deal from these star players, after all, if they can do it, so can you. All you need is the formula that they use, the time to study and understand it, and the attitude of mind to put it into practice because you want to improve.

The formula for a peak performing team can be broken down into six elements. These six elements are in every effective team. Let me take you through them.

1. **Clear Objectives:** All effective teams work with clear objectives that are correctly interpreted by each member of the team. Everybody needs to know exactly what needs to be done, when it needs to be done by, and, here's one of the motivational elements, why it has to be done. Involving every team member in the objective stage eliminates misunderstanding and misinterpretation. It allows people to ask clarifying questions and to understand where their role fits in with other team members. Clear objectives help people to see just what impact they will be having on the whole process. If people can see exactly what is meant to happen then they are more able to use their initiative for the good of the team and maximise their effectiveness.

2. *Good Decision Making Processes:* When people are involved in the decision making process they are more willing to get involved in the actions that need to follow the decision made. People can either be part of the problem, or part of the solution. If every decision is always made solely by

The Pillars of Successful Management 83

the team leader then they will feel that their opinions and ideas count for nothing. The whole thing quickly becomes one of those do or die situations and you begin to increase your problems and stress accordingly. It's a team objective, it needs to be a team decision where possible. It's true that the leader must make some decisions alone, but even these can be handled far more effectively by involving the team with the sub-decisions of how best the main decision can be implemented. There are many decision making processes, find them out, make sure you use the one or ones you feel best suit your team, have a structure, set out the ground rules and follow it.

3 *Trust, Co-operation, Support and Constructive Dissent:* It is not always easy to trust people to do what needs to be done, but once instilled it is extremely powerful. It is where respect comes into being. If I trust you, I respect you. If I trust and respect you then I am more likely to co-operate with you, and offer my support whenever I can. When this exists within a team, we call it team spirit and camaraderie. As a leader of a team, it is one of your key responsibilities to develop this. Breaking down some of the deep-seated cynics within the group is not easy. A way of dealing with the cynic is by focusing on their behaviour and how it is detrimental to the team as a whole. It is important to note that as you will never achieve agreement on all issues all of the time, dissent will rise to the surface now and again (more so in the early team development days), but one of the golden rules is that all disagreements must be constructive. If someone doesn't agree with an issue or proposed action then they must offer an alternative. Disagreement for the sake of it, or without being thought through, must not be tolerated. This helps keep the focus on the positive.

4 *Clear Roles, Responsibility and Effective Leadership:* In order for people to consistently perform at their personal best, also known as Peak Performance, they must have a totally clear understanding of their role. Where their role fits into the bigger picture, what happens prior to the task coming to them, what happens after it leaves them. They also need to know exactly what they are responsible for and the consequences to the whole team, the task and themselves if it is not carried out as it should be. If you have someone in your team that is consistently under-performing then it is up to you to check out the key elements that could be causing this. If someone is unclear about the role they are carrying out, de-motivation sets in. They could also be in a role that does not suit them; maybe their strengths lie elsewhere. This would be a classic case of a round peg in a square hole. Effective Leadership is about being aware of these factors and making sure that moves are made to remedy the less effective elements. People much prefer to know where they stand, so make sure your people know specifically what you expect from them, including trust, support and co-operation.

5 *Relationships With Outside Groups:* As John Donne said: "No man is an island." And neither is a team. We need to establish good relationships with the outside groups, departments and other teams that we often rely on at

different times in order to get our tasks completed. Using empathy is a good way of establishing a rapport with other groups over time. You never know when you may need to ask for a favour. And any way working with co-operation is always easier, less stressful and more effective than working with conflict and confrontation. I have always found that co-operation is more effective than competition. If you are currently experiencing, problems with teams outside of your own then begin working towards a solution. You will greatly benefit in the long run. And so will your company.

6. *Evaluating The Teams Performance:* Analysing your team's performance on a regular basis will pay high dividends. It doesn't have to take a great deal of time, but it does need to be done if you want an effective team full of 'want to' people. Think of the way sports teams do this. They review their last match by evaluating what they did well and what they need to re-work. Periodically it is a good idea to get the team together and review the areas that are going well and that people are pleased with. This also allows you an opportunity to give out deserved praise and recognition for work well done. You then ask the question: How could we improve our performance even further? What procedures do we need to fine-tune? What processes need removing, replacing or re-working? The whole team then gets involved with the improvement process, which is essential, because at the end of the day it will be down to them to implement any changes. And people are far more motivated in working on ideas that they had a hand in creating.

How does your team currently compare to the above six characteristics? Highlight what you are currently doing. Well done. Now highlight what you need to work on. Now slow down.

It is important that whatever you decide needs changing you do it one step at a time. If you were re-learning how to walk, the one step at a time programme would ensure that you eventually get to the other end of the room. It would be slow and it may be a little frustrating at times, but the alternative, of attempting to run the course, would only result in you falling flat on your face and maybe never getting there. Remember success by the inch is a cinch, by the yard it's hard.

Let us pull all this together into an outline plan that you could work with. This last section will lay down a strategy for creating a 'want to' team of people. It is not cast in stone. Your particular situation will be unique to you; so use the information in the strategy in a way that would best suit your current circumstances. Just remember to have faith. All of the tactics and strategies I have taken you through really do work, but people need time to adjust to different attitudes and behaviours before they begin to adjust their own with encouragement from you. Have a plan and quietly work away at it.

Keep your awareness raised to the fact that *behaviour breeds behaviour* and *like attracts like*. With these fundamentals in your possession, you can fashion a team of highly effective 'want to' people. You should aim to become their role model.

Leading by example means behaving by example. That will only happen of course, if you really 'want it to'.

Creating and Putting into Action a 'Want To' Team Strategy

The following plan is an outline for you to use as a place to start your own unique plan of action. If you learn what needs to be learnt, understand what needs to be understood and then do what needs to be done, success will be yours. Just be sure to give more than thirty minutes.

Developing A 'Want To' Team Strategy

Understand Your People

Get to know your people. Discover what makes them tick. Every one that works for you is a unique individual and they have a part to play in your team. If they don't, then why are they there? Talk to them. Acknowledge them. Pay them attention. Ask them questions about what really interests them.

So many managers have no idea just what a gold mine of skill they preside over every day. They accuse their workforce of being only interested in money, of avoiding responsibility and work. They then deal with these people with an attitude that matches their beliefs. The fundamentals of behaviour breeding behaviour and like attracting like then takes over. This is also known as the self-fulfilling prophecy. It is a fact of life and in its negative state is not desirable. So beware, your attitude is always on show and will always be reflected back to you.

On my training courses and workshops I come across hundreds of shopfloor workers who have outside work interests that would surprise you. One was a treasurer for a large charity organisation. They were responsible for thousands of pounds and spent hours keeping the accounts up to date and accurate. And guess what? They did it for free. Yet, their manager wouldn't trust them with putting money into the coffee machine. They were definitely a 'want to' person outside work.

Seek to understand the behaviour of your staff. If they behave in a way which goes against the team's objectives then positively challenge it. Remember they are behaving that way for a reason. Find the reason and you find the solution. Maybe their interpretation of the objectives is incorrect. Maybe they can't see where their job fits in. Maybe they are in the wrong role.

The information you begin to gather through working to understand your people will help you with completing the next interlinking step.

Turn Motivation Theory Into Practice

By working your way through step one you begin to address Maslow's hierarchy of needs. The key to creating a 'want to' attitude in all of your team members lies within this area.

Here's another example of how naturally Maslow's theory fits in with real life. Whenever companies and departments within companies have attempted to increase productivity, they have tried many tactics. One of those was based on getting the people on the job to spend less time talking with one another and more time working. This, they believed would result in higher production levels. They were very wrong. They had failed to take into account Maslow's third level ~ social needs. Socialising is an important aspect for many people in work; it's often the only place where it really happens. The managers had not picked up the social need because it didn't include them, well you don't socialise with people you have no respect for, do you?

If your team is currently focused on the money aspect of work then you need to work on the higher levels. Giving recognition, through praising a job well done, and encouraging new learnt skills and allowing people more involvement will, over time, begin to shift this money focus.

People crave feedback. Make a point on your own personal development plan to learn how to give constructive feedback. The untrained manager will often give feedback couched in words of criticism. I have yet to meet anyone who enjoys being criticised. Criticism, even when it is merited, causes people to become defensive and highly emotional. Those two elements are the key ingredients of conflict and confrontation. The behaviour breeds behaviour element comes out too, they criticise you back. Not necessarily to your face maybe, but it still undermines your position and further entrenches the 'have to' attitude.

I recommend that you read some of Tom Peter's material. This guy has a whole wealth of real work situations that all managers could learn from. One of the methods he advocates and I've put this into action, so can vouch for it, is MBWA.

MBWA is Management By Walking About. Get out of your office and walk amongst the people whom you expect great things from. After all, they are your ticket to the results you want. Involve them; show them that you recognise that they are human beings with feelings, families, and fears. It's all feedback. Two way communication. You have to get to know people before they can respect you. You have to communicate with people to build a rapport with them.

Respect and rapport. The two greatest motivators around. Think of the people in your life that you were willing to work beyond the call of duty for. I guarantee that you will find respect and rapport were present. You know it works so why aren't you practising it?

I have always found that by treating people as I would wish to be treated was always a good place to start and quite easy to implement immediately.

Create A Climate For Team Success

You now know that even a neutral climate still creates a great deal of wasted energy. So encouraging team members to co-operate and support one another should be a top priority. Your regular team briefings should be highlighting this key issue.

Team briefings are a great forum for communicating the key points and involving people. It allows you to update people on the important work issues, give out some deserved recognition and allow some feedback. Team briefings should be what the name implies ~ brief.

You should also create opportunities so that people can offer their ideas on how to improve the team's processes and procedures. These are best run periodically and depending on the logistics and working patterns may be a little harder to initiate but do pay back well. Another option is getting feedback on team performance improvements on a one-to-one level. The key is getting team members involved in the maintenance and development of their team. This also allows you to create that important sense of belonging need.

Characteristics of Effective Teams

Does your team have clear objectives to work to? Do they know what is expected of them? How do you want them to behave? Remember the essential behaviours should be; co-operatively, supporting, and trusting.

Work your way through the list of six characteristics of effective teams. Some of those elements will be easier and quicker to implement than others. Remember the re-learning to walk analogy, you shouldn't be judging the speed of the journey, only the direction of the progress. Positive and forward.

You can see that all of the steps in this Strategy are interlinked with each other. They all have a positive knock on effect as and when applied constructively.

While this makes it powerful, it also makes it impossible to rush. All of the good things in life, in my experience, suffer in quality and effectiveness if they are implemented at too fast a pace. The critical word here is patience.

Re-read this chapter and note down what you need to learn more about. Then draw up two plans.

The first plan should be for your own continuous personal development. This is essential is becoming an effective and progressive leader of people.

The second plan will map out how you intend to transform the 'have to' people into 'want to' people. To ensure that you are practicing the six characteristics of effective teams. To develop a clear understanding of your people. To utilise Maslow's hierarchy of needs in the workplace to the best effect at all times.

Give yourself a realistic deadline for achieving each key element and monitor your progress regularly.

Once you start this vital process to make your life as a leader of people easier, less stressful and highly successful you will begin to see the benefits. And you won't be alone. As I promised earlier in this chapter you are free to call me or write to me with any questions or queries and I will endeavour to answer them to the best of my ability.

Now go out and create the ultimate 'want to' team.

Key Summary Points

Understand Your People
Learn what makes the people you manage tick.

How To Turn Motivation Theory Into Practice
Discover how to apply Maslow's Hierarchy of Needs to the workplace for higher motivation.

Establishing A Climate of Team Success
Develop a proven 'success' climate to increase your team's performance.

Practising The Characteristics of Effective Teams
Discover and learn how to apply the key elements that top performing teams practice.

The 'Want To' Team Strategy
Create your own action plan for developing a high performing 'want to' team.

6 How to increase sales – The Artist sales process

Introduction

As David Sandler the founder of the Sandler Sales Institute once said, **"to conquer the art of professional selling you need to learn a system"**, with this mind I have produced what I believe to be one of the most effective sales systems currently available.

Over the years there have been dozens of "new" ways, "mega" ways, "effective" ways and many other superlative ways to describe the latest fad selling crazes, (usually emanating from the selling guru's in the States) . Each one promising riches beyond your wildest dreams if you just follow the magical steps guaranteeing your fame and fortune and the certainty of winning the golden briefcase award for Salesperson of the Year.

For as long as there are salespeople there will always be an interest in new and improved techniques to help clinch that extra sale, and close that one more order. I have found after many years as a salesman (having been introduced to many, many methods of selling), that not one method does it all. One aspect of one technique or model would be useful, and then one piece from another and one piece from yet another.

This became rather frustrating and inefficient not to mention confusing!.

So I have developed a model that encompasses what I believe to be the best of what are accepted to be the best sales models around.

Why another system?

As with all things there is always room for improvement .

It was said in a report for the Sales Qualifications Board (1993) that "... *Many suppliers will have to invest substantially in training, organisational reforms and knowledge building if they are to remain one step ahead of their customers and competitors".*

Simply there has never been a model quite like this one. Of course, in parts it bears similarities to others, but when (as I hope you will) you internalise this method and practice it in the real world as I have many times, you will increase your credibility, your success and your bank balance in the space of only a few months.

There are numerous credible ways of selling, but let's not forget that (and there are no figures for this, it is only by my estimation) only one in 10 salespeople use any form of method at all, let alone this one.

All of the latest methods have something in common and that is they show a greater understanding of the **buyer** than previous models. However I believe that there are fundamental gaps within all models and it is these gaps that as an accomplished **A.R.T.I.S.T.** salesperson you will exploit and use to win over the competition.

How much of a competitive advantage will you have if you & your people use A.R.T.I.S.T.

It is my opinion based upon my sales experience, that the majority of salespeople (over 400,000 in the UK currently selling for a living) have never had any formal training by a competent sales trainer. Many are trained by their managers who themselves have never received any quality training.

Few if any sales books ever reach the higher echelons of the best seller list even though if you think for a moment we are all in sales in one way or another.

> So, it is without fear of contradiction, that I can say if you practise and become expert in the use of **A.R.T.I.S.T.** questions you will by default put yourself in the top 5-10% of salespeople in the country if not the world.

Where does ARTIST come in the sales cycle?

ARTIST only represents part of the sales cycle and I believe it is important to point out at this stage just where it fits in. We do not have the space to go into detail about the other stages listed here.

The **first stage** is Preparation and Planning.
"If you fail to plan you plan to fail", never a truer word was spoken. It has been said that the success of a sales call is directly proportional to the amount of prepara-

tion and planning that goes on beforehand. I certainly believe this to be the case. How many great sales are ever made on a cold call?

The **second stage** is Qualifying.
You may be saying, surely you must qualify a prospect **before** you even get into the preparation and planning stage. Of course you are right. However, I always qualify again just to make sure that this is the right person who can make a decision, or (if access to the buyer is strictly limited) is at the very least a major influencer in the purchase. I also check if they have the finance in place and that **nothing has changed** since the last meeting or phone call.

The **third stage** is your introduction and benefit statement.
This usually takes the form of introducing yourself and your company and explaining very simply the reason why you are there in the form of a benefit to the buyer.

For example "I am here today to establish your current and future photocopying requirements, to provide you with some cost effective and efficient options."

The **fourth stage** is questioning using the **A.R.T.I.S.T** model.
Covered in full here.

The **fifth stage** is to summarise the findings and the **pain** found, and then pre-close.

This should be very straight forward and is simply a re-cap of the information found, together with a full description of the pain and discomfort that will be felt (if allowed to continue). The pre-close asks the buyer if, on you providing a solution to their problems and helping them to remove the pain, they are in a position to take action and go ahead.

The **sixth stage** is to present your product.
Whole books have been written on the subject of presentation so I will simply summarise by saying present your product with strict reference to the benefits that can be realised by the buyer. Don't spend forever on these benefits as the competition almost certainly has the same ones. So this is NOT where the sale is usually made.

The **seventh stage** is to close.
If you have correctly carried out the structure as outlined later you will have very little need for closing techniques. You will be working much more closely alongside the buyer in a position of trust and respect almost like an internal employee and never from a combative position that may give rise to disagreements or objections. You are not selling from your position or for your reasons as in the past, you are providing a solution strictly that matches what the buyer is searching for and has agreed at each stage.

There should of course be no surprises when it comes to where the order is going.

There is no specific stage for objection handling because I believe as previously explained objections only arise out of a buyer defending himself from the seller. If you have been truly collaborative, and not tried to **sell them** something but tried to **solve their problems**, I guarantee you will rarely encounter an objection.

How Buyers Buy

There has probably been more research carried out on this subject within the sales process than any other. I have seen dozens of different explanations of what mental journey the buyer goes through during the buying cycle and all of them claim to be the absolute answer!

The stages I will briefly explain here are not revolutionary, simply the ones I have found to be the most accurate and true.

The stages of decision making a buyer goes through
For a buyer to purchase a new product or service, I believe they must clearly understand two things:-

1 What they currently have in place either a) no longer provides what they need now or b) will not provide what they want in the future
2 How this new product or service will fit into their environment and be accepted by the current staff, politics, management and aligned systems.

Stage 1	What is the current environment? What have I got now?
Stage 2	What does the environment need to be and what is the cost to us if we don't?
Stage 3	What are the internal resources? What have we got *now that could fix it?*
Stage 4	What do I need to do to get the environment to where it needs to be?
Stage 5	Decide I need to get help from outside
Stage 6	What exactly will this help need to provide me with
Stage 7	Which one will I choose
Stage 8	When do I need this to be in place
Stage 9	Buy the solution

If you accept that these stages of decision making are true, then I am sure you will agree that the buyer has always gone through this process, only as sellers we have allowed them to go through this process ALONE.

The difference by using **A.R.T.I.S.T.** is that you will take an ACTIVE part in each of these stages, rather than what happened in the past, you simply presented your solution and waited till the buyer came back to you with a hopefully favourable decision.

You will notice soon how similar the **A.R.T.I.S.T.** questions are closely mirrored to the process the buyer goes through toward the purchase of the solution .

The most important stage is undoubtedly stage 2. This is where the **problems** are discovered and more importantly you find out the cost to the buyer of **not** changing.

Questions are the key

It is not for the first time I am sure that you will have heard the phrase "telling is not selling". It is therefore the art of listening and asking questions that is at the heart of a great selling method. **ARTIST** is no exception. Someone once said "take a tip from nature, your ears are not designed to shut, your mouth is!" and my favourite "when your talking you're not learning", it's so true isn't it?. If power comes from knowledge, and knowledge comes from listening, listening gives you power.

It has been said that traditional salespeople talk as much as 70 percent of the time when in fact it will be shown that 30 percent may be seen as too much.

That phrase "no-one cares how much you know until they know how much you care" could not sum up more accurately the process by which all good sales should follow.

There are of course many reasons for asking questions, for example:

1 You get the buyer to do most of the talking
2 Questions help you gather information, which lead to more questions
3 Questions also allow the buyer to become emotionally involved, and as we know buyers make decisions emotionally and justify logically.
4 Questions help you to gain credibility in the eyes of the buyer, as you are obviously trying to understand his position and gain empathy. To gain true empathy it is said you must walk four miles in the buyer moccasin's. It is also said, that "to put on another man's shoes you must first remove your own."
5 They also shift the focus from you to the buyer, which is really where the focus belongs.
6 Questions of course help you to think and focus on the buyer and his arena. They give you time.

> **ARTIST** has been designed to give a structure to the flow of questions that will help both you and the buyer realise: what the problems are, the cost of not solving them, how to solve them, who to solve them and when to solve them.

7. It is of course almost impossible (if you are asking quality questions), to fall pray to that most dreaded of salesperson habits bombarding the buyer with information!
8. Many successful salespeople use this time when asking questions to build rapport via their body language. This technique is called "mirroring and matching" and is an excellent way to get the buyer feeling at ease with you and help develop that all important trust.
9. To find the implied needs

The buyers problems discovered by your excellent **A.R.T.I.S.T.** questions usually manifest themselves in one of two ways.

1. Implied needs or
2. Specific needs

The **implied** need is one of unhappiness with the current situation with regard to the future.
   "I'm unhappy with how long it takes for the engineer to turn up."
   "We always seem to run out of toner towards the end of the month"
   "It would be awful if we couldn't get x on time"

The **specific** need is a clear expression of a buyers want to solve an issue.
   "I am ideally looking for a 2hr response time"
   "I need to keep a backup stock of toner"
   "I want a guarantee that you can deliver on time"

When questioning you are searching initially for **implied** needs. These are usually quite subtle and will need careful listening out for.

Self Test

Which of the following are **Implied Needs** and which are **Specific Needs**?

1. I am very dissatisfied with my present speaker units
2. I'm looking for help in preparing next years VAT returns
3. Our present training takes people off the job for too long
4. I want to be able to take underwater photographs at a depth of 20meters
5. We'd like to reduce the delays in delivery
6. The trouble is that whenever the power drops the humidity gets too high
7. I'm fed up with invoices always going out late
8. The microphone picks up too much background noise
9. I need a replacement widget that costs 20% less than I'm paying now
10. The staff haven't been at all happy with the canteen food recently.

Answers at the end of the chapter.
We will be referring to these again later.

How do I get an implied need?

Work Backwards!!

We have established the benefits in asking questions, and the implied needs that we hope to get from them which then lead to the specific need that our product or service can solve.

But how do we start?

Simple. First write down the problems that your product or service solves. This is often quite a foreign concept to most salespeople and even some Managing Directors so let me explain.

As we discussed earlier the reason a person buys any product or service is to solve a problem that they can't fix internally. (see **Why Buyers Buy**) . You therefore need to think of your product or service in terms of a solution provider, or problem solver.

What problems then might they have that your product or service can solve?

The A.R.T.I.S.T Questioning Process

A is for ARENA Questions or "A-Questions"

Arena questions are designed to investigate the facts and the background behind both the present arena and the future arena of the buyer. They are also to help the buyer begin to discover for themselves the difference between where they are now and where they want to be.

For example "what are you doing in the way of health and safety training in your company right now"

"How many people work in each area"

"How many offices and satellite's do you have now?"

"What do see as a reasonable return on investment?"

"How do you currently recruit your staff?"

"What percentage of your business is retail?"

The way then to structure your questions should be with the intent on uncovering background information but also to highlight any problem areas in the form of **implied needs** to you that may exist in your buyers environment with regard to their future plans. This moves away from the old adage about just asking "open" questions which were taught as the most valuable questions to use for opening up the conversation.

I am suggesting that you ask questions to help the buyer **realise for themselves** that there may be a difference between where they are now, and where they want to be, thereby realising that there may be a **problem that requires a solution**.

Whether there is or not, how much of a problem, and exactly what the implications of that problem are we establish in the next stages. We are simply concerned here with ascertaining background information at this stage.

Having then helped the **buyer** start thinking about their environment and provide you with information based upon it, you should have in the back of your mind that there may be problems or dissatisfactions which you may be able to help with.

For example, if you ask your buyer "What percentage of your business is retail?" and the answer comes gloomily back "about 40%, *unfortunately* ", you should mentally pick up on it, as it is a big clue to environmental dissatisfactions.

However if you are not thinking about problems and actively listening at this early stage the clues will pass you by and opportunities for sales may be lost for good.

It is important that the buyer starts to see you as a solution provider not a salesperson. It has been said that "the salesperson who goes out trying to solve solutions will sell considerably more than the salesperson who goes out trying to sell product".

All the time you are seen as a salesperson the buyer believes you are doing everything for your gain not his! It is the difference between on the one hand a buyer genuinely trusting you and giving you the order and on the other seeing you as a box pusher . . . and there are many of those!

The interaction must become more collaborative, working together jointly to find a solution, rather than a battle for the seller to overcome the buyer and provide an instant fix that they possibly didn't want. Is it any wonder that salespeople are labelled in the way they are?

It has been established that the most successful salespeople ask good quality Arena questions. That means they are questions which (as well as helping the buyer to begin to discover his own needs) are likely to provide you with interesting and detailed information about the buyers environment, both now, and in the future, (not basic facts that could be answered by someone far more junior than the buyer.)

Many a senior buyer has been subjected to questions about hobbies, or asked to give them the basic details on the company that you could have asked the receptionist.

This of course will only irritate the buyer and not help in your attempt to build rapport.

It is essential to ask assumption free questions, or else the buyer will defend themselves against the predictable pitch on it's way rather than thinking about the genuine answers.

How do you eliminate unnecessary Arena questions?

1. Ask yourself, does this question have a clear purpose?. In other words is it relevant?

2   Ask questions that are specifically related to problems your buyer may be experiencing or about to experience.
3   Could I establish this information from a more junior person.

The do's for Arena questions

1   Ask them early on. These help build rapport, set the scene, and uncover implied needs.
2   Ask them especially when there has been some time since you last saw the buyer, or there has been some company change or restructure.
3   Ask them to establish important info about new customers.

The don'ts for Arena Questions

1   Do not ask them in the latter stages of the call. Either you have enough information or you don't. If you find yourself at the end of the call and you don't have enough you will have to start again. Don't try and just stay where you are and "fill in" with some extra information.
2   Do not ask questions that generate information a) you cannot use or b) doesn't help the buyer toward the goal of self realisation.
3   Do not ask too many. If you do not have a plan or structure (see working backwards), you are likely to a) run out of time b) irritate the buyer c) not achieve your goal of discovering implied/explicit needs.

R is for Realise Problem Questions or "R.P Questions"

This is probably one of the most important stages in the whole **A.R.T.I.S.T** process. The reason simply, is that I believe that buyers don't buy unless they have a problem, or more accurately they don't buy unless they have been made to realise themselves they have a problem.. If the problem is big enough, there will be huge pain attached to it, and they will do almost anything to get it resolved. The bigger the pain the more someone will pay to get out of it or better still, prevent it from happening in the first place.

Your job is to take the buyer (by way of your **A.R.T.I.S.T** questioning techniques) into the areas of as much pain as possible. These areas can be separated into three main areas:-

1   Pain in the past
2   Pain in the present and
3   Pain in the future

When exposed to pain the buyer will usually uncover their **implied needs** (see earlier section).

You will therefore need to listen extremely carefully as these may be very subtle. Your **"Realise Problem"** questions may well include words such as:

Unhappy
Satisfaction
Concerned
Trouble
Difficulty
Too slow
Too expensive
Cope
Happy
Adequate
Worried.

For example "what concerns do you have about the productivity schedule?"

"What difficulties exist currently in the staffing levels?" or "Is it difficult to employ qualified people?"

When people make a buying decision – unconsciously they are either moving toward a pleasurable situation or they are trying to get as far away from pain as possible.

It has been said many times that people make decisions logically but they BUY emotionally. In other words, we can go down the route of reduced costs, increased profits, ease of use etc. which appeal to the logic but does not tug on the emotional heart strings.

What I would suggest to achieve greater success in your selling career is that you go the easier way, and dig out the pain, as this is such a strong emotion that buyers (if it is done effectively) will make decisions much faster than they would have done under any other circumstance. Lead the buyer to **experience** the pain especially in the present and then show them how you can end their unhappiness by providing a solution for them. If you do this you will be just that little bit closer to the signed order that gets you that "Golden Briefcase Award"!

It was said to me once that the way to sell is to: "Find Someone Happy, Make Them Unhappy and then Make Them Happy Again."

This just underlines perfectly the encourage the pain – provide the pain solution analogy.

So, before trying to elicit the pain, you should already have an idea of what pain they may be experiencing. This of course goes back to planning.

The pain they reveal to you must be in the terms of an implied need. For you to expose this implied need, you must first think of your product in terms of what problems will it solve (see **How do I get an implied need**)

The Pillars of Successful Management

For example:
If you sell double glazing, the problems potential customers might experience could be . . .

a badly fitting windows giving uncomfortable drafts and high heating costs
b low level of security so easy access for burglars
c old, peeling wooden windows making the house look generally unattractive reducing it's resale value.
d single pain glass windows providing no protection from high external noise levels
e painted wooden windows requiring a high level of maintenance and care.

Would you agree that if you were going to buy new replacement windows it is probably for one or more of the reasons above? Are the problems listed above implied needs, or explicit needs? Yes, they are **implied** needs.

Would you agree that if they did utter any one of the above you are in quite a strong position to sell, why?, yes because they are starting to show **pain?**

For example some **REALISE PROBLEM** questions that may help to uncover implied needs or the problems as listed above may be . . .

a What is the difference between the heating bills you get in the winter, and the bills you get in the summer? Or, which part of your house is the worst for drafts? Are you happy with the amount you pay on heating bills at the moment?
b If you were a burglar how easy would you say it is to gain access to your valuable possessions?
c When do you expect to move house?, or, How much do you think the overall look of a house effects the sale price?
d How much are you effected by the noise of the traffic outside?
e How much time and money do you spend on the maintenance of your windows?

The statements I usually hear from the salespeople trying to convince their customers are these:

a The company has been established for over 60yrs
b We make our own products
c We have hundreds of happy customers
d We offer a very personal service

Can you see now how ineffective these are?

When to avoid asking "Realise Problem" Questions

There is usually some degree of risk associated with asking these questions and the areas you need to be very careful about are the following:

1   When talking to a current customer. If you already supply a product or service it is possible you could raise dissatisfactions about the service you provide, (even if it is the best solution currently available)
2   Delicate areas. If the buyer has a large degree of emotional or personal involvement, or there is conflict internally in the company.
3   Recent decisions. Your questions in this area may be seen as inappropriate if they come from a position of criticism. So, be careful!

Conversely there are three low risk areas in which it is positively encouraged to ask Realise Problem questions.

1   Specific areas of importance to the buyer.
2   Very early on in the sale process when you have developed a little rapport and you have enough Arena questions .
3   Areas where you have the solution to the underlying problem.

Self Test

Arena Questions or Realise Problem Questions?

1   Mr Smith what is the proposed deadline for this project to be completed?
2   Have you also come to some agreement with regard to the integral phases?
3   How confident are you of meeting the first integral stage?
4   What would you define as sufficient staffing levels?
5   Will you have any problems regarding systems compatibility
6   Are you sure you will receive your allocation on time
7   Who will you receive your expenditure budget from, and when?
8   How sure are you that he will approve your CAPEX budget?
9   When will he be available to speak to?
10 Do you have any issues you need to raise with me now?

High Risk or Low Risk Realise Problem Questions?

Now that you know which type of questions are which, of the following questions RP Questions are low risk and which are high risk?

1   Last month the buyer bought three cars for his fleet from a competitor

2   You have discovered an explicit need for your product (see implied and explicit needs) and are entering into the last phases of the selling cycle.
3   You've used some basic Arena questions about the company and you are not sure what to do now.
4   You are seeing a current customer and he has asked to see you for a repeat order.
5   The buyer has been experiencing some problems with a major competitor in that they are not providing the service they were promised.
6   Whilst asking Arena questions you discover that the buyer has been supplied for the last 5 years from a company who happens to be your major competitor.

It is absolutely fundamental that before you move onto the next phase of the process, you discover at least one Implied Need. Without this you are going to get unstuck and not be able to apply the leverage that is the next stage.

Some less experienced but well meaning salespeople when asking Realise Problem questions sometimes find the temptation of providing a solution just to much to bear and launch into a presentation along the lines of "well, have I got a product for you! . . ."

This of course can have devastating effects and in the majority of cases you are sent packing!

Patience is the key with Realise Problem questions. It may be of course there is more than one problem, and that may be even bigger than the one you have just uncovered, so it pays to wait and see.

I'd like to tell you a story that describes this process very well.

It's a story about two fisherman, one amateur, and one professional.

The professional planned and so knew where to fish, he had put bait there the night before and so maximised the chances. As a result he always came home with a string of fish.

The amateur on the other hand, just dropped his line in and as a result rarely caught a fish. The amateur was getting a little tired of this particular hobby, whereas the professional couldn't get enough!

The professional watched the amateur one day and offered his help. It was accepted and the two began to evaluate what the amateur was doing wrong.

The amateur said "I get a nibble, pull up the line and usually the bait is gone but no fish."

The Pro said "Do you know what is actually happening when you get a tug on the line?"

"no" he replied

"The fish is killing the bait" the pro said. "He has yet to take a bite out of it, so if you pull on the line now, all you have is dead bait and no fish. Make sense?"

"So, he has to kill it first, then he eats it?" asked the amateur.

"Nearly", the pro said. "The other fish want a piece of the action so they gather around and want some of the bait too."

"Because they are hungry?" the amateur asked

"Absolutely, now would you want to eat your meal watched by a hundred hungry people?" asked the Pro.

"Of course not" said the amateur

"well, neither do the fish, so what would you do?" asked the Pro

"I'd take the bait somewhere I could eat by myself" replied the amateur attentively.

"Exactly, so the next time you get a nibble, let the fish go, and give a little line. Then when your line tightens up again, strike then . . . OK?"

The amateur tried this new way, doing what he had been told, and by giving a little slack when he got the nibble he was able to land more fish in one day than he had ever done before in one week.

The parallel to be drawn here is the amateur salesman strikes as soon as he hears a buying signal and the result is very often no sale.

The buyers of today are like the wise old fish and they have seen too many hooks to be caught out by that old technique.

So, how do you "let out the line" in a sales call, and so hook the fish?

Imagine the buyer reveals an implied need and says something like "I wish I could find a way to cut those costs and make the department more profitable"

The amateur would say "Let me show you how we can do that . . ." Pulling the line in straight away.

The buyer is now under pressure and realising that the amateur is trying to sell him something goes on the defensive and starts to say things like "Well, of course I would need to think about that." The frightened buyer runs for cover! The amateur salesperson sensing the buyer slipping from his grasp chases even harder and with more enthusiasm hoping this will bring the buyer back to him. It all of course goes horribly wrong.

Could this have been done any better?

Yes, the buyer says something like "Yes, I like the sound of that . . ."

The professional, acts very cool and "lets out more line" by saying "That's great, however, are you sure this is what you want?" or "Let's not do anything now but meet up again in a week?"

No threat, no pressure. If this technique is continued the buyer will eventually hook themselves.

T is for TROUBLE AHEAD Questions or "T.A Questions"

Trouble Ahead questions are those that build upon the seriousness of the buyers problems.

They add momentum to the sale and put the buyer in the position of realising pain in the future. TA questions look at the consequences and implications of the problems that you have uncovered. In other words, if you have just uncovered the fact that the buyer maybe losing customers because of delayed deliveries, the follow up TA question, would be "what could be the effect on the business if this were allowed to continue?"

What this will do is to have the buyer think through the implications of each lost customer and how the business will be effected medium to long term.

Notice, you are not telling him the effect, he is. This is an important point. If you were to tell him something such as "obviously the loss of these customers will have a dramatic negative effect on the business", the buyer I am sure would agree, but they have not felt the pain that they would if they were made to think it through for themselves.

Good TA questions will therefore get the buyer to verbalise the PAIN he will go through if the problems you have uncovered are either a.) allowed to continue or b) forecast to happen.

The best way to avoid the price objection is to spend time on these questions.

If you regularly get the comment "It's too expensive" then you must get practised at using A.R.T.I.S.T questions, and especially the TA part.

The Maths

If you are selling a sales training course to a company priced at £3000 then you need to find out how many calls they are making, what the sales ratio is (how many calls to sales) and how much it cost to keep them on the road (ARENA questions)

Divide total cost by Total calls (ARENA questions) and you have how much it costs for the salesman to make each call successful or not. If they are currently selling one in five calls and it costs on average £161 per call (*The costs and effectiveness of salesforces in Britain report 1993 SQB.*) then they are getting one sale for every £805 spent, and the company is spending £644 per salesman on unproductive calls.

If we assume they have 5 salesman and they each make an average of 4 calls per day (*The costs and effectiveness of salesforces in Britain report 1993 SQB*) then they are making a total of 100 calls per week of which 20 are successful and 80 which are unsuccessful.

So, to find out how much money the company is spending in unproductive sales calls we simply times the 80 calls by the cost (£161) which equals £12,880 per week. If we get agreement that the salesman work on average 40 weeks a year then you can times that figure by 40 giving you a yearly cost to the company of unsuccessful sales calls of £515,200.!!

How difficult would it be to sell a training course that (worst case) improved the effectiveness of the sales people by 1% (£5152) for £3000? This however may have looked expensive if you hadn't gone through this exercise.

The secret of TA questions is to get the BUYER to give you his figures. It is VITAL that you do not make them up or assume them yourself or else when you get to the end the buyer will just turn round and deny it all. So, even if he doesn't know how many calls his salespeople are doing (in this example), you must agree together on a number before you move on.

Self Test

TA Questions or RP Questions

1 It's a busy office for this time of evening John, do you have people staying late often?
2 I see . . . What's the most common cause of this paid overtime?
3 Does that lead to problems in meeting pay budgets
4 When systems crash does it mean that you get involved personally
5 Are there any particular machines that crash more often
6 What happens when you can't get work done on time due to systems being down
7 Have these staff problems led you to lose any customers
8 In what way would you say the shortage of staff has effected the business with regard to response times?

TA questions are often more difficult, and certainly require a lot of concentration if you are to do the exercise as mentioned earlier, but they are worth it! You will rarely get the price objection when you have proved how much the current or the future problem is/or will cost them.

When you have discovered your implied need/s it is this step that helps transform that implied need into an explicit need (which, if you have planned it correctly should be the buyer clearly stating that they want to solve or prevent the problem that your product or service can solve or prevent!)

Research in this area has found that questions of this type are directly linked to success in large sales.

The key phrases you will need to remember when starting TA questions are these:

- "What does that result in . . ."
- "So, what happens when that occurs . . ."

The Pillars of Successful Management   105

- "What effect does that have on . . ."
- "Do you ever get . . ."

To ensure that you do not sound like a broken record, you will need to vary the way in which you ask TA questions. The amateur if asking at all may well get stuck in the groove of continually saying " What will happen if that problem is allowed to continue?" this will become a little irritating to the buyer.

It's important to realise that to be effective at **A.R.T.I.S.T** questions they do not (and almost certainly) won't follow in perfect sequence.

It is quite common to do some **Arena** Questions then RP questions then TA Questions them back to more Arena questions. Provided you are focused on helping the buyer uncover their problems and more importantly THE COST of those problems should they decide not to do anything about it you can't go wrong.

As with RP questions there are low-risk times to ask TA questions and there high risk times.

The low-risk times are:
- When the buyers problems are unclear to you
- When the problems need explanation
- When the buyers problems are substantial

The high-risk times are:
- At the beginning of the sales cycle
- When you can't sell a solution to the impending problem
- When the problem is of a delicate or political nature

I is for Internal Resource Questions.

I believe that buyers only buy when they can not solve their own problems with their own resources. It is only when these internal resources have been explored and found to be lacking that the buyer will turn to a solution to be provided by an outside supplier.

Let's imagine the buyer has expressed an explicit need that you can solve (yes!). Can you imagine asking the buyer a question such as "What internal resources do you have at your disposal that could satisfy this problem?" or "Are there any departments or other offices that could supply you with a product that would solve this problem?"

How do you think the buyer will react? Exactly, shocked, but pleasantly surprised!

I would suggest that it is unheard of for a salesperson to ask whether or not there is a way the buyer could solve their problem without selling them something.

I can just hear you saying "Hang on, surely, if I ask them to look to see if there is some other way internally of solving the problem I will do myself out of a sale!?". To answer, just ask yourself, would they have found that solution anyway?

Of course they would! The only difference is that this time they will find it while you are there. In other words saving you hours and hours of work providing a proposal that will be redundant along with the other ones who failed to ask the same question.

If they do find an internal solution, how will you be seen? Yes, you will be seen as having integrity by the bucket load, The one who saved them from having to buy anything. This cannot be a bad thing for referrals and future sales with that company can it?

So, in order for a buyer to make a decision about buying the seller's product or service, there must be a clear view of the product or service at the time the prospect discovers he has reached a pain plateau. A plateau he would really rather not endure any longer or experience at all. If the buyer is introduced to the product or service before he has undergone any pain about his current or future situation I believe he will reject the product wholeheartedly

S is for Specification Questions

This part of the process comes into play when you have:

1   Discovered the basic information (ARENA)
2   You have found indications of an implied need (REALISE PROBLEM)
3   You have examined and helped the buyer realise the implications that not solving this problem will have (TROUBLE AHEAD)
4   You have helped the buyer translate that into an explicit need (TROUBLE AHEAD)
5   You have helped the buyer search for a solution internally (INTERNAL RESOURCE)
6   You have reached the point where the buyer now confirms they need an external fix

How will the company decide which company to go with? Hopefully you if you have followed the stages as described and have built up such excellent rapport with the buyer that they wouldn't dream of going anywhere else. But, just to make sure, you need to go through this penultimate stage.

Unlike the other stages there are not many questions to ask in this section. Your questions will seek to establish what you will need to highlight from the product or service that will solve the buyers problems and what will the company need from you to satisfy their buying specifications

The question to the buyer is "What is the SPECIFICATION or criteria that you will use to choose an external solution?"

This often meets with blank faces only simply because the buyers rarely go through the process consciously.

The Pillars of Successful Management

You may hear answers such as;- "Before we invest, you would have to speak to our systems guy who would determine that what you had to offer would be compatible" or "We would have to make sure we were going to get a good service with the possibilities of penalties if the standards were not maintained"

These you may realise are not objections, the buyer is simply stating what SPECIFICATIONS he expects from you before the deal can go ahead.

Do not waiver off the specific point they want you to answer, as they are going through a thinking process that just needs you to dovetail with it to arrive at a satisfactory outcome.

Remember that the buyer will usually need to be sure of a number of things not just price before they can go ahead with your proposal so it's best to find out what these things are now.

These can include political implications, system compatibility, personnel compatibility, staff training implications, and budget implications with respect to whose department etc.

When you know what these are you will simply have to produce a solution that fits with their SPECIFICATION.

T is for Time Frame Questions

This last and most simple phase addresses the **TIME FRAME** the buyer looking to bring about the external fix? To establish this ask a question such as "How will you know when your company is ready for the change we have talked about?" It's a little more subtle than "when do you want it?"

A good tip I was told once was that the best clue as to how the buyer buys is to look at the steps that were taken for a previous purchase.

It sounds so obvious when someone says it to you. But, if they took three months deciding to spend £3000 how long will they take to spend £10,000? It is not always comparative but there well maybe clues that you can follow.

For example: First, the general idea was floated past the office manager, then with that approval, it would need to be in written proposal form for the director of sales to see. He would then after reading it call for you to do a personal presentation to the board, they meet every two months.

If this is how major decisions are made, it is as well you know what the form is, so you can follow it!

You will notice I am sure that the product has remained in our case up to now and even this may not be the time to do your presentation. Many salespeople choose to leave at this point and put together some ideas for a return visit. If your product or service does not warrant a return trip, now is the time to get the product out of the bag and and bring into play your presentation skills.

Summary

> ARTIST has been designed to give a structure to the flow of questions that will help both you and the buyer realise: what the problems are, the cost of not solving them, how to solve them, who can solve them and when to solve them.

The A.R.T.I.S.T Questioning Process

A is for ARENA
These questions are designed to investigate the facts and the background behind both the present arena and the future arena of the buyer.

R is for REALISE PROBLEM "R.P Questions"
These questions are designed to encourage the buyer to verbalise his problems in terms of implied needs.

T is for TROUBLE AHEAD or "T.A Questions"
These questions are those that build upon the seriousness of the buyers problems.

I is for INTERNAL RESOURCE
These questions are designed to establish whether or not the problem can be solved internally.

S is for SPECIFICATION
These questions are designed to establish the buyers criteria for the product/service

T is for TIME FRAME
These questions are designed to examine the previous buying patterns of the buyer.

Self Test Answers

Implied/Specific Need
1.Implied 2.Specific 3.Implied 4.Specific 5.Specific 6.Implied 7.Implied 8.Implied 9.Specific 10.Implied

High Risk/Low Risk
1   High Risk – The purchase was only a short while ago, so it is very likely the buyer will defend his reasons for making the decision. This is very dangerous ground!

2 *High Risk* – The reason for asking **Realise Problem** Questions is to uncover implied and explicit needs, once you have found them, move on!
3 *Low Risk* – This is a great time to ask **Realise Problem** questions, straight after establishing details from **Arena** questions.
4 *High Risk* – If you ask **Realise problem** questions at this time you may inadvertently uncover dissatisfactions about your own product/or service, and then you will be on the defensive.
5 *Low risk* – If ever there was an ideal time to ask **Realise problem** questions this is it. The more pain you can attach to this the better. Don't forget, that the greater the pain the more the buyer will pay to get rid of it or prevent it from happening in the first place.
6 *Low risk* – The purpose of **Realise Problem** questions is to uncover dissatisfaction, but if there aren't any, you do not really have anywhere to go except back out to the car park!

TA or RP Questions
1.RP 2.RP 3.TA 4.TA 5.RP 6.TA 7.TA 8.TA

7 Increasing Shareholder Value

Introduction

There have been many papers written, and expensive seminars staged on the sale and valuation of businesses. Excellent value if you are about to embark on the process of releasing the value in your business by selling it. I nevertheless sometimes wonder if these means are used as business gathering tools for consultants, accountants and lawyers. The dispensation of this knowledge is for use in what may possibly be a once in a life time situation. The subject of this chapter covers a much more than a once in a life time occurrence as it deals with the prime responsibility of the CEO and Board of Directors, namely increasing the value of the business on an ongoing and repeating basis.

This is applicable to all types of businesses whether they are in public ownership quoted on a stock exchange, or a private business of any size. Size is an issue in relation to corporate priorities particularly where large public corporations may be involved. In this instance financial engineering may dominate the management ethos and subsume the real objective in the minds of the career executives involved in 'running' such enterprises. The key words 'running the business' give a clue to performance as the business will perform below potential if this is seen to be the objective. At the other end of the scale in the case of the owner or family managed business a similar under achievement may occur for the same reason whilst arising from a different source. Many owner managers 'run' their businesses as a means of generating income to create a life style without achieving the understanding that their role is to continuously improve the value of the business whilst drawing income from it.

Why try to maximise performance for a corporate year end to impress the Stock Exchange or as you come to the realisation that you are going to sell the business? These are short term situations not necessarily in the best long term interests of the business. The overriding long term objective must be to create business processes and cultures which on a continuous basis improve the business and shareholder value no matter what the nature of that business. Implicit in this quest is the involvement of all of those who can affect the performance of the business. This means that we are discussing the realisation of the overall reason for the business existing. It is objectives, actions and cultures that affect all parties who in any way are touched by the existence of the business. Customers, suppliers, employees and shareholders.

In the large corporate or the smaller private enterprise there may be inadequate skills for the task of growing shareholder value. This limitation may be caused by the different cultures. Yet whilst both cultures arise from the differing perspectives described they are common and widespread in the business community. That which should predominate, the objective of increasing shareholder value, the value of the business, its worth as an entity are not widely recognised. The skills are not therefore developed to meet the overall need, which means that performance does not match what should be the overall purpose, how can it, if that purpose is not widely recognised? It follows therefore that if the fundamental purpose was recognised by all of those with responsibility for the management, development and value of these enterprises the performance of many businesses would be enhanced because the recognition of the need would lead to the progres- sand acquisition of the skills required.

In this chapter we will develop an objective view, techniques and processes which will show the way to achieving the objective of increasing shareholder value. This can appear mechanistic if it is not at all times understood and kept very much in mind that a business is the collective interaction of customers, suppliers, employees and shareholders and that success will only come from the effective management of the resulting variety of priorities and relationships. This determines that the management styles of 'only tell them what they need to know', 'mushroom management' and 'elitism' must be outlawed. If we are honest we have all suffered from it, done it and witnessed it. I write from the experience of a lifetime in business and the last twenty-five years of leading companies to improved performance. There are tactics to be adopted in given situations and the ability to develop the appropriate strategy is vital. However, we are discussing the maximisation of effectiveness with the objective of increasing shareholder value. This will not be achieved without the willing support, services, skills and positive input of all involved with the enterprise.

The start of the process

We are proposing to take a business performing at a particular level with the intention to alter the performance so that the value of the business is increased on a continuous basis. To embark on this process it is necessary to establish the performance of the business at the outset. It would be mis-leading to think that a valuation should be made of the business and that is the starting point. It is worthwhile creating a starting reference value based on an objective quantification, but only as a reference for measuring progress in the longer term. What is of most importance at this stage is to establish an objective quantification of current performance and trends;

How is the business performing?
What trends are evident?
Understand the markets in which it operates.
What products and services it offers.
What resources, human, physical and financial, it has available to carry on in business.
To do this a particular mind set needs to be created and this mind set will be central to the success of any efforts to increase the shareholder value.

If you arrive new to the business and you know what you are looking for you are objective because you are appraising the performance before you have formed any emotional attachments and have been influenced by the opinions of existing personnel. If however you are working in the business as say the owner manager, it will be more difficult to look in from outside on the business and see it as a number of interacting processes. Interacting processes, which you have to dispassionately assess to see how well they are performing individually and collectively. You have to learn to look at the business in this way and think dispassionately and objectively. So that you can quantify the effectiveness of the constituent parts, and of the total, with a view to devising ways of maintaining and improving the performance of the business by taking decisive considered action. Moreover you have to maintain this ability to give perspective as you progress with the challenge of improving the performance of the business and increasing its intrinsic value. This means that regularly reviewing progress and building on the gains made to date becomes a part of the ongoing approach to the management of the business.

I try to illustrate this by asking you to imagine your car engine not running correctly. The performance is not what it could be. If this is the case you analyse what is wrong – let us say the engine is mis-firing and you identify that a spark plug is not working. Having established the current performance you then work ON the engine to improve the performance, you may then work ON the tuning of the engine to obtain optimum performance. As you use your car you monitor performance (perhaps sub-consciously) to maintain on a continuous basis optimum performance. With the example of a car there is clearly a limit to performance improvement when you reach the optimum. Even so many of us try continuously to improve the car's performance and condition.

Working ON YOUR BUSINESS is a similar process for which you must have a range of skills coupled with the vision of where you want the business to eventually be. Please note the requirement for a range of skills rather than a specific specialist expertise. Only by firmly adopting such an objective stance and setting out to identify and develop the skills, with perhaps external assistance, will you achieve success in concluding an independent diagnostic review from which you develop and implement an ongoing programme for improvement. This review process will also be assisted if you can clear your mind of the organisational confusion and emotional attachments to individuals which seem to dog many businesses, more about this later.

The Review

At this juncture it is difficult not to get into an extremely detailed technical description of the review process and the detailed financial information necessary. The review process will therefore be dealt with under key headings, which may involve you in some future research.

Basic Information:

A profile of the business covering:

- Main (Owners) objectives for the business.
- What the company does, key activities, overall performance.
- Key Issues.
- Problems, Current and Anticipated.
- People:
  - Organisation Structure with names.
  - Directors responsibilities.
  - Key Staff.
  - Major skills in the business.
  - Team management, morale.

Marketing and Sales:

- Customers.
- Products/Services.
- Competitors.
- Promotion Media.
- Service Levels.

Finance and Administration:

- Business plan.
- Managing the business – objectives and monitoring.

- Monthly trading performance.
- Accounting procedures.
- Computer utilisation.
- Costing/Pricing policies.

Operations:

- Site, premises, offices.
- Equipment, machines.
- Workforce.
- Quality.
- Controls.
- Purchasing
- Distribution.

Analysis:

- Strengths – Weaknesses – Opportunities – Threats. [SWOT]
- Financial.
- Key financial data must cover: Trading Analysis Trends. Covering, the last financial year, the previous financial year and the current year forecast.
- Turnover.
- Gross Profit%.
- Operating Profit%.
- Cash Flow.
- Current Assets.
- Current Liabilities.
- Funding, capital.
- The Bank.
- Net Worth.

In this way key trends are established to determine the current situation which can be used as the point from which decisions can be made on action planning and assessment of risks. It is the starting point for the improvement programme which needs to identify opportunities for improving current performance and improving the use of resources which can if desired also be part of a long term strategy.

Principles of Control

Before embarking on any forward programme it is vital that the means of controlling the business are in place. Any enterprise from the home/one man business through to the large corporate should have a means of effectively controlling and monitoring progress.

The minimum standard practice is: A one year business plan/budget covering profit and loss account and cash flows. A small detail is that I prefer to talk about the annual plan as opposed to budget. This indicates the need to think ahead and plan what is going to be made to happen. Rather than spending the budget.

The Plan:

- The budget – look at the past and learn from it, note the trends.
- How can we maximise our resources?
- Involve supervisors and management
- Get commitment to the plan
- Always control costs and margins.

Cash Flow:

- Profit does not always mean money in the bank.
- Maintain Strong Credit control.
- Forecast Debtor receipts in detail and set payment policies accordingly.
- Capital expenditure can drain cash – be careful to estimate all costs.
- Eliminate obsolete stock.
- Make sure that stocks and work in progress are controlled and minimised.
- Turn unused assets into cash.
- Eliminate Borrowings.

Management Accounts

Monthly detailed management accounts showing month and year to date actual against plan. Management accounts should be produced without fail at the end of each monthly accounting period. A detailed considered review of the current performance should be conducted and corrective action decided upon, if necessary.

More broadly, to drive the business forward it is necessary to be able to work from a position of certainty in which it is known that the management information up to date, reasonably accurate and the correct controls are in place and working. The controls needed can vary with the level of activity of the business and the nature of its activities. So many leaders in business get impeded by the priority of Corporate Accounting deadlines and monthly reports, which can become to be seen as an end in themselves. Others get lost in the excess of accountants jargon and detail. The net effect is loss of impetus and focus on the agreed objectives. Yes management information meeting all of the above criteria is all important and needed, but it is information which must be seen as a providing of an indication of the continued health of the business from which conclusions can be drawn and further actions decided.

The effectiveness of a business is rarely established totally from conventional accounting packages alone and supplementary management information will be required. As a general rule the old adage 'if you can't measure it, you can't manage it' is an excellent principle.

Control Means No Surprises
The Way Ahead

We have completed the review, decided on the action plan, assured ourselves that the accounting information is accurate and that effective controls are in place and working.

At this point we must perhaps remind ourselves what we are seeking to achieve. We could now get distracted by considering the very interesting and tempting topic of strategic direction, many wish to talk in general terms about what is right for the business but taking action and bringing about enhanced performance is what counts at this juncture. The immediate strategy is to create a business which is improving in performance and which will continue to improve. Strategic direction is vital in the context of overall longer term business development and will be progressively developed as the growth in shareholder value occurs. The purpose of this chapter is to create a means for you to take an existing business to another level of performance to 'increase shareholder value'. We will therefore put aside the topic of strategic direction and concentrate on **Company Effectiveness.**

Many people in organisations will initially resist the principle of 'if you can't measure it, you can't manage it' so one of the key culture changes is to get people to understand the importance of management information through simple measurement as sound business practice. Which means sharing the key information and using it as a motivational spur. When this occurs the information (the production and use of which was probably initially resisted) invariably becomes adopted as a means of people measuring their own progress. This is an ideal situation because the collective focus becomes performance and how to improve it. As improvements come through morale rises throughout the organisation.

There are many facets to the quantification and action plan processes but it is of vital importance to fully understand the principles of LEVERAGE. In this context Leverage is the art of applying the least effort in the correct place at the appropriate time to gain maximum effect. The action planning following the review will have established where effort for improvement is required and the correct priorities will be set by objective quantification. The quantification process allows you to set your priorities so that you work on that which is going to give you the best benefit. Get the biggest pay off as fast as you can. To get the maximum effect it is necessary to identify the areas to affect. Examination of Exhibit 1 shows in 'family tree' format the ingredients which impact shareholder value. Plainly all will not have the same effect and improvements will be achieved over differing time periods. It is necessary to identify priority actions which give rapid short term perhaps one off benefit, as distinct from those of a longer term nature which may require a different approach to achieve. Exhibit 2 is based on a fictitious company turning over £1million, this to illustrate the principle of Leverage. The effect on the business of a 10% increase in selling prices far out ways any other action in terms of the Profit earned, whilst a 10% reduction in cost of sales lowers the break even. The striking order would be; increase selling prices whilst reducing cost of sales as the top priorities. Too many executives have opinions on what is needed when a little objective quantification identifies of the Leverage Effect which will focus every mind and allow development of agreed actions which everyone understands. Simple quantification shared with those that impact on results rapidly creates consensus, which saves time spent on endless debate.

Total Company Effectiveness has now become the issue as we progress from the current performance following the review, which established, how the business is performing, what are the dominant trends and what actions are needed.

The Organisation

In an earlier paragraph I briefly touched on the issue of whether the organisation is 'confused' and suffering from 'organisational road blocks'. These terms I use in relation to the organisation of the Management Structure and the efficient working of the whole in fulfilling its primary purpose which is in turn a measure of the 'performance of the people' within the business. The often used phrase *management of people* in business is itself mis-leading. If you are managing the people you are fundamentally missing the point.

The structure without exception has three legs; Marketing, Operations, Finance.

- Marketing and Sales – Wins the Business
- Operations – Processes orders/contracts.
- Finance and Administration – Handles Accounts, Administration and Management Information.

In professional practices and small businesses, all of these activities occur, though sometimes done by the same individual, but not at the same time. In larger organisations there are activities within each of these functions as shown on the sample organisation chart Exhibit 3.

There is here a vital principle which should never be overridden but which invariably is.

Many businesses have the organisation designed around the function and not the people.

Why?

The principles of designing and maintaining an organisation structure are not widely understood, so when the business is progressively equipped with resources (humans) the situation often gravitates from one of how does the organisation integrate this new additional activity/task to one of 'who shall we get to do this?' Hence the structure becomes corrupted. Allowances are also made for friends, favourites, old hands, relations, poor performers, characters etc. This can only have one outcome, an ineffective management system which has allowed the creation of an organisation not capable of best completing that which it is there to do. Tasks carried out and organisation of the human resource within the three functional legs must be set to meet the needs of the clients and the business only. These must be determined dispassionately to define the purpose of each particular position in the organisation. The individual who fills the position has to be fully competent in the work requirements of that position with a clear understanding and acceptance of the responsibilities and authority of the position whilst understanding and accepting the importance of its relationships and effectiveness in the wider workings of the business. It is my contention that in a correctly designed management structure each position will have a relevance to the whole business and no matter how apparently junior the role may seem the incumbent has to reach an acceptable level of performance and be accorded the respect this deserves. If people would more widely understand that performance in the role is what deserves respect rather than expect respect from apparent seniority many of our businesses would perform better. It is of great importance that the minimum standards required of any position are met. Objective appraisal of performance coupled with direct action to bring about improvement is essential. This can involve training or some hard decisions. A business embodying the principles outlined will operate with flexibility and will effectively achieve more when the overall structure is understood and everyone readily accepts their part in the workings of the business.

In some organisations because of size it is necessary for some individuals to carry out a number of complimentary tasks. This need does in no way change the functional structure. In my view this is where much confusion arises, for some reason many people find it difficult to see a business as a number functions carrying out processes needing to effectively work as part of a system which is in itself the complete process. In any business you secure orders/instructions, you process those orders/instructions and you count the results of the transactions. This happens within functions, departments, sections, and to individuals and is where the resistance to quantification often arises as people initially do not like to be measured in terms of their performance because they see themselves as individuals. They think they know better or are insecure and resist. Weak management allows under performance and corruption of the organisation structure to satisfy the individual.

It happens time and time again and yet, when this natural resistance is logically and fairly overcome and the individuals accept the satisfaction of monitoring their own and their functions performance, from the company information generated they start to see the contribution they can make. They progressively gain satisfaction and confidence from making a growing contribution to the performance of the business. Confused organisation must not happen if the business is to operate at anything like optimum performance.

How many businesses have you known that do not have a widely understood organisation structure?

How many businesses have you known where the work needing to be carried out was not fully understood by the immediately responsible supervisor/manager?

How many businesses have you known where because of this lack of understanding the incumbent never had his or her responsibilities clearly explained?

How many times have you seen someone promoted without training for the new position?

Should we then be surprised that businesses do not perform to their full potential?

Simple but obvious truths often ignored. The key point is that, people correctly developed working within a defined organisation will perform well because they understand how the system is intended to work. By having a clearly defined organisation it is possible to determine the skills required and the level of competence for the effective execution of the duties and the responsibilities within the particular position and the overall system.

Returning to the car engine analogy.

We would not let an untrained, unskilled operator loose on our expensive cherished possession – would we?

Why then do we take chances with our business organisations?

Based on personal experience I can confidently assert that it happens all of the time. People get thrust into positions not because they are fitted perfectly for the role with the right skills, attitudes and experience and with capacity for further development. The overriding criterion invariably is that they are acceptable to the person making the selection, or need to be appeased in some way which means that subjectivity overrides objectivity, and the higher you go in many organisations, particularly large corporates, this is more prevalent. I could write a chapter on theories of why this is so but this is not the purpose of this particular exercise. The point is the organisation structure needs to be designed functionally for the needs of the business and people with the appropriate attributes placed in the correct positions to let the system work. It is our task to optimise the overall performance. This will invariably be way ahead of the current performance particularly if 'organisational road blocks' are removed and the 'organisational confusion' is eliminated.

Focus and Direction

In setting the scene at the beginning it was indicated that the CEO is primarily responsible for increasing shareholder value. To do this he or she needs to recognise that clear focus and direction needs to be achieved and understood throughout the business. Focus and direction are about the future which involve some strategic thinking and strategic action to create five ingredients in harmony with each other.

1. Mission – our mission is to continuously grow shareholder value through operational effectiveness. If this is the clear purpose of the business and the people in the business understand the mission then they, the people, behave progressively in line with the spirit of the mission. (Not to be confused with a mission statement)
2. Vision – there is a clear picture of the future which people recognise. When in place your people seem to find ways of moving towards the vision.
3. Core Skills – what the business is good at, core skills in terms of how customers are won and profit is made – are clearly identified. The business develops core skills into new opportunities.
4. Environment – being aware of the trends of change, the business constantly accurately identifies threats and opportunities. It is very rarely taken by surprise, and uses this information to move towards emerging customer needs.
5. Key Resources – assets critical to the business's continued performance. It has identified and ensured a regular supply of key resources. The business will not be stifled by the lack of critical resources.

A significant deficiency in any of these areas will limit the business's ability to shape its focus and direction. Key is the issue of resources and here I would like to define these a little more clearly as we are talking of the vision, meeting the customer's needs and their relationship.

	Important to the business	*Those of which an effective supply exists*
	A	B

* People and Skills
* Raw Materials
* Energy
* Information
* Equipment/Technology
* Capital
* Customer Base
* Contacts
* Collaborative partners
* Company image
* Know how and intellectual property

By ticking as appropriate current resources are assessed and a future supply plan can be established by considering the gaps between A and B.

The Growth Challenge

So far we have considered the importance of establishing the performance and characteristics of the business. In so doing we have discussed the importance of control and working from a secure base to ensure no unpleasant surprises. We have reviewed the need for objectivity to allow the development of action plans embracing the principle of leverage whilst emphasising the vital importance of the organisation structure, freedom of information and the performance of people with clearly defined roles in the organisation. There is little to be gained from reviewing in detail the differing types of operational means of fulfilling orders which operate in the myriad of businesses that exist. We will pass on with the assumption that we have a business, which is capable of meeting its customer's needs effectively. Suffice it to say that all of the principles that have so far been outlined, apply to any complete business. No matter what the nature of the operational methods of the business the review process, control principles and culture development all applied in a focused action driven manner will give a performance uplift. I am basically saying that in any business, constant improvement is possible. This is undoubtedly so, provided the design of the information systems and organisation structure are sound and coupled with the correct amount and type of human resource. Under pinning all of this is the need for acceptance of change arising from constant review of performance and the consequent development of improvement action plans. Moreover the ready acceptance of changes to existing practices is so vital because the personnel within the enterprise will respond to the challenge if they are shown the purpose, more, as the processes become established and the culture is developed they will develop confidence and start to initiate change. The culture for this comes from the vision and desire of the CEO.

We are not to lose sight of the purpose of this chapter and it is time to consider the subject of growth. Earlier I mentioned the distinction which needs to be made between 'running the business' and 'growing and developing' the business by 'working on the business.' I also outlined the principle of leverage showing as an example the relative effect on margins resulting from action on selling prices and direct costs. These examples are valuable and considerable early opportunity may exist, it is worth noting that these may be one off opportunities, particularly the selling price adjustment. The principle of leverage applies wherever you are deciding on priorities. However, building on operational improvements we need growth of turnover and this has to come from Marketing and Sales performance. Let me illustrate the need to capture the importance of sales performance as an ongoing activity key to the growth in shareholder value.

Consider the example company;

		%		%
Turnover:	1,000	100	1,200	100
Total CoS	750	75	900	75
GM	250	25	300	25
Fixed Costs	190	19	190	16
Profit	60	6	110	9

In this illustration sales growth of 20% results in profit growth of 83%. So that there is no confusion let me explain. Cost of Sales in each case is 75% of the sales value covering basically costs which are only incurred in the execution of the additional business. i.e., materials, labour, power etc., resulting in a growth in Gross Margin of 25% in line with the turnover increase. Where it now starts to get interesting is as we look at the effect after the deduction of the Fixed Costs/Overheads. These have not changed and are reduced as a proportion of turnover, resulting in growth in profit of 110-60 = 50 which when expressed as a percentage is 83%. This is yet another example of quantification of the possible effect to allow decisions based on fact on where to apply the effort. We are now in the situation of deciding on how to obtain the desired growth without the addition of any fixed costs. Many will express opinions on what to do, and many will set off following their hunches but once again there are opportunities available which can be exploited. The golden rule is to follow the dictates of our old companion Leverage.

Sources of Growth

Acquisitions.

This route can give a leap in size if executed successfully. Many fail to live up to the projections leading to the conclusion that the glamour and excitement can send common sense out of the window. The post acquisition integration process is extremely difficult to cope with and a great drain on management time and resources. There are many advantages if the process can be accomplished successfully including increased market share, extension of a range of services or product, additional capacity, protecting supply sources and adding sales outlets.

Mergers and Demergers.

Mergers may be particularly relevant for smaller companies and professional partnerships. It may be desirable to merge to create size to offer additional services or products in line with market demands. It is a tactic used to accelerate entry to the stock market or overcome problems caused by lack of management succession.

Conversely, demergers are used to release non-core and/or loss making businesses, releasing funds for reinvestment, and in the case of loss making businesses improving the return from the retained business.

Collaborations

- Licensing and Royalty Deals.

This can be a quick and relatively straight forward tactic for the company which does not have products or services which allow it to push for export growth. There are numerous examples of Japanese and US companies establishing a European presence through this route.

- Franchising.

This is very much dependent on the nature of the business – service – product. It has become increasingly popular in the past 30 years and can be the driver for extremely rapid growth.

- Joint Ventures.

Very often used on specific projects to augment the resources of a business which could not tackle a project alone. Co-operative arrangements for sharing marketing costs can be successful. This method is very dependant on the chemistry between the participants.

- Organic Growth.

Even if any of the foregoing are being pursued the need for the business to grow organically is always present. Effective organic growth means developing the business internally by encouraging people to come forward with new ideas and variations for products, services, market segments and sales opportunities.

The process needs to be on-going as it can be long term. Many organisations toy spasmodically in this whole area where in fact a tight dedicated approach is required. We will deal with identifying the major elements contributing to this form of growth and the understanding required. We will conclude by more setting of priorities for attack using objective review and Leverage.

Take stock of your market

- identify the market segments and geographical territories currently served which can be entered

- evaluate each one by analysing the relevant history
  identifying and evaluating trends and likely developments
  compiling future projections

This whole process starts with the idea that the business becomes market focused as opposed to being product focused. By becoming market focused it becomes possible to establish what are the major market segments that will provide opportunities.

As a result many ideas for opportunities will start to occur;

Should we...
- promote a limited edition of a product?
- focus on a major customer?
- focus on a newly identified major target?
- offer to create different products or services for a selected major customer/
- transform a specialist service into a branded standard product?
- adopt a low-cost no-frills approach?
- concentrate more on product design and point-of-sales presentation?

Should we...
- take our existing technology to a different market?
- enter an existing market with different technology?
- enter an existing market with a different product?
- enter an existing market with a different service?

This is all good value in establishing policy. It will however all be wasted if certain basic actions are not part of the routine operations of the business. In describing them as routine, I am not in any way wishing to imply or give the impression that they can be taken for granted. I am of course coming to what is the make or break for any business, the customers. The routine being that of nurturing and protecting the existing relationship whilst winning
more business. I expressed fairly clear views in relation to personnel recruitment and assessment earlier. These views are nothing compared to those that I hold in relation to the general approach taken by much of British business to customer relations. We are appalling. We have it seems to me just got past the 'what do you want?' stage. True there are many companies that are paying attention to this whole area of customer contact for generating additional business but there is still a long way to go before we can truly claim that British business is truly achieving fully effective customer relations. British companies abuse their customers in so many ways. The latest example being the introduction of new financial services at higher interest rates than existing accounts, and the staff in the institution being 'advised' not to inform existing account holders.

The problem is that such policies are possibly doing irreparable harm. Turn this the other way round. Your company can win out if you get the whole process of customer contact/relations right and a sound system of lead generation in place.

Let me at this moment give an example from a British manufacturing business, this is from real life experience when a director of the company was asked to describe how the business went about getting orders:

- Planning – no plan, reactive to enquiries.
- Getting enquiries – no active plan. (I know but this was what was written down)
- Achievement control – the existing order book.
- Incentives – money on invoiced sales.
- Advertising – almost none.
- Literature – much of average/poor quality.
- Product range – 50 'prime products', 250 others listed.
- Product mix – Machines for sector 1, Machines for other industries, Consumables for sector 1
- Control of product sales – None, reactive to client demands.
- Sales staff – 1 person   80% on customer contact.
  10% on documentation.
  10% on reception duties.

Willing and competent, not currently motivated, no direction or ability to plan. Can be ponderous with paperwork. Well thought of by clients.

I accept that this may be extreme case but it is in part typical. The area where it represents what is evident in so many of our companies is in relation to the products and the stance in relation to the market.

The company illustrated clearly needed to become market focused. To enable any organisation to become market focused some fundamentals need to be addressed.

Are you offering   – a product? – specify them all.
  – a service? – specify them all.
  – a mixture of both? – understand the mix and their relationships.

Many people confuse this issue and do not clearly differentiate between products and services, clarity is vital in the minds of the people doing the marketing and selling. Define all products and services in total, even in established businesses this exercise brings forward offerings which had not been previously recognised. Next identify the market sectors to which the products and services apply. You already have an existing customer base which can be divided into the applicable sectors. Over time it will be possible to identify all of the businesses in each sector and thus extend your target market.

We are setting out to continue with the growth of the business and it is necessary to decide where to apply the effort which is going to give the best chance of success for the least effort. Yet another example of leverage. The following illustration shows very clearly where to devote your selling effort.

This allows a very clear set of conclusions to be drawn:

a: The best source of additional business is from existing customers, old enquirers and old contacts.
b: By keeping close to your best source for additional business you reduce the risk of losing the customer by lack of contact.
c: By keeping in regular contact with your existing customers you are responding to the buying influences and are in a position to obtain referrals and intelligence through the word of mouth process.

It is necessary not to drift away from this method of working. Indeed structured programmes for regular contact with major customers are essential. How do you decide who are your important customers? Grade them;

The reality:

Sources of NEW Business	%	Reasons for LOSS of custom	%	Company Buying INFLUENCES	%
Chance	5	Misc	9		
Referrals	15	Enticed by competition	15		
New names	20	Product not satisfactory	9		
Existing customers Old enquirers Old contacts	60	Lack of contact	67	Actively seeking inf.	68
				Buy from those that keep in touch	60
				Actively look forward to receiving post.	70
				When seeking new product or service use word of mouth	50

Source: Henley Centre for Forecasting.

A customers – Probably the 20% who are 80% of your turnover, who warrant around six visits per year.

B customers – Those of a size which is sufficient to warrant around 3/4 visits per year as they make significant impact on your turnover and could grow to be A's.

C customers – Those that place a small amount of business with you each year and have no real loyalty or prospects such that you are probably best to adopt a reactive stance.

Having defined the full range of your businesses products and/or services and understood where you are going to get the best return you now need to go forward with 3 objectives.

This is the critical action mode which is going to truly determine the growth in shareholder value.

1   Increase the average order size.

Tell your existing customers about the full range of your products and/or services and when you have explained the full scope of what you can provide sell them and keep doing it to get maximum penetration.

2   Increase the average order frequency.

By selling more to your existing customer base plus lapsed customers etc., you will increase the order frequency. However what you also need to do is create additional ways for the customer to take the services or products more frequently.

3   Increase the number of active accounts.

We do this by adopting a strong market orientation taking our full extended range of products and services to existing customers, lapsed customers, previous enquirers and old contacts. Whilst continuing to seek new business.

An increase by any one of these three means is going to be beneficial, a combination will give exponential growth. A 10% increase in each would have the following effect on our example company.

		%		%
Turnover	1,000	100	1,333	100
Total CoS	750	75	1,000	75
GM	250	25	333	25
Fixed Costs	190	19	190	14
Profit	60	6	143	11

A turnover increase of 33% coming through as a 138% increase in profits.

If you employ a sales force in your business it is essential that they are achieving in line with this method of attack on the market in an action oriented programme. You are requiring of them that they do their job in a focused, controlled and disciplined manner. This is an anathema to a salesman and will require dedicated management on your part.

Take Action – Develop an effective business generating system using the following process:

1. Calculate; target annual sales
2. Calculate; average order size from historical records.
3. Calculate; number of orders per year.

$$\text{Calculation:} \frac{\text{Step 1}}{\text{Step 2}} = \text{Number of orders.}$$

4. Decide on how many orders will come from existing customers. Buying customers.
5. Determine how many orders are required.

   Calculation: Step 3 – Step 4 = New orders required.
6. Calculate conversion rate.

   Quotations to orders(e.g. 3 quotes to one order).

7. Calculate the number of new orders required.

   Calculation: multiply Step 5 by Step 6. Divide the answer by 12 to give the new orders required per month. Build in any seasonal effect.

8. Determine the conversion rate of new prospects to quotes.
   (e.g. four new prospects to one quotation).
9. Calculate the number of prospects required.

   Calculations: multiply Step 7 by Step 8. Divide by 12 to obtain monthly figure.

This is the arithmetic of the Business Generation System. Now you need to work out how to create the business on a regular basis.

10. Determine how new prospects are best created in your business (i.e. mailshots, telephone calls, advertisements, exhibitions etc.).

Plan to undertake this activity monthly to create the level of prospects required at step 9.

It is necessary to collect the data of activity on a monthly frequency and work on the performance of the group and the individuals. Progressively performance will improved and the business will be growing profits progressively. Which means that the value of the business is being enhanced and if you have used the pointers in this paragraph it will mean that everyone in the enterprise is contributing to the growth and in so doing leaving you free to work on the business to continue the process.

Summary

I have illustrated parallels which exist between public and private enterprises. The common goal of increasing shareholder value has been identified and reasons why many companies fail to perform at the optimum level explored. Recognising the need for shareholder value (the value of the business) to be enhanced I have described where to start the process and the nature of information required with the controls necessary to allow the development of quantified objective action plans. Action planning involves the identification of priorities and the principles of leverage were explained with examples. The importance of a sound management structure was outlined with information on what pitfalls to avoid as the structure develops when the business grows. The importance of the CEO's vision and clear focus on the objectives was followed with an explanation of the sources of where the growth will come from. Targeting on the most fruitful areas of the markets following the development of the full product and services portfolio was illustrated. Examples of what may be achieved are set out for additional understanding and as illustrations of techniques that have been developed, tried, tested and proven in real company situations in a variety of sectors and differing circumstances. In this chapter I have hopefully been able to create a flavour of what may be possible in the quest to raise the value of a business for the shareholders. I use the word quest because that is what it is. I have worked in the public and private sectors for 25 years leading companies to increased value through some of the techniques briefly outlined. The quest is so interesting and rewarding because it is also a continual learning process with measurable results as you progress. In increasing shareholder value you can focus on the single objective of a business and embrace all of the constituent facets of business in total. So many of the currently fashionable topics are but just a part of the whole. Setting out to increase shareholder value allows you to devise your own solutions to the many and varied obstacles and questions encountered, and you can try many alternatives. I hope that a flavour of this comes through in the text and makes you want to set out on the interesting and rewarding journey. I have enjoyed setting out some of my thoughts for you and hope that you will find some spark for ideas to try in your own situation. To progressively improve a business is a very rewarding process which can also be fun. I wish you substantial success in your endeavours and would very much like to hear of any major successes as they occur.

Good Luck!

Michael Harrison

The Pillars of Successful Management

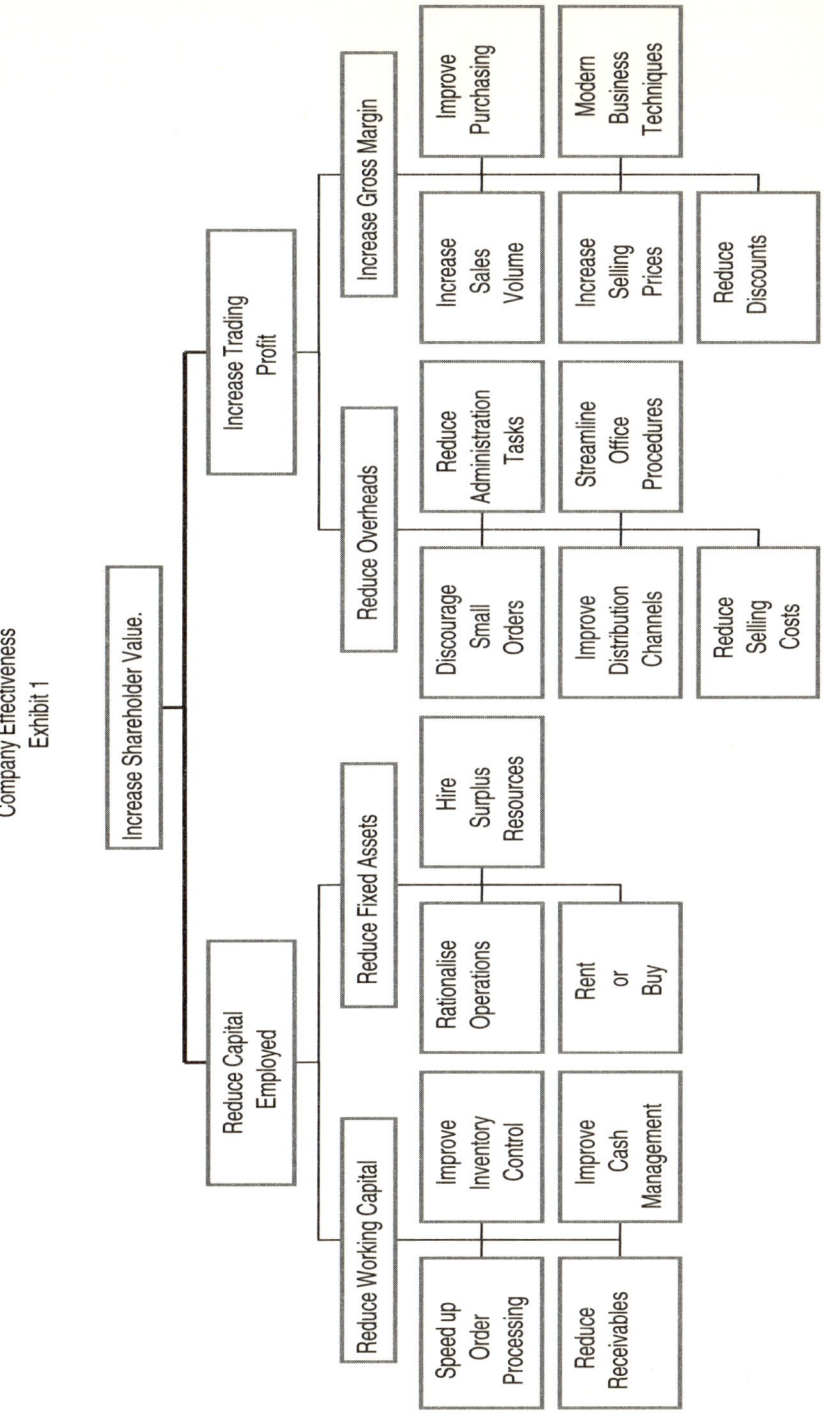

Company Effectiveness
Exhibit 1

```
Increase Shareholder Value
├── Increase Trading Profit
│   ├── Increase Gross Margin
│   │   ├── Improve Purchasing
│   │   ├── Modern Business Techniques
│   │   ├── Increase Sales Volume
│   │   ├── Increase Selling Prices
│   │   └── Reduce Discounts
│   └── Reduce Overheads
│       ├── Reduce Administration Tasks
│       ├── Streamline Office Procedures
│       ├── Discourage Small Orders
│       ├── Improve Distribution Channels
│       └── Reduce Selling Costs
└── Reduce Capital Employed
    ├── Reduce Fixed Assets
    │   ├── Hire Surplus Resources
    │   ├── Rationalise Operations
    │   └── Rent or Buy
    └── Reduce Working Capital
        ├── Improve Inventory Control
        ├── Improve Cash Management
        ├── Speed up Order Processing
        └── Reduce Receivables
```

GAINING LEVERAGE.
Exhibit 2

£000's

	Current	%	Increase Sales by 10%	%	Decrease CoS by 10%	%	Decrease Fixed Cost 10%	%	Increase Sales Price 10%	%
Turnover	1,000		1,100		1,000		1,000		1,100	
Cost of Sales	800		880		772		800		800	
GROSS MARGIN	200	20	220	20	278	28	200	20	300	27
Fixed Costs	190		190		190		190		190	
PROFIT BEFORE TAX	10	1	30	3	88	8.8	30	3	110	10
BREAK-EVEN POINT	950		950		679		855		704	

This analysis is at the heart of rapid profit improvement, which is often, though not always, possible in a company.

The Pillars of Successful Management

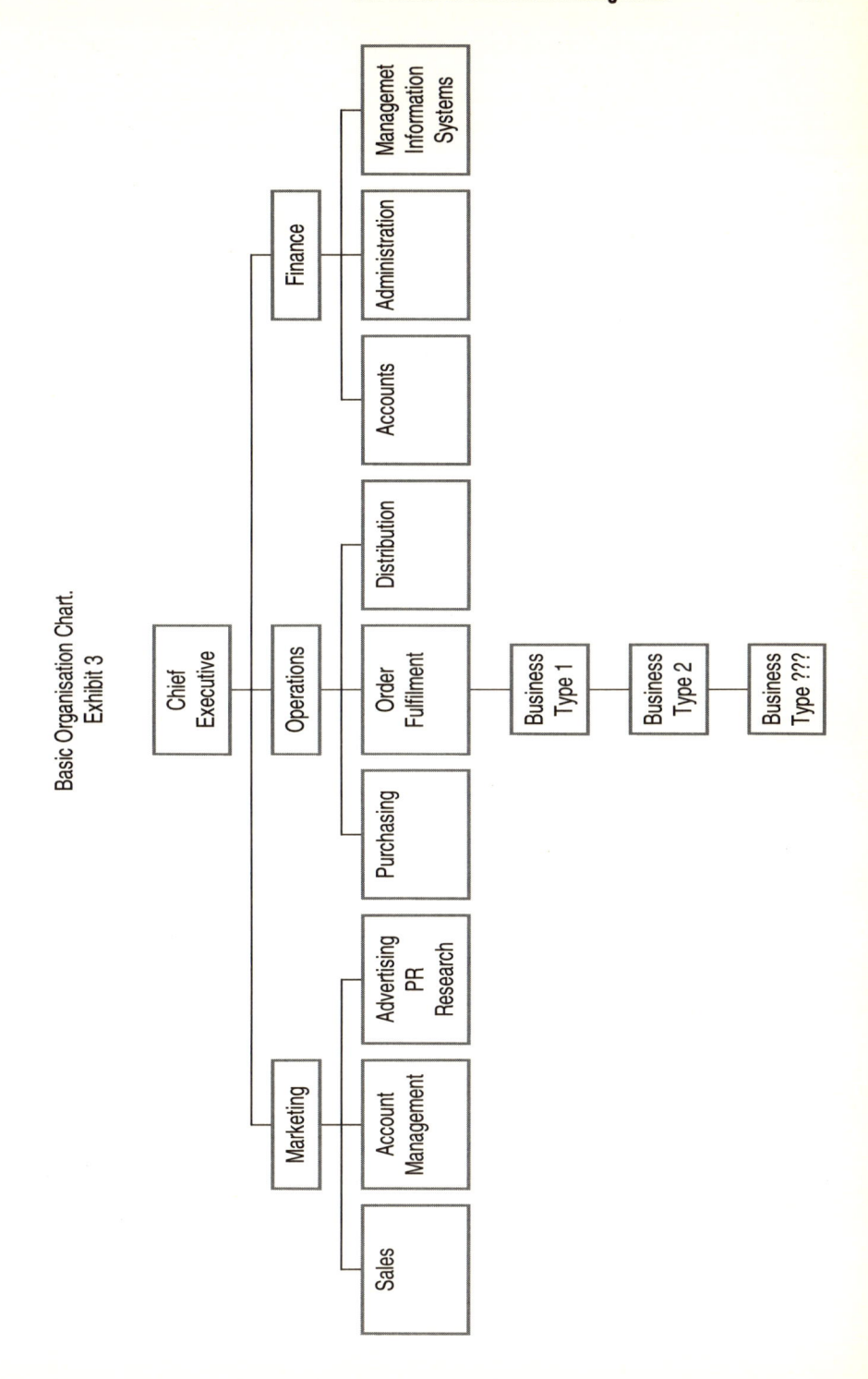

Basic Organisation Chart.
Exhibit 3

```
                           Chief
                         Executive
                             |
        ┌────────────────────┼────────────────────┐
     Marketing            Operations            Finance
        |                     |                    |
   ┌────┼────┐         ┌──────┼──────┐       ┌─────┼─────┐
  Sales Account Advertising Purchasing Order Distribution Accounts Administration Management
       Management   PR                 Fulfilment                                  Information
                  Research                                                           Systems
                                        |
                                  Business Type 1
                                        |
                                  Business Type 2
                                        |
                                  Business Type ???
```

8 Stress management for managers

Stress. Is something that happens to other people right. It doesn't happen to me, I'm not stressed. OK well I do get a bit short with people from time to time and well I've had those spells where I can't sleep properly. But me stressed.... not a chance. Maybe Fred from accounts, speak to him.

Would this be your reaction if I suggested that you may be suffering from, or could suffer from stress. I think its fair to say that we have all suffered from the effects of stress at one time or another in our lives. Yet how many of us realise the potential effect it can have on our health and also our performance as effective managers or business owners.

Stress itself is not a new phenomenon its been with us for centuries. In fact stress in its purest and healthiest form was experienced by our caveman ancestors. The fight or flight response to threat or danger. The effects are becoming more and more prevalent however. The number of days lost to businesses worldwide through stress related illnesses are growing daily. Indeed the majority of the average GP's daily round is directly attributable to the strain of modern living. The coughs, colds, aches, pains and the insomnia. In fact virtually everything that seems to have no apparent physical cause. So much so that we are living in what will probably become known as the 'Century of Stress'.

Sadly most people only become aware or admit that they are suffering from the effects of stress when the effects or symptoms have reached an advanced stage. This normally means that their performance at work, their family life or health is suffering. At this stage the average person goes in search of 'the quick fix'. Like free lunches, I'm afraid there is no such thing, it takes time and dedication to return to a normal healthy state. However, don't be disheartened the journey itself can be very rewarding and the prize is that once begun it will continue and all those symptoms will occur less and less frequently.

Before I go any further its important to note that not all stress is bad. Imagine you are crossing the road when suddenly a car careers round the corner, travelling at speed heading straight for you. I imagine that like any normal person your body would take immediate and probably very rapid action to reach safety. In doing so you and your body have been subject to stress, which has very quickly produced the correct mental and physical reactions necessary for survival. This is an example of the fight or flight response mentioned earlier, in this case flight.

What is Stress?

The dictionary defines it as 'emphasis, strain, impelling force, effort, tension, accent. Not very helpful in the context that the word stress is most commonly used. The London Institute of Stress Management use what I believe is the most useful definition of stress.

Stress is
'OUR INTERNAL RESPONSE TO EXTERNAL EVENTS'

Take a moment to consider this definition. What does it mean to you? Has a lightbulb come on? It is, very important that you have a clear understanding of this as it is the cornerstone of dealing with the effects.

Let's break the definition down a little further.' Our internal response.' This indicates that what happens around us will have either a direct or indirect effect on our lives. These events do not in themselves cause us to suffer stress rather its the way our mind processes them that can cause stress.

Imagine that you have just been given a major assignment by your boss. You already have a hundred and one things to do and the deadline is the next day. How do you feel? Angry, resentful, 'why me I'll never get it done'. Maybe you feel 'OK it's not what I wanted right now, but it will be interesting, I'll be able to get it done in time though it will mean a few hours extra work. It will certainly help with my next promotion.'

Two different internal responses to an external event. If your thoughts had been along the same lines as the first person you would most likely suffer the effects of stress much more than the second person whose more positive approach to the same situation kept them calmer. Which brings me to the most important concept in the management of stress. This concept is all to do with choice.

You may not believe it but everyone that suffers from stress made the choice to do so. At this point you are probably very sceptical and thinking that you don't have that much control over your thinking. You're probably right, not many people do. What I'm trying to do is help you understand that if you realise you have a choice about how you react to things then you can begin to minimise the effects of stress.

Lets look at the next part of the definition. 'To external events'. The first thing to note at this stage is that external events can be both real or imagined. An important point. Think about something that caused you great anxiety in the past. Maybe it was a presentation you had to give, maybe it was the last time you asked for a pay rise. Was the event itself as bad as you imagined it to be? Probably not, yet your imagination almost certainly ran riot constructing all sorts of disasters or undesirable outcomes. These imagined disasters would have increased your stress levels enormously, and may have had a detrimental effect on your desired outcome. Yet they were not reality but what you imagined that reality would look like. Why do we invariably look at the worst outcome and not the outcome we desire.

Another important point about external events is there are some things you can change and some you can't, yet many people get very stressed indeed, reacting badly to things they have no control over. Why are we so unfair to ourselves?

What are the early warning signs of stress?

I know it sounds strange but the vast majority of people don't know how to recognise the indicators and early warning signs of stress. More importantly many people that have suffered major illnesses as a result of stress continue to do the very things that caused the illnesses in the first place. Its like driving down the road when the oil warning light comes on. Do you go to the garage and get them to remove the bulb or do you get the problem fixed? Or do you just think 'what an attractive light I've got on my dashboard' A lot of people remove the bulb when they apply the situation to their own health but wouldn't dream of removing the bulb in their car.

The early warning signs can be broken down into two categories, physical and emotional.

The physical signs usually manifest themselves as a general feeling of being below par. Mostly headaches, indigestion, inability to sleep properly, tightness of the chest, palpitations and a whole host of unexplainable aches and pains. In some cases the effects can be severe enough for people to suffer from diarrhoea.

All of these symptoms can be dealt with once we realise that they are connected to our situation and the way we are currently handling it. What is most important here is that we deal with the cause and not the symptoms themselves. In the case of stress related complaints the result of dealing with the symptoms and not the cause is temporary respite, which can lead to more severe manifestations at a later stage.

A good indicator that the symptoms you experience may be attributable to stress is to see if any of the emotional signs are present at the same time. An inability to relax properly, intolerance of noise or other disturbing stimuli. Poor memory. Inability to concentrate. Reduced willpower. Uncontrollable emotions. Inability to finish tasks. Impulsive behaviour and overreaction to little things. These signs may occur individually but it is more common to experience more than one at a time.

If you notice any or all of the above early warning signs both mental and physical then it's likely you are suffering from stress. Don't panic, the good thing is that you are now aware that there is a challenge to overcome and that it is within your power to do something about it. In this realisation alone and by accepting the challenge you are already well on the way to overcoming the problem. We will look at what you can to combat stress in more detail a little later.

Before we go on to look at the ways to reduce stress and restore the balance you need in your life to be healthy its important to consider that some people appear better able to cope with stress than others. There are a number of reasons for this. However for our purposes the main reason is that these people all display certain characteristics.

Those people that show a strong commitment to what they are doing and view it as important and valuable will be able to withstand higher levels of pressure. Those who are functioning as robots, mechanically doing their set tasks, waiting for the weekend or the holidays will be less able to cope with their situation and will feel generally unfulfilled and restless. Such people tend to moan about their lot in life but have no suggestions as to how improve.

The people that have control over their lives generally handle stress better than those who stand and watch as events happen to them and respond with the poor me, its awful, attitude. Be very careful here with the word control. Control in this context means how we react to what happens to us and how we can affect these events. It does not mean we must control all of what happens. It would be impossible to do this and would probably drive us mad in the process.

The next quality is challenge. Those who enjoy a challenge and create suitable challenges in their environment can withstand higher levels of stress because they are happy to stretch themselves and derive satisfaction from doing so. Those who do the minimum necessary to get by, to avoid the wrath of the boss, will in most cases be building feelings of guilt with the result that their stress levels will be fairly high.

Clarity is the last of the qualities and also the most important.

'Would you tell me, please, which way I ought to go from here?'
'That depends a good deal on where you want to get to,' said the cat.
'I don't much care where.......' said Alice.
'Then it doesn't matter which way you go,' said the cat.
Alice in Wonderland, Lewis Carroll

People who know where they are going in their lives, deal with stress a great deal better than those who don't, simply because they know at any given moment what their next task is. They are able to compare their present situation to their desired situation and assess the deficit. Such people also have a clearer sense of how, what they do, relates to the results they get and tend to be better communicators. It is very difficult to articulate exactly what you want or need if you don't know yourself.

Do you have these qualities? If not, its likely that you are more suffering from the effects of stress more than you need to be. At this stage it would be useful to take a while to reflect on your position. If what you have read has struck a chord, make a promise to yourself to do something about it. Not just an idle promise but one you are totally committed to.

Psychological Outlook also has a great deal to do with how we handle stress. Are you one of those people who always look for the silver lining, or do you look for the cloud. Henry Ford once said 'If you think you can or you think you can't you're right' Its amazing how we limit ourselves so much in everything we do.

The human mind is capable of staggering achievement, the problem is we rarely trust it sufficiently to do what it is capable of. There is mounting evidence that what we think about we become or put another way if we expect things to go well they will or if we expect things to go badly then they invariably do. Why is this? The answer is simple. The subconscious mind alerts our conscious mind to look for signs that support or actions that will make our original statement happen.

People that are positive and optimistic in their outlook tend to get what they want, and are happier and healthier than those who have a negative or pessimistic outlook. Pessimistic people get what they expect to get but suffer as a result, as it is not what they really want. Pessimists also tend to suffer more from ill health.

Our perceptions play an important part in what we actually experience. It works like this, the subconscious mind will try and prove any statement that it is given. So if you say to yourself this will never work then the subconscious will look for past evidence to support this at the same time as being receptive to external stimuli which reinforce the original assumption. When the mind is doing this it is blind to other evidence that contradicts the original statement thus preventing you from taking advantage of breaks that occur. This is true even when the contradictory evidence in overwhelming.

As a result of the negative programming we receive daily throughout our lives we tend to look for reasons why we can't do something rather than reasons why we can. Have a brief audit of the people you know both socially and at work that you look up to, respect and are successful. Which way do they think? What is it you admire about them and do you have the same qualities.

Which way do you think. Can you see any patterns in your thinking that are holding you back, stopping you achieving what you want? If you are like most people you probably can. Write these patterns down now and review them carefully. Are they real or imagined? Now for each negative pattern replace it with the opposite and imagine that it is already true. Hold that image and repeat it until you believe it and start to see the results it is bringing.

By thinking in a negative pessimistic way we increase the stressors that act on our lives as we do so we activate the bodies defence mechanisms and use coping strategies to combat these effects. If the coping strategies work we return to our normal state and no harm has been done. If the strategies don't work we start to descent into a highly stressed state and our health begins to suffer.

Personality and Stress

Personality has a lot to do with stress and the way people handle pressure. We all have certain characteristics and patterns of behaviour which have a bearing on how we react to situations that involve pressure. These patterns when grouped together are believed to create distinctive personality types known as Type A and Type B.

It's important to note that the characteristics of each personality type are only generalisations and shouldn't be taken as absolute. The theory of personality types dates back to the work of Friedman & Rosennman in 1959.

People with a Type A personality are commonly noted as;

Constantly working, indeed striving for their next promotion and having to prove themselves in the eyes of others.

Generally aggressive when challenged. Impatient with others that they see as not working at the same pace as themselves. Also very likely to finish others sentences.

Very hard workers, generally doing two or more things at once. Often displaying a frantic sense of urgency. They tend to measure the success of everything they do purely in terms of numbers. They also tend to feel guilty when they relax.

Type B on the other hand tend to be the exact opposite of the Type A. Type B personalities tend to be much more relaxed, good listeners and not prone to creating artificial deadlines. Type B also have a much lower rate of heart disease. The Type B also tends to be more popular though at times frustratingly casual especially to a typical Type A.

Type A people tend to suffer from the effects of stress more then Type B with the result that in the past it was felt that they should change their personalities to become more like Type B. I don't know how you would feel about that but I and many others believe that it is an unrealistic aspiration. The process of change itself would probably lead to even more stress for the already potentially stressed Type A.

Most people have a mixture of Type A and Type B characteristics, it's the ratio of each type to the other that will help indicate your tolerance to stress. It is quite common for managers to display more Type A than Type B behaviour. Current thinking has now broken Type A behaviour into Type A (Impatient/ Irritable) and Type A(Assertive/Striving). Have a look at the following characteristics of both and decide which are most applicable to you. Its important to be honest as you need to see how you truly are not how you think you are. If it helps ask a friend that you trust and you can rely on to give you an honest assessment.

A.II	Joyless striving. Permanently tired Frustrated. Perfectionist Reactive. Slow to recover.	A,AS	Get things done Challenging, productive, creative. Enjoys process. Balanced. (Work/non-work) Curious.

Dr Andrew Stewart of Brunel University, who made the above classifications argues that extreme type A's should work at becoming more AS rather than undergoing a complete personality change to type B.

So if you have decided that you are an high type A then keep the good traits and begin to change the not so good II characteristics to the better AS characteristics. Be curious about what happens to you and around you as you do this. Take exercise. Get your life in balance enjoy both work and non-work. Create systematic change.

At this stage you need to make a decision about your priorities. If you want to change, get more out of life and really get on then make the time to do so. If you are happy the way you are now move straight to the next chapter.

How do we cope with Stress

Talking.
Now you have a better idea of what stress is, how it can affect your health and the early warning signs to look out for its important to look at the various ways you can deal with stress.

The methods I'm about to describe are designed to be used as a whole, not in bits and pieces. If you look at and work on each area then your stress levels will decrease dramatically. Should you decide to use only some of the methods and not others you will notice a difference but why not commit yourself and enjoy the full effects. Not only will you benefit but those around you will notice the change and respond accordingly.

In overview the system looks at how we communicate with both ourselves and others, how to relax effectively, our activity, our interests and nourishment.

Firstly, let's look at how we communicate. We spend our lives in constant communication with other people, how else do we express our desires and feelings. A lot of this communication is automatic and follows well established pathways that were learnt in childhood and refined as we got older. These pathways are so ingrained in our subconscious we are no longer aware of their structure, with the result that we do not notice any flaws.

Yet these flaws exist and can have a detrimental effect on our daily lives. What I'm talking about is not only what we say but how we say it. Would you describe your present communication as positive and full of conviction. Does it express your ideas and values or those of other people? If it expresses those of other people then you will lack conviction and even though you are saying the right things the other methods you use to communicate will let you down.

Body language plays a major role in how we appear to others. It unconsciously transmits our true feelings about what we say and is received in a similar manner by others. Have you ever instinctively felt, without evidence, that another person is lying and subsequently been proved right? If you have then your subconscious has read that persons body language accurately. Yet how often do we heed these feelings and act on them?

As all sales people know its vital to build rapport with others in order to communicate effectively. This is done largely unconsciously using various techniques such as mirroring, matching, eye contact and body pointing. Taking this a stage further if we are negative in our approach to others they will tend to respond negatively having accurately read the mismatch in our speech and our body language. On the other hand if we are positive we will get a positive and more open response.

Not only is this true of other people it is also true when we communicate with ourselves. If we are negative about what will happen to us then is usually does. We have already discussed the power of the subconscious and the effect positive and negative outlooks can have on our stress levels but are you aware of how you speak to yourself? For the next few days deliberately note exactly what you say to yourself and then ask yourself if you would talk to your partner or best friend in the same way. What I'm getting at is the times you tell yourself you're stupid/clumsy/ wrong/foolish/not capable etc etc.

We all do it, its a form of programming. So... if we can programme ourselves to be negative we can also programme ourselves to be positive. From now on every time you are aware that you are being negative in your self-talk immediately replace the negative with the corresponding positive. It will take a little time but you will begin to notice a difference, you will find that your confidence will improve and your outlook begin to get brighter and brighter.

Next be conscious of how you talk to other people. Look for the silver lining not the cloud. Instead of saying 'I won't be able to get to that until next Tuesday' say 'No problem, I'll be able to do that for you by Tuesday'. The result is the same but the meaning is different. 'Won't' opens all of the problem, defence files within us whereas 'able' opens all the co-operation, help files. It has taken you years to develop your current communication system so its not unreasonable to expect that it will take time to correct it. Don't be hard on yourself, relax, treat the exercise as fun and watch for the results.

Something else that we have all been guilty of at one time or another is making false assumptions and believing them without question. Next time you're automatic assumption is 'I can't' – challenge it! What is the real answer? It may be that you have the ability but choose not to carry out that particular task. There are very few things we 'can't' do and to combat the effects of stress, it's important to understand the distinction.

To effectively challenge the 'cants' in our lives I would recommend that every time you use the word write the sentence down. When its written down immediately rewrite it another way eg 'Do I really want to do this? Look at the answer carefully. If yes then explore what you need to do, what you will have to learn or read about etc. to make it possible. If the answer is that you don't want to do it, then look for other avenues, outlets to get you to your goal.

Most people will have some things in their lives that they feel they can't do and build a completely negative failure system around them. I have found, when working with these people that the simple re-phrasing of the can't do's to I don't choose to do, opens new areas of confidence and dramatically reduces stress.

So next time you feel stressed out and are suffering from the symptoms already described, have a very careful look at what you are saying to yourself. Catch yourself saying all the wrong things and then say the right things. To start, I would strongly recommend that you write it all down, this will help your conscious mind to grasp the technique. Once the conscious has grasped the technique it will pass over control to your subconscious when it will become automatic and your stress levels will decrease. As Jack Black says 'Try it, it only works'.

Relaxation

The next and probably the most important technique to be mastered in combatting the effects of stress, is relaxation. Relaxation means many things to many people and is for the most part only partially effective in the stress context....unless of course it is done properly!

I would like you to ponder for a moment the effect that an extra five days holiday every year would have on your stress levels. The condition is, that these extra five days holiday, you are about to award yourself, will in no way affect your work in a negative sense. In fact once you have begun to take advantage of this extra time you will begin to notice a very positive effect not just on work but on everything you do.

What am I talking about? I'm talking about setting aside twenty minutes a day for proper relaxation. I don't mean twenty minutes a day when you have time. I mean twenty minutes each and every single day. Sadly this causes people a major problem because they consign it to the bottom of the daily 'to do list' even below such important things as chatting around the coffee machine or other forms of social grazing.

If you make the time for this personal time, you will find that you will begin to function much more effectively which will in turn mean that rather than taking up your valuable time you will actually create more time for all of your activities. At the risk of teaching you to suck eggs I cannot stress this enough. Why do we give everyone and everything more time than we give ourselves.

Society has taught us that to do anything that is purely for ourselves is selfish and wicked. If you want to make someone else feel special and valued then what do you do. Perhaps you take them out for a meal, take them on holiday, buy them something nice, compliment them on their appearance or just pamper them generally. People love to feel special and appreciated and you are no different.

However, you can't always rely on others to make you feel the way you want to, they are mostly too busy with their own lives. So if other people can't be relied on all of the time why is it so bad to rely on yourself? I personally regard this time as essential not selfish. The better I feel, the better I function and the better able I am to be of service to others. More importantly the better I feel, the less stressed I am.

Modern management can be extremely stressful mainly because it is focussed on the wrong things. There are the constant deadlines, the pressure to produce. I'm not saying these are bad, in fact I regard them as good, if treated correctly. It's the implied threat behind them that causes all of the damage. Its the consequences of not meeting the target or deadline that stresses us. The deadlines won't go away but we can lessen the threat of them, simply by using relaxation as our weapon.

So how do we relax effectively? We can relax in a number of ways and I would suggest that you use all of them, as and when, you find them appropriate. Initially I would suggest that you use the shorter ones first until you get into the habit.

First the car exercise.(As you will see it is essential the car is stationary!) I'm sure that like many managers you spend at least part of the day in the car or on a train. This exercise is for you, it will not only help you to relax but can also be a great deal of fun. It's important, that during the exercise you suspend judgement on what you see sense or observe.

Close your eyes and take three deep breaths, inhaling and exhaling slowly. As you inhale notice that your breath is slightly cold. As you exhale notice that your breath has been warmed by your body. Continue to breathe normally but now begin to notice your breathing cycle. Is it short, does it catch or is it slow and easy? It is important, not to try and change it at all . . . just notice it. As you settle down you will find that your breathing will naturally settle into a smooth rhythm. Once your breathing has settled down, begin to notice what is going on around you. Notice the sounds, even the small sounds, notice the smells, is it warm or cold, is there a breeze? Notice everything. Do this for as long as feels comfortable. I would recommend three to five minutes initially.

You will find that this time spent purely observing without judging, or trying to control your environment will have a calming effect. More importantly, the act of observing will distract and eventually silence the inner voice. It is this inner voice that beats you up all the time and causes the stress.

In order to relax more deeply you can continue with the above exercise. For this I would recommend that you either sit or lie down in a comfortable position. Make sure that you don't have your legs or arms crossed. Once you have settled down and become aware of the external things slowly start to observe your internal world. Starting from your toes, slowly check out each area of your body. Can you feel any tension, if so, consciously let it go. If you find this difficult initially grade the tension on a one to ten scale. Ten is the agony end. You will find that using the scale in conjunction with a conscious instruction to the body to reduce the score to zero or as near as possible will release any tension that you might feel.

Once you are completely relaxed start to observe the thoughts that come into your head. Don't do anything else just observe them as they appear and disappear and then wait for the next one and so on. Eventually the thoughts will slow down and you will begin to feel warm and peaceful. Enjoy this sensation for as long as you like. To return to reality just count from one to ten, on ten open your eyes and you will feel refreshed and ready to take on the world.

As you will have gathered by now, relaxation is not just doing something that you enjoy such as reading or going out with friends. Relaxation is a Neuromuscular skill and as such, has to be learnt. One of the most effective ways to relax deeply is to progressively tense and relax all the major muscle groups in the body. The technique has been around for years and when used with a visualisation will produce great results. But like all skills it has to be mastered and then practised.

Take a deep breath, close your eyes, and begin to relax. Begin to notice the sounds and smells around you. Notice your breathing but don't try to change it. Take a few moments of being still and feel yourself slowing down. Notice your thoughts, as before don't judge or consciously process them, just be aware.

Once you are comfortable tense your feet and hold for a few moments then release. Tense your calf muscles . . . hold . . . and release. Next tense your thighs . . . hold . . . release. Feel your lower body relaxed, beginning to feel warm and heavy. Notice any residual tension draining away.

Tense your stomach muscles . . . hold . . . release. Tense your chest and shoulders . . . hold . . . release. Feel the tension just flow away. Now tense your arms by making tight fists . . . hold ....release. Continue to notice the warm feeling and the heaviness in your body. Finally tense your neck and face . . . hold . . . release. Notice any tension and deal with it.

Now you are deeply relaxed take a few moments to enjoy the sensation. Notice your breathing once again. It will be slow and smooth with no jerks or catches.

Now imagine that you are walking along beside the shore. You are on the landward side of a row of sand dunes, it is a warm sunny day and you are feeling relaxed and at ease. As you walk along you come to a gap in the dunes. The gap leads down ten steps to a beautiful sandy beach. See yourself going down the steps, count them, ten, nine, eight, seven, six, five, four, three, two, one. At the bottom of the steps you step onto the golden sand. Feel it between your toes. Feel the warm refreshing breeze that is blowing. Watch the sun sparkle on the sea, see the small white clouds high in the sky. Hear to sound of the water on the shore. Hear a far off seagull cry as it wheels and glides. Watch it for a moment.

Walk slowly along the beach until you feel you want to sit or lie down. Continue to notice what is going on around you, enjoy the sensations you experience. If you feel like it go into the warm refreshing water, feel it against your skin. Enjoy the support it gives you as you swim lazily.

Enjoy being in this special place and when you are ready to leave place you thumb and finger together as a way of remembering all the peace and beauty of the place. Slowly get up and walk back to the steps. Climb the steps counting from one back up to ten. When you get to ten open your eyes and slowly return to the present feeling relaxed and refreshed.

Each time you visit the beach you will build more detail into the visualisation and it will become more and more real. Of course you don't have to use a beach as the setting for your own exercise, you can use any place where you feel warm and relaxed. It is however important that you place your finger and thumb together during the exercise as this becomes what is known as an anchor. To feel relaxed at any time in the future all you need to do is use the anchor and the subconscious will automatically and instantly recreate the feelings of peace and relaxation you experienced at the time.

Whilst this exercise is useful in itself, it is much more effective when it is practised regularly. I would recommend you use it once every day for about ten to twenty minutes. In time, the effects will increase greatly and you will get to the stage where you will look forward to this time for yourself.

All of these exercises are even more effective when soft instrumental music is played during the session. I would recommend that you make up your own tape for the length of session that you feel most comfortable with. It is important that it is instrumental music as words will activate the subconscious to process them and distract you from your relaxation.

Finally once you have relaxed deeply use the following energiser exercise to get you back to full awareness.

Sit upright and put both feet flat on the floor. Rest your hands comfortably on your knees or thighs. Keep your spine straight but not stiff. Keep your chin up and breathe easily. As you inhale slowly raise your chin and gently arch your back until you are looking at the ceiling. Hold for a few moments then slowly breath out as you round your back and lower your chin. Repeat the exercise four or five times.

As I have already said relaxation is a neuromuscular skill that has to be learnt and practised. Be patient with yourself, if it doesn't work first time or you don't begin to feel the effects immediately. Some people have difficulty building pictures. Whilst pictures help the important thing is that you follow the exercises. They will provide more benefit than you realise.

If you have difficulty with the whole concept and don't feel ready for the above exercises then I would recommend the occasional walk in the country where you can escape the noise of the traffic and fumes of the town or city. Being in the countryside will refresh and delight your senses with its natural sounds and smells.

Activity

Next we come to activity or as some people refer to it exercise. It is my belief that if we think of exercise we automatically think of something that will involve a lot of effort and almost certainly pain. The word activity does not have the same associations, it suggests something that is both pleasurable and interesting. As an aid to combatting stress I would suggest that activity is a better description than exercise.

It has been suggested by the sports council that as many as seven out of ten men and eight out of ten women between sixteen and seventy four do not do enough exercise to keep them healthy. Our bodies are designed to be used. Designed for the flight or fight syndrome. If they are not, then like anything else that is neglected, they deteriorate. For us humans that means a build up of harmful chemicals that can cause disease and tension.

Apart from all the medical reasons why activity is good for us it also has many other advantages: it gets us out and about, helps us deal with anger, can be fun, helps with weight control, calm us down, helps us sleep better and gives us energy. I am sure that you can think of many more reasons why it can benefit us but I think the point is made.

The technical reasons activity is beneficial are: at certain intensity levels it improves cardiovascular efficiency, reduces blood pressure, reduces blood sugar levels, raises levels of endorphins, releases muscle tension and may retard furring up of the arteries.

Sadly activity is like the relaxation exercises mentioned earlier, the benefits cannot be stored for later use. People that have been very active in youth have no greater health benefits than their less active counterparts if they become inactive as they grow older.

Activity will involve some effort but it certainly does not need to be painful to be of great benefit. In fact the opposite is usually true, if pain is experienced the body is telling us we are going about our chosen activity too hard. A balance has to be struck. Also if people associate activity with pain what incentive is there to continue with a fitness programme. So select an exercise that is both enjoyable and beneficial.

It is generally accepted that there are three general criteria for physical fitness: strength, suppleness and stamina. As far as dealing with stress is concerned the most important of these is stamina. The more stamina you have to better able you are to cope with the stresses and strains of everyday life.

To improve stamina you will need to do at least ten minutes activity three times per week that will raise your resting heart rate. More than this is recommended but if you are very unfit then start at the ten minute level. Any activity will do as long as it raises your heart rate. However not all stamina building activities will benefit your strength or suppleness. The following table is a good guide to pace yourself.

Age	Resting Pulse	Minimum Rate to Benefit	Safe Maximum Rate
25-39	60 – 75	115	150
40-60	65 – 80	110	140

It is vital that you never exceed the maximum heart rate for your age or level of fitness. To do so may be both counterproductive and also dangerous. As your fitness improves your resting heart rate will fall enabling you to exert yourself more. Remember that the benefits of any activity will begin to tail off after three days.

REMEMBER IF AT ANY TIME YOU FEEL DISCOMFORT OR PAIN WHEN FOLLOWING A FITNESS PROGRAMME STOP IMMEDIATELY AND SEEK MEDICAL HELP IF APPROPRIATE.

For those of you, who have neither the time or inclination to follow a structured programme to get fit I would recommend walking briskly as often as possible. Walking has many advantages and is inexpensive and safe. The main advantage that walking has for many people is that it gives them personal time and space. A lot of very profound and innovative thinking has been done while walking.

Interests

Another very effective way to combat stress is by having a balance of interests within your life. Imagine your body as being like a sports team where each individual member has a vital part to play. If a member of the team is injured or unavailable then although the team may continue to function it will do so at less than its maximum efficiency.

Treat your interests as the members of your team. Again it is important to be honest. What are your interests? Write them down. Another way of looking at the question of interests is by looking at what is really important to you. Look at each of the following categories in turn: Career, family, finance, spiritual, sports, hobbies, social, community. There are many more than this so please feel free to add to the list as you see fit.

Here is another set of questions you may find useful as you define the major areas in your life. These questions look a little deeper into why things are important to you. This aspect is as important as the things themselves because it makes us redefine decisions that we made some time earlier. In many cases a great deal earlier, with the result they have become an unquestioned habit. Some people find that on questioning these areas of importance they loose some of their impact and can be replaced with newer updated areas. Holding onto an interest that is out of date is unnecessary and in many cases can add considerably to your stress levels.

Who are the most important people in your life and why?

What values and ideas about life would you not compromise under any circumstances and why?

What events in your life have most affected you and why?

What activities give you the most satisfaction and why are they so satisfying?

If everything was taken from you what would you miss most?

Finally ask yourself the question which is vital to all managers. Do I balance my work with my family and other interests or do my family and other interests take second place? If the latter is the case then for your own sake do everything in your power to restore this balance. You may be the best manager in the country but you are failing to effectively manage the most important thing you have. Your life.

Nutrition

Finally I would like to touch on nutrition. As you should be aware of by now the key to stress management is balance and this is also true of diet. As we saw earlier one of the signs of stress is unbalanced eating habits. Most people will acknowledge that it is common sense to eat a balanced diet and also the importance of eating enough fruit and vegetables. However, as with so many other things doing it and saying it are two separate things.

Improving your diet will not only make you feel better, but you will reduce your stress levels and therefore benefit your health in the long term. Look very carefully at what you eat on a daily basis. What does it consist of? I suggest that once again you write it down and analyse it. What does it show? Hurried meals, meals that consist of highly processed foods, fast food. All of these things have a detrimental effect on health if they are the bulk of your average daily intake.

There are not many areas of life that you have total control over. Other people may let you down, the weather may be foul for that all important outdoor event etc. You do have total control over your diet. It may mean a little extra care or a little extra time but the results far outweigh the price. As I have already said people tend to give everyone and everything priority over their own health and well being. Why is this?

The fitter and healthier you are the better you will be able to look after others and the more reward you will get from life. I don't propose to go into diet in any great detail here however I will cover the basics as a type of revision. The main element of a healthy diet is water. We do not drink enough water and as a result do not cleanse our systems of the toxins and general debris we accumulate daily. Experts advise at least 8 glasses of water daily. I would also suggest that you drink good quality bottled water where possible. Tea and coffee are not substitutes for fresh water.

On the subject of tea and coffee, try and keep your intake to a minimum. No more than three or four cups per day and then decaffeinated if possible. Caffeine is a natural stimulant too much of which can cause anxiety, irritability and heart palpitations. Whilst on the subject of fluids be very wary of your alcohol intake. It is wise to stick to government guidelines on weekly intake avoiding beers and mixers if possible. Red wine is particularly good when taken in moderation

Finally some general rules for healthy eating;

- Reduce fat consumption, particularly saturated fats.
- Decrease consumption of sugar and alcohol.
- Increase amount of dietary fibre.
- Eat a varied diet.
- Maintain a desirable body weight.
- Eat regular meals particularly breakfast.

A word of caution. The body needs both vitamins and minerals to function efficiently. However without the correct minerals the body is not able to absorb the vitamins provided. The caution is that not all foods which are traditionally high in vitamins and minerals actually contain them. There are a number of reasons for this including over processing, use of chemicals and overcropping. There are many more but this subject is better dealt with elsewhere.

In view of this I would recommend a good supplement be taken regularly. Advice on this is generally available from your local chemist. It is also felt that organically produced food is richer in vitamins and minerals. The drawback of organic produce is cost. It is up to you.

Diet is very much a personal issue and there is a wealth of different ideas on the subject. Suffice to say that a healthy diet will reduce stress levels and help you to operate at maximum efficiency. Of course it goes without saying, stop smoking. Enough said!

In summary then for busy managers to combat stress effectively it is necessary to take an overall view of your lifestyle. However, before any significant changes can be made take the time to assess exactly what you want to achieve in each area of interest and then balance these interests.

One very effective method of "kick starting" the whole process is to engage the services of a coach. A professional coach will assist you throughout the entire process and provide you with an extra conscious to enable you to stay on track. Coaching is available on a face to face basis with groups or individuals. Coaching is also available on an individual basis via the telephone. Telephone or virtual coaching has many advantages amongst which is convenience. There is no need to travel to see your coach.

If you have found this section of value to you and would like to know more about any of the topics or would like help finding a coach, please contact me directly, I'll be delighted to assist you. John Lennon is reputed to have said that 'Life is what happens to us whilst we decide what to do with it'. Don't delay for a minute, if you feel that your life and situation should or could be improved. Just do it. Procrastination is not only the thief of time it also destroys our will to succeed and increases our stress levels. One final hint. Pick the thing you least want to do next and do it. The feeling of achievement is enormous. If you don't believe me try it once.

As you will have gathered by now I have only been able to give an overview of this important area. Stress affects us not only at work but in every area of life. It doesn't pick on just one age group or any other grouping. It is important as a manager that you not only recognise the symptoms of stress in yourself but also in those that work for you and in your colleagues.

With what you have learnt in this chapter you will be able to assist others and yourself to overcome the negative effects of stress and become more productive and alive. I strongly believe that if we spend more time communicating effectively with others we will find we are able to take gigantic leaps forward at the same time as maintaining the balance that is essential to our lives. People like to be liked. If you genuinely like others and help them through their challenges then they will help you in their turn. What's more your likeability factor will increase tenfold.

Summary

Know what stress is and what it means to you.

Spot the early warning signs of Stress.

Know what to look out for both physically and emotionally as indicators that we may be suffering from the effects of stress.

Know how your personality affects the degree of susceptibility towards stress in your everyday life.

Know your Coping strategies. Pay attention to How you talk to yourself and others and the effect this has.

Use relaxation to combat stress and improve effectiveness.

Take Regular Activity to reduce stress.

Have a balance of interests to keep stress to a minimum.

Provide the correct fuel for your body.

9   How to define priorities, set and meet deadlines

There are two keys to meeting deadlines successfully:
A – Begin at the end;
B – Have a MAP.

How often have you found yourself partway through a project only to discover that you need more resources? Or found yourself working like mad, day and night, with no opportunity to do anything else, in order to meet a deadline? Or, worse yet, after all your effort, you find that the product is not what your customer or manager really had in mind?

Completing a project or task successfully, on time, in budget and with expected results happens every day. It's not magic. It simply requires a plan.

By knowing where you want to go and what your objectives are, you put yourself in a much better position to efficiently manage your time and consistently achieve successful results. Imagine having more time to enjoy life, build confidence and credibility in your ability to achieve project success, reduce stress and improve your health.

Psychology, since the time of Freud and before, has suggested that our lives are organised into three key areas: our job/work/career (that thing we have to do to sustain our way of living); our self (personal well being, health, religion, education, etc.); and relationships (others in our lives such as colleagues, friends, and family). By defining an objective or vision, for each of these three key areas, you work more efficiently and thus have more time to enjoy life. One customer said to me after having implemented this approach, "I now have more time to spend with my favourite person and I'm never too tired to have sex!".

It's a simple process that allows you to define priorities and set and meet deadlines successfully. It can be used for anything that requires more than one step, or task – from deciding what contribution you want to make to the world, to selecting and implementing a new computer system for the company, to redecorating a room. It's called The MAP – My Achievement Plan – and this is how it works.

1   Envision the result
2   Set the date
3   Write down your Statement of Objective using my special technique, the DART rule
4   Chunk it into actions
5   Validate it
6   Schedule it
7   Carry it through
8   Reward yourself for succeeding.

1 – Envision the Result

Begin at the end. It sounds odd but, in actual fact, it's what any creator does. The artist envisions the painting or ceramic pot before starting. The architect envisions the house before building begins. Think about what you would do when given a new address that you have to get to for the first time. If you're like most people, you pull out a map. Once you find the address, you then begin the process of figuring out how you're going to get there and what you need to do it.

Let's take, for example, something that you have done or will do at some point in your life: redecorate a room. What is the first thing you do?

Well, you might decide on the colour scheme you want. Then you might decide whether you are going to have new wallpaper or just paint. Do you keep the old carpet, or do you pull it up and maybe restore the hard wood floor? If you decide on wallpaper, would you want matching curtains – and so on.

Take a project at work. Your boss comes in to see you and says there is a new project that needs to be done and he or she would like you to head it up. What is the first thing you do? Hopefully, you will ask, "What is the project about?", "What needs doing?", or "What is going to change?"

You want to know the outcome – the expected end result. You are defining your objective.

Have you ever just found a tin of paint lying around and said, "Hey, I think I'll just take this and go paint my bedroom with it – who cares what colour it is? I wasn't really going to redecorate. In fact, I was going to just going to wash the dishes, but hey, here's this tin of paint sitting here doing nothing and I might as well use it." Not if you are serious about redecorating!

Yet everyday, people everywhere get out of bed in the morning, get dressed, go to work, come home, turn on the telly, crash on the sofa and then say, "Oh, yeah, I was meant to start on that project today." Or, "I was meant to wash the car today", or go to the grocery store or whatever it was. But you didn't. Instead when you got to work, you got side-tracked because somebody needed you or something arrived on your desk which you decided to deal with.

Have you ever set New Year's resolutions? How many of your resolutions have you achieved? If not many (and you are like most people), you feel discouraged with yourself because you didn't follow through. But if you did achieve some resolutions, you probably feel pretty pleased with yourself.

It has been proven by research that people who set clear objectives and define goals more often achieve what they set out to do and feel more satisfied about their lives.

The first question you ask is "WHERE AM I GOING?" Setting objectives and defining goals in nothing more than beginning at the end. What is the address I want to arrive at? What does the room look like when it is decorated? What is accomplished as a result of this project?

Visioning can be used as part of the process. Close your eyes. Imagine exactly what your goal looks like – as if it has already happened, the goal has already been achieved. Get a clear picture of it in your mind. What does it look like, down to the smallest detail? What does it feel like, smell like, sound like, taste like?

Try this now. Think of something that you have been wanting to do, something that you have wanted or needed to accomplish. A work-related project, such as implementing a new computer system, establishing customer service levels, or maybe just reorganising your office and filing systems. It could be a personal project, for example, restoring an old car, organising a party, or planning an exotic holiday. Take that project or goal and think of it now in terms of it being completed. Look at it as if it is the finished result. Look at it in detail in your mind. What does it look like? What colour is it? How big is it? Does it have a particular smell or odour? Is it something you can touch? How does it feel? Does it have a sound? What does it sound like? Imagine also what other people are saying about it – how would they describe it?

In the 1960's, Jan Leschly was among the world's top ten tennis players. His goal was not to be world champion. It was to play on Wimbledon's centre court. Every time he practised, he would imagine it: the smell of the grass, the sound of the crowds. In 1969, Leschly reached Centre court where he was defeated by Rod Laver.

According to psychiatrist David Myers, in experiments, people who imagine themselves succeeding outperform those who expect to fail,. By the time you face the real challenge, your mental rehearsals will have given you confidence and will power.

Scientific tests have shown that whenever you are imagining an object in your mind, your electrical brain patterns are very similar to as if you are actually looking at it. Through the technique of visualisation you simply picture in your mind's eye whatever it is you want to achieve.

Step 2 – Set the Date

Now that you have a picture in your mind, you know where you are going. Next you need to determine by when you want to get there. Notice the use of the word "decide" rather than estimate or calculate or assume. Make a determination of when YOU want to arrive and then build a plan to accommodate it.

Why do you do this? Because it's part of the visioning, it's part of the objective. The date and time may have been set for you. For example, if your company or a customer has tasked you with a project, they may designate the date. That's okay, as long as they give you the opportunity of planning the project so that you have some control over what goes into it and what you need to accomplish by that date.

Take the example of a business meeting at a new address where you have never been before. You and the person you are to meet probably decided together what date and time to meet. You decided. The point is that you negotiated with each other around diaries, etc. When you plan on a deadline you should try to have some input as to when you will finish.

There will be situations when you will not have the luxury of setting the original deadline. One of the key functions of an IT department is doing projects such as replacing older computer systems with new ones and writing new systems and implementing them. At one time, I worked with the IT departments of banks and financial organisations. When they said they needed a project completed on a certain date, I had to deliver. Otherwise they might lose money or customers or both. I might not have won the business if I could not commit to their deadline. I worked together with the customer on step 1 (envision the result). Taking the target date they set, I then had to determine what was needed to achieve it by that date. In IT project management, what do you think is the number one reason why projects don't get done on time? (And if you think about it, it's the number 1 reason why any project doesn't get done on time.) Because there is deviation from the plan during the project – staff numbers are reduced, new results are described, or funding is cut.

A key part to setting the date is to be realistic. How do you define realistic? You might say you have a gut feel, intuition, or instinct. But there are some guidelines you can apply.

There is a maximum amount of time you should apply to a project. I suggest that it is 5 years. There are some exceptions to this, for example when planning your retirement. If you need to plan on funding and investment for your retirement, unless you are in your 60's and just now thinking about it, it will most likely be more than 5 years.

Is there also a minimum amount? Well, I believe there is not. This process could be applied to a task that may be accomplished in one day or less. For example, you walk into work in the morning and on your desk is a note from the sales manager saying you are having customers in the office today. Please ensure that the office is tidy and in good order. (This could even apply to your housekeeping at home.) First ask yourself, "What is my objective?" Second, "By when does it need to be done?"

If the project requires a new process or behaviour, remember that it takes a minimum of six to eight weeks to change a habit.

Research by management experts has highlighted that people who manage their time well always stop and ask these two questions before they start any task, large or small. They are the same as your first two steps in planning. "What is my objective?" (Envision the result.) "By when does it need to be completed?" (Set the date.)

Step 3 – Write down your Statement of Objective using the DART rule

The picture in your mind needs to be written down so that your eyes can now begin to see it as we begin the process of making it real. This written description is called the Statement of Objective.

Notice the word objective rather than goal. According to the Oxford dictionary, goal is a structure or area into which players try to send a ball in certain games; a point scored in this way, or – an objective. An objective is defined as having real existence outside a person's mind, not influenced by personal feelings or opinions; something one is trying to achieve or reach or capture. You take the vision you created in step 1, and create a real existence outside of your mind.

Writing it down gives you an anchor. It exposes the objective to more than one sense. Studies into how you learn have proven conclusively that the more senses you can expose to a situation, the more likely you are to remember it and thus retain it. If you think about experiences in your memory, you can probably recall many more than one sense – in addition to what it looked like, how it sounded, felt, smelled, etc.

Writing down your objective takes the image you envisioned from inside your mind and puts it before you – in black and white, if you will. Seeing it creates a more likely opportunity for it to happen.

You may be familiar with Scott Adams, the Dilbert cartoonist. He spent 17 years working in corporate America where much of his work involved the sort of endeavours he now lampoons. He wanted a change. He imagined in detail what he wanted to accomplish. Then he worked out how to go about getting there. He used affirmations – repeating over and over both in words and in writing what his end objective was. Then he began to observe things happening that made his objective more likely to materialise.

This phenomenon is called optical reticulation. You have probably experienced it. Perhaps you decided to purchase a red car. Suddenly every other car you see is red, whereas you never noticed them as often before!

When I first started working for myself, I recognised that one key area I needed some additional training and guidance on marketing. I described my objective and set the date for when I wanted to issue my first marketing campaign. I wrote down in detail the objective and within a matter of days I started to meet marketing experts. People, either whom I had never met before (in one case), or had known previously, but who now came back into contact with (in two cases). These three people were instrumental in helping me learn and prepare the campaign and thereby achieve my objective.

Some people use the term synergy to describe when this happens. The key point is that once you have nailed down the details of your exact objective, the more likely you are to be aware of opportunities that help you move forward in achieving it.

When you write your objective, you want to apply what I call the DART rule. If you think of your objective as a bulls eye on the dartboard, then this is the dart you are going to throw to hit it. You can apply it to both personal as well as business objectives. DART stands for *D*etailed, *A*s we speak, *R*ealistic and *T*ime-stamped.

Detailed because it needs to include all those details you described in your mind in step one. The more detailed and specific it is, the richer, more vibrant the vision, the more likely you are to achieve it because your brain thinks it's real. Have you ever woken from a dream in a daze and had to take a few minutes to determine if it was a dream or if it was real? It was so vivid, so detailed, it seemed real and it fooled your brain. The more of it you can see, the more of it you can experience, and the better prepared you will be in defining the details of the plan required to achieve it.

The Statement of Objective can be more than one sentence. But the main point is to make it detailed. Use specific numbers and characteristics to describe it. For example, it's better to aim for eating 20 grams of fat per day than to say you'll have a healthy diet or to say the project is completed within a budget of £10,000 rather than just within budget.

The A in DART is for "as we speak". When writing your statement, write it as if it is already happening – it is active at this moment in time. Use the present tense – what I call the AH'S: AM ... HAVE ... IS. I am the department manager. The office has a new computer system. The project is completed on the 21st of February 1999.

Tests performed with university graduates over a period of several years showed that those who had written goals were more likely to achieve them than those who did not. And of those who had written goals, those whose were detailed and written in the present tense were even more likely to achieve them.

The brain uses a process called conditioning. The way you train a pet to behave a particular way for example is conditioning. Once the animal has performed the activity you require, that experience is logged into the brain. It is further reinforced by your reward to the pet. Knowing that your brain can interpret a detailed vision, like a dream, as if it were real, but telling the brain that the activity has already occurred, you condition it to accept it as fact.

So simply by saying "I am ...", you condition your brain to believe it is true.

The Pillars of Successful Management

The more you can convince yourself that it is in fact true the more likely it is to become true.

I'm sure you have heard of the self-fulfilling prophecy. The more you believe something, the more you convince yourself that it is true, the more likely it is to happen.

The R in DART is for realistic. When you define your objective, you want the outcome to be positive. In fact, the whole reason you are going through this 8-step planning process is to improve the chances that you will be successful in achieving the objective.

Realistic can be a relative measure. Especially if your goal is personal or it is the first time this project has been attempted. But by going through the process you do have the opportunity to adjust once before you complete the final plan and begin to implement.

Realistic can be tested by asking these questions:

a) "Do I, or the people involved in achieving this objective, have to give something else up to achieve this objective in this timeframe? If so, how much of a loss will it be? Can I (the team) live with that loss?" If the answer is NO, your goal is not realistic.
b) "Is there a possibility it will impair or harm my health or any member of my team if I attempt to achieve this objective in this timeframe?" If the answer is YES, your goal is not realistic.
c) "Do I need more resources (time, money, people, equipment) than I have available or can afford to achieve this objective in this timeframe?" If the answer is YES, adjustment is necessary.

One of my customers uses this technique for all of her project planning both at home and at work. She boils it down to one question – "Do I have a prayer of achieving this goal in this timeframe?" – and if she's too embarrassed to pray for assistance, she adjusts.

The final piece of the DART rule is T – time-stamp. Time stamping is important for two reasons. One, because it focuses the target for you (so you know where you have to be at a certain time) and it helps you look forward. Two, because it helps you look backward. By evaluating how you have done and looking for ways to learn from past experience, especially if you are dealing with an objective that is going to occur again in your life – like a work project or decorating the house. You can see if it did take as long or as little as you originally anticipated and include that result in the next project.

Time stamping is very specific. It needs a day, a month and a year. Remember that your mind likes details. The more details, the more it believes it is real the more likely it is to happen. It's like the bulls-eye on the dartboard. If you simply say, "I am the department manager by February 99", you have made the bulls-eye vague and out of focus. So when you do throw the dart you might be lucky and hit it, but it's more likely to hit somewhere outside of it, if even on the board at all.

Be specific, be detailed and assign a day, month and year. For personal goals, some people prefer to choose an anniversary, such as their birthday, or maybe a holiday. For business goals, you may have more specific requirements. When I worked with IT projects for banks, we always scheduled the implementation of a new system over a bank holiday to give us a larger window for the actual process of converting the data, verifying it and so on.

Step 4 – Chunk into actions

Using the business meeting example from earlier, at this point in the process you will have pulled out your map. You have found the exact location. You know the address, what the building looks like, and how you feel when you get there. You have decided what time you need to be there. Now you need to look at how you get there.

Step 4 is to chunk into actions. You may be familiar with the term chunking. It means breaking a large item into smaller more manageable parts.

Begin brainstorming. What actions or activities must you accomplish in order to achieve your Statement of Objective?

For example, you may be implementing a new computer system. The Statement of Objective might read "A new computer system to monitor customer activity is implemented and running productively by 10 February 1999". You brainstorm each activity required to make that happen on time. Activities may include documenting specific operating requirements, evaluating eligible systems available on the market, selecting a system, and so on.

For each activity, apply the first three steps. Envision it, set the date and write it down applying the DART rule.

This is important because it is not enough to just focus on the end result. What makes success is focusing on what is required to get there. According to new research on athletes, if your eyes are on the prize, they may not be on the ball. Research found that those athletes who play in order to understand the game better, or to develop, or improve their skills, played better than those who played simply for the end result – the prize or the win. Their vision was sharper and their reaction time faster because the concentration crucial to acute vision is more available to those deeply immersed in the activity. These are the type of people you would call self-starters. They draw on the energy generated by their own goals and aspirations. They became aware of what is valuable to them about the game and then use that as a motivator.

Thus, for every plan, you will have a Statement of Objective and a list of activities. The Statement and every activity is written using specific details, in present-as-we-speak tense, and with a realistic time-stamp.

Step 5 – Validate it

At this point you have developed the plan. You have identified what you want, when you are going to get it and how you are going to go about getting there in quite some detail. But you are not done because now you need to reconcile it. That is, now you need to verify your objectives. You do this by asking a series of questions that you apply to the original Statement of Objective: What, who, where, how, when, and why.

1   What do I need to accomplish this objective?
2   Who will support me, or not?
3   Where will I be if something goes wrong?
4   How do I deal with problems?
5   When do I re-evaluate?
6   Why is it so important to me to succeed?

The first question you need to ask is what resources are needed to achieve this objective? What equipment, training, types of individuals or professionals, funding, etc. is needed in order for this to succeed. One of the main reasons why projects fail in business is because those who are responsible for planning did not think through all of the external resources that would be required. A large well-known company was responsible for implementing a new computer system that was chosen for its ability to enhance employee productivity and improve customer service. Much design and planning went into the project. Millions of pounds were spent on decisions, planning and implementing. Within about two months, the system was causing more chaos and havoc with employees and customers than the old system. A team of consultants were brought in and more money was paid for them to investigate the cause.

At the end of their assignment, the consultants asked the company's executives to meet and they reported their findings. In all the designing and decision making and planning and implementation and testing, nobody had thought to ask the employees who were to actually use the new software for their input. Management had been involved, but no actual end users. Even though they knew it was coming, when it was coming, and they had been given some instruction manuals on how to use it, they had not been involved.

When you think of what resources are needed, look through the activities you have defined and for each one ask, "Is training needed?", "Are any particular groups of individuals required?", "Is this going to cost extra money?" And for each of those resources identified, you will need a new activity statement with a time-stamp.

The second question is who will support me, or not. This question focuses on specific people – not types of people or groups of individuals (like end-users, managers, etc) but those like your wife, husband, parents, friends, etc.

This question relates to attitude. Who should know in order that they can support you? Whenever you work towards achieving any sort of goal, there will be specific individuals in your lives whom you know will help you, even if it's just by being there for you with a positive or encouraging word. These people will help you, as an individual, to succeed.

However, there are people who will do everything in their power to stand in your way. So the less they know, the better off you are. A few years ago I set a new goal to leave a rather good job after 15 years with the same company and start my own business. I applied this 8-step planning process to it and worked out all the timing and details. One person in particular I wanted to tell was my mother. Her reaction was to say rather worriedly, "Are you sure you want to leave a good job with good pay to take such a risk?" From that point on, I knew that I could not count on her to help me through or support me because of her own concerns.

It's important to focus your energy on achieving not on worrying. A famous blues musician, Duke Ellington, said, "I merely took the energy it takes to pout and wrote some blues". Think about the energy you use for negative activities, like worrying, feeling guilty, angry, sorry for yourself, etc. If you used that time and energy for achieving your goals, how much more successful would you be!

The third question forces you to analyse what could go wrong. It asks "Where does it leave me if something goes wrong?". Think first of what is the absolute worst thing that could happen. Write that down and then create a list of anything else you can think of that might go wrong. For example, the worst thing might be financial ruin – you have to live on the street. Other potential problems might be that you lose your job and can't get re-employed. Your family leaves you. You go bankrupt.

Set yourself a time limit to do this. It should be no more than 30 minutes to really brainstorm potential worries.

You then move straight into the next question – How do I deal with problems? Take the list from above and for each issue, write down how you would overcome it. For each item, think how you might solve the problem and then once solved, how you would get back on track and move forward. I call this technique "negative reversal".

Thinking and working positive is very important and keeps you focused on moving forward with your goals. But there is a time and a place for looking at negatives and this is the time. This is the one time you want to really focus on potential problems.

This is an important step because if you can take all the worries and set them aside, that leaves room for you to focus on making it work and achieving the objective. It sets your mind into the positive avenue you are striving for.

And if something does go wrong, (and you know things do), it's more likely that you will already have thought through it and be prepared for it. You can then react faster to it and get back on track as quickly as possible.

Let me share with you an example. A friend of mine was in the process of starting up his own business. He and his wife had been investing the majority of their savings and pension into the venture. The first day of trading began and he became very ill. He was diagnosed with a serious disease and was put straight into the hospital where he was watched over and had total bed rest. At the end of a couple of days of tests he was released home but within a matter of days he had to report back and was again admitted to the hospital. The doctors basically told

The Pillars of Successful Management   161

him that he needed to stay in bed and do absolutely nothing for three months. Of course he was devastated. Especially since the business was just new and struggling and his wife was required to spend all of her time on it. But he did as they advised. And the more he lay there, the more time he had to think and the more worried he became. He got into such a state that he rang me in the middle of the night in a frenzy, worried about the health of his wife, the future of the business, the financial security of his family, his own health, what if the disease progressed, what if he went through all this and then was permanently disabled or died?

I spoke to him for awhile until he calmed down and then I asked him to try my negative reversal technique. "Try", I said, "to think of absolutely everything that could go wrong. Think about how you would feel, how your wife would feel. Write them down. Then for each problem, go back and think about how you would deal with it? What would you do? How would you react? How would you get through it?" I asked him to spend just 30 minutes on these issues and the rest of the night on the resolutions. He could dwell as much as he wanted to on the problems but after 30 minutes he should stop and work through each issue. Then put it out of his mind. Stick the paper in a drawer or even throw it away. But get it out of his mind now. And think only about good things, taking care of himself, making the most of this time to catch up on reading or doing something positive for the business. Think about when the company reaches a million pounds in turnover, taking a well deserved holiday to an exotic location with his wife, or sharing an easy retirement with her and so on.

The next day he rang me quite late in the evening. He sounded quite different than the night before and back to his former good-natured self.

"Thank you", he told me. "I did what you said. I got it all out of my system. Every last little problem and worry I could think of. I dealt with each one, worked through it. I feel like a great burden has been lifted and it seems like the sun is shining brighter today and everything just feels better."

Several months later, after a full recovery, he was back in the business and soon he and his wife celebrated their first million pounds in turnover. He tells me he still uses this process whenever he starts to worry too much and every time it helps clear his brain and get him focused on moving forward. And once or twice when something has happened, he was prepared for it and it wasn't the end of the world. Just another part of the project that had to be dealt with.

Your fifth question is when to evaluate. It asks you to define some points in your plan to monitor your progress. These strategic monitor points, or SMPs, ensure that you take a look at how the plan is moving and help you to adjust if needed.

Simply schedule the SMP dates at various points in your plan. I suggest you use once per week for a project of 3 months or less; once a month for a project 12 months or less, once a quarter for 5 years or less; and once a year for anything more than 5 years. As the project moves forward and gets nearer its deadline, increase your SMP dates according to the above suggestions.

Six – why is it so important to you to succeed? This question gets you back to a positive point of view. Make a list of why this project is important. Write down how it will make you feel, what you will have accomplished, who or what you will have helped (including yourself!) and in what ways.

Keep this list handy to refer to when things are going through a tough patch or priorities are conflicting due to external causes. Communicate these positives to the team involved in the project.

Step 6 – Schedule it

At this point, you take every time stamp in the plan, including the Statement of Objective's, and put them in your diary or project schedule. At each date, include the written statement of the objective and activities.

In addition, (and this is the key to this step), repeat the written statement in a date prior to the deadline. This is the pre-completion date. It is a reminder that the deadline is looming. It is an advance warning for you to evaluate your progress and prepare the activity, if it has not already begun.

I suggest the pre-completion date should be at least one week before the deadline.

Step 7 – Carry it through

Execute, mobilise, maintain – whatever you want to call it, this step is about making it happen. The MAP is now complete but it is only half the job. Now you want to see the project through to a successful completion without the rest of your life going awry.

First, you need to develop a self-maintenance program. It is simple but requires consistent and demanding attention. It is this: before you do anything, start any task or begin any effort, STOP and ask yourself this question:

Does it fit within my objective or is it a detour on the MAP?

The answer will fit into one of these four responses:

1 – YES – it fits within my objective and does not require a detour.
2 – NO – it does not fit within my objective and does not require a detour but a whole new MAP.
3 – GET HELP – it does not fit within my objectives and will require a detour.
4 – NOW – it does fit within my objective but also requires a detour to make it happen.

The Pillars of Successful Management 163

	MAP	DETOUR
1	Yes	No
2	No	No
3	No	Yes
4	Yes	Yes

If the answer is YES – it does fit within my objectives and does not require a detour, you should carry out the activity. This is the ultimate response you are working towards and the one you want to answer the majority of the time. This is your most important priority.

If the answer is NO – it does not fit within my objectives and it does not require a detour – don't do it. It is not important and there is no pressing deadline. So forget it. This is your lowest priority.

If the answer is GET HELP – it does not fit within your objective for whatever reason, it will require a detour. The best way usually to accomplish this activity is to throw more resources at it. It assumes that it is so urgent that the deadline cannot be changed. However, it may not be your objective at all. In this case, you should delegate it, quickly, to someone who cares. This is not your priority.

If the answer is NOW – it does fit within your objective but a detour is required to accomplish it. It may be an activity you accidentally missed during your planning, or more likely, an activity you kept postponing and rescheduling and now has reached urgent status. It requires some re-prioritising and adjustment to the MAP. It is a high priority only because the deadline is quickly closing in. So you must deal with it, now, and then adjust your MAP accordingly.

If you had been following the process and the plan as directed, this will rarely happen. This is where you never want to find yourself. The best way to ensure that, is to follow the second part of "carry it through" – or maintenance.

	URGENT	
	GET HELP	NOW
	NO	YES
	IMPORTANT	

Monitor, Adjust, Review
You set SMPs throughout your plan. On a regular basis you are evaluating your progress. This is the opportunity to check off the completed activities and look forward at the activities still to do. Based on your progress so far, if you are on schedule, no adjustment is necessary.

However, there are two instances when adjustment may be necessary. And when it is (you guessed it), there is a simple technique for how to adjust.

The first reason you may need to adjust is when you reach the deadline on an individual task and you have not accomplished it. Reschedule it, noting at that time that this is the first rescheduling. But don't just stop there. Now review the remaining tasks to see if any of those deadlines are impacted by this change. If so, reschedule those activities, again noting if this is the first or subsequent rescheduling of the task.

The second reason you may need for adjusting the plan, is when you become aware of any outside influences that could change the plan. For example, loss of a resource or unexpected and urgent demands on your time which arrive to you unplanned. Use the same process described above for each impacted activity. Reschedule it noting the rescheduling occurrence.

The rescheduling occurrence is extremely important. It is very likely that you need to postpone and reschedule an activity once, especially if you are inexperienced at this planning process or it is the first time you are planning a particular type of project.

You may need to reschedule an activity a second time. This should be a less likely occurrence if you are managing the planning process carefully.

But should you find yourself needing to reschedule an activity a third time, stop and question it. Why is this required? If it is procrastination – you just keep putting it off – you need to analyse your motives again in achieving the overall Statement of Objective. Go back and look at your list from the answer to "Why is this so important to me to succeed?" If it is not important any more, you need to re-evaluate the objective and maybe scrap the plan.

If you are rescheduling a third time because of genuine external influences consistently interfering, you may need to consider evaluating those influences. Perhaps you need to go back and think through, "Where does that leave me," and ensure you have identified, "How I deal with problems", more thoroughly.

Anytime you have to adjust the plan, look at the reasons for the adjustments and ensure you include them in your "Where does that leave me" list. Learn from the solutions you come up with in "How do I deal with problems". Remember the focus is to learn from problems and move the project forward!

Step 8 – Reward Yourself for Succeeding

This step should not only happen at the end. It should happen along the way, especially when a difficult or challenging activity has been completed.

Celebrate achievement. Taking pride in your accomplishments builds a sense of self worth. When something goes wrong, don't despair or gloss over it – focus on why it happened and what you can do to make it better. Then move forward.

You must learn to celebrate your successes. Celebrate with those who assisted, the project team, your family, friends, or anyone who supported you.

Reward is important to maintain motivation.
Reward prepares you positively for the next project ahead.

Summary

Some people believe that having a process in place to do anything takes away from impulse, fun and enjoyment of life. But I find that it is those same people who (a) never finish what they start, (b) find themselves chasing their tails and never actually achieve their goals and (c) reach a point in life where they say "where did all the time go – I haven't done xyz yet!"

Having a process in place for any event that occurs regularly – like how to plan a project – in actual fact leaves you more time to be impulsive with the fun things and to enjoy more of what you want to enjoy in life.

Once you have set your Statement of Objective for each of the three key areas of life (work, self and relationships), all other projects will begin to fit in better because you will have defined your priorities.

How can you enjoy life while being responsible? Buddhists advise "Act as if the future of the universe depends on what you do, while laughing at yourself for thinking that your actions make any difference".

Remember to . . .

1. Learn this process for planning – start with the three key elements of your life and continue to use the process for any project in life
2. Begin at the end – vision
3. Build a MAP
   - Define the required tasks and resources
   - Set the dates
4. Before beginning anything new, always ask
   - Does this fit within my objectives?
   - Does it require a detour on the MAP?
5. Monitor, adjust and review
6. Reward yourself for succeeding.

10 Effective Coaching in the Workplace

>"A good coach is one of the greatest assets an organisation can possess."
>
>The Industrial Society

Ordinary people achieve extraordinary results in business. For many people these extraordinary results are achieved through, and with, the support of coaching. The term coaching has been around in business for much of the 1990's, and yet still has many and varied interpretations.

Simply defined, coaching is one person guiding another through a process, leading to performance enhancement. Coaching can mean different things to different people. It can mean giving a person support to achieve a specific project, helping them to do *better*, what they already do well, or it may mean teaching someone to perform a specific task or develop a skill, which they don't yet possess.

Why use Coaching Inside Organisations?

Coaching is the lever for unleashing potential! The tool for unlocking performance! An approach to change! It can be used to enhance performance to a level beyond the current dreams of the coachee. Once that incredible performance is released, it automatically means 'change'. A change of thinking, doing, acting and ultimately being.

Take a look at any of the extraordinarily successful companies in the world today – IBM, McDonalds, Federal Express. These companies, along with many others, are continuously going through change and this results in employees owning their own work systems. They take responsibility for their own functions, which opens their thinking to new and more effective ways. In companies such as these, coaching supports new thinking, which leads to a continuous and never-ending change process.

Focussed coaching can, and does, improve performance of individuals, teams and the organisation itself. Over the last two years there has been a widespread growth of interest in one to one coaching, and that interest is huge. There is an emerging pattern of people seeking individual coaching.

1   Company directors and senior management

Company directors and senior managers, whose role has recently changed *from* that of technical or professional *to* managerial or commercial, are caught up in the swift pace of organisational change. They are looking towards personal coaching to help them unlock potential in these new, often challenging and isolated roles.

Due to the pace of change, directors and senior managers may find themselves working outside their area of influence, knowledge and comfort, sometimes operating in unexplored areas; areas of concern and uncertainty. Isolated from others, these senior people are looking for a sounding block – a safe environment outside the organisation. A personal coach, who can release their blockages and move them towards action and desired results, is paramount to their continued success

2   Middle managers and teams

More and more requests for coaching are coming from managers or teams who are stuck or paralysed in an organisation double bind. On one hand, their job description requires them to work in a particular way; to have a set of operating values which support their approach to working. On the other hand, the behaviour and values of the organisation, and their immediate seniors, operate from a diametrically opposed base of behaviours and values. In this situation, a supportive outsider, with coaching skills, who is well-versed in understanding people behaviours, can help to move the teams or the managers forward, developing patterns and strategies which constantly deliver success.

3   Job stressed individuals

The term stress is an umbrella word, which covers a wide range of factors in the 90's. Stress and stress-related illnesses have their root cause in fear, which *causes* the nervous system to use massive amounts of negative energy, which the body fails to replace. This can lead to exhaustion and to the nervous system shutting down, in some cases, breaking down. Stress levels run high inside many businesses in which employees are working under great pressure to produce results. Stress is a *reality* in many workplaces rather than a business bonus!

Physical signs of stress can include headaches, backaches, shoulder tension, heightened adrenaline flow, racing heart, heightened cholesterol or other general aches and pains. *Mental* signs of stress include lack of sleep or too much sleep; waking up feeling exhausted; lack of energy, drive and concentration.

Stressors are the experiences, situations, environment, and behaviours that cause, or lead to the cause of, stressful symptoms.

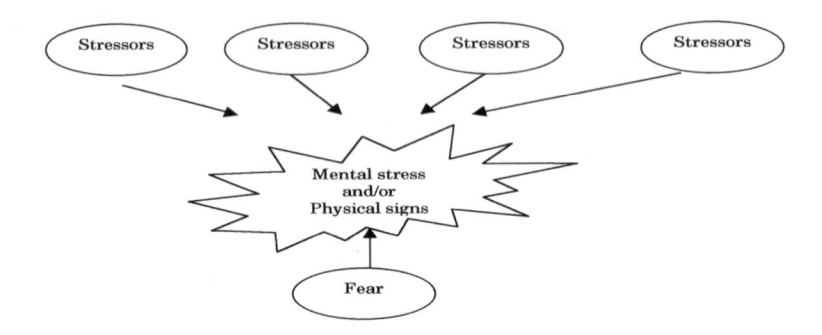

```
  Stressors    Stressors    Stressors    Stressors
         \        |        /         /
          \       |       /         /
           \      |      /         /
            ↓     ↓     ↓         ↙
            Mental stress
              and/or
            Physical signs
                  ↑
                 Fear
```

Stressors in the workplace include situations such as insufficient support or resources; lack of recognition; lack of employee control; conflict of values; constant change and low employee support within that change; too much or too little work.

Above and beyond relieving physical and mental signs of stress, coaching puts you back in control, *at cause*. It gives you an improved focus on business and personal goals, along with increased motivation, confidence and self-image. Coaching develops strategies for peak performance, producing extraordinary results time, after time.

Working with stress, through effective coaching, is about changing beliefs and behaviours; releasing the root causes of fear, and eradicating patterns of limiting decisions which hold individuals back. If you always *do* what you always *did*, you always *get* what you always *got*.

Repeated behaviours are, in fact, habits. Stress inducing habits may exist undetected for a lifetime. The more behaviours are repeated, the more they become habitual. The longer they exist, the more ingrained they become, and so the more difficult they are to remove.

There are people who have made a fine distinction between motivational pressure and stress. They believe that having the correct amount of stress *is* the motivational pressure they require to perform and achieve. Because of this belief system, their stress is relieved and becomes non-existent. When you believe something, then it becomes true. Beliefs drive behaviours.

4 Learning organisations

Learning organisations need support if they are to *be* learning organisations. The learning, development and change that follows, requires support. Often managers have no time or energy left to offer that support. People within this type of organisation, are expected to take responsibility for their own learning, which reminds me of a story of a young man who got his first job as a sales rep, in a large multi-national organisation.

After going through a training and development period he finally went out on his first sales call and very soon he was selling full-time. One day he made a mistake, which cost the company millions of pounds. The Chairman of the company asked to see him the next morning and the young man, full of trepidation, knocked on the door of his office and walked in.

'Well, what have you got to say about this situation?' asked the Chairman.

'I'm sorry', said the young man, 'I made a mistake and it went *very* wrong. I expect you're going to fire me.'

'Fire you', repeated the Chairman, 'why no, not at all. I've just spent millions of pounds on your development. So, what have you learned from this situation to make sure it never happens again?'

This is where the role of the external coach comes in! A supportive outsider who understands the way organisations work or fail to work; who understands the way teams work or fail to work; who understands the way individuals produce results or fail to produce results, is key to the success of a learning organisation.

In business, coaching can be used for many things including:-

- Motivating staff
- Building teams
- Performance improvement
- Building relationships
- Performance enhancement
- Resolving personal issues/problems
- Developing individuals
- Enhancing and accelerating learning

Organisations who are dedicated to remaining competitive and successful are organisations who have visionary leadership and an entrepreneurial spirit. The people at the top of these organisations work *on* the business, not *in* it. Part of working *on* the business is working on the people *within* the business –

coaching people to change the way they think which, in turn, improves performance which produces consistent results time, after time, after time. Ordinary people achieving extraordinary results, through coaching.

What is coaching?

Coaching focuses on *future possibilities* and utilises learning from *past experiences*. Coaching is more about *how* things are done rather than *what* things are done. It is the process of doing, rather than the content of deciding. It is about unlocking a person's potential and maximising their performance. It is about helping people to learn rather than necessarily, teaching people.

In the last 20 years we have learnt more about the brain than in the whole of the previous history of mankind. Each of us has the potential within us to produce magnificent performances in every area of life but, from time to time, we may need or require encouragement and support. This support can come in various forms, one of which is coaching.

As a generalisation, the term coaching has become interchangeable with the term mentoring and to some degree, workplace counselling. It matters not what we call this process of support, what counts is the results that the process produces. The measurable enhancement of performance in individuals, teams, and businesses.

Coaching works on resolving problems at the level *below* where they occur! For example, beliefs and values drive behaviours; and beliefs and values come from our identity. Therefore, working with a problem that manifests itself at the level of behaviours, necessitates the coach working at the level of beliefs and values. It's rather like peeling away the *top* layers of the onion, only to find the cause of the problem is in the heart of the onion; the core. Coaching, done well is about working with the core of the onion which resolves not only the presenting problems, but also those which, at the time of coaching, are not even manifesting themselves yet.

As a coach you need to have positive beliefs about your own potential, in order to unblock others, as well as unlimited beliefs about the potential of each person you coach. As human beings we are limited by our own thinking – our own belief system – about what is possible or impossible.

When Roger Banister, for instance, became the first person to break the 4-minute mile, within 12 months 24 other runners had achieved the same feat. Suddenly, their belief system had changed as a direct result of Banister's conquest!

Following other discoveries and achievements – the creation of the light bulb; the telephone; man landing on the moon etc., a global belief system changed, to open up unlimited thinking. Our beliefs can directly impact upon those we work with, those we coach.

Coaching is about using a conglomerate of skills, styles, approaches and models. It is about being aware and highly skilled in many approaches and strategies, and using whatever is needed to support each individual, in achieving their goal. People are *more than* their behaviours, *more than* their performance. Whatever we think we are, we are always *more than that*! Coaching is about releasing that 'more,' that hidden, possibly untapped, potential.

Coaching is about building a relationship which is based on choices rather than based on advice. For me, at least, coaching is holistic, taking into account the whole person and the complete range of issues which require resolution and improvement. Coaching is a way of thinking; a way of being; a way of accelerating development. It is *much* more than a process; *much* more than a technique!

A Blueprint for Coaching

There are various fundamental stances from which an effective coach operates. A good coaching approach would utilise the following before and during each coaching session.

1   Reasons or results

Empowerment means always having *results* in life. The *results* you choose to have. Individuals who achieve *results*, achieve their goals. They have no excuses, no reasons. *Reasons* are for the faint-hearted. They exist as excuses for what's really holding us back.

The people who achieve consistent results in life have no reasons for lack of achievement. They just do it – produce the results they choose – time, after time, after time. Man had no excuses for being unable to fly – he just went ahead and kept trying until the aeroplane came into being. It was the same with Eddison and the light bulb or Alexander Graham Bell and the telephone. These people knew the end result they wanted and they just kept going until they got it. No excuses, no reasons. Simply results driven!

Coaching is a way of empowering the coachee to achieve excellent performance by discovering the limiting patterns, and reasons, that hold them back. By releasing these reasons, these excuses, the coachee can start to get the results they desire.

2   Cause and effect

The English language encourages thinking in terms of cause and effect. *'You've caused me to lose my job'*, *'She makes me feel very angry'*. Both these statements are a shorthand way of expressing a very complex relationship. To believe that someone else is responsible for *your* emotional state, is to give power to others and so put *you* at the *effect* of others; others thoughts, actions, behaviours and beliefs. You are the only person who has direct control over your emotional state. *Your* emotions are *your* responsibility. Thinking that other people can force you into different moods, different emotional states, is very limiting, and can cause a great deal of distress.

With a cause and effect pattern you can become either the victim, or the nursemaid, of others emotions. Either way they are *reasons* for non-achievement of results. Coaching helps separate the *cause* and *effect* and builds in the idea that each of you has a choice in your emotional response to *every* situation.

Coaching works with you, the individual, to assume responsibility for your own feelings and choices – moving each of you from *effect* to *cause* and causing you to stay there!

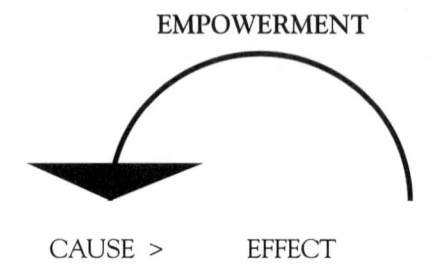

EMPOWERMENT

CAUSE >   EFFECT

Once empowered you can and will, cause yourself to get the results you desire, to achieve your goals. Your emotions *are* your responsibility.

3 Education and intervention

Often there are two distinct approaches to the mental skills part of coaching – *education* and *intervention*. *Education* is about working with the coachee to develop skills, to enhance performance and to create new strategies. It's about educating the coachee how to deal with issues; perform tasks better, more effectively, and even to speed up learning. *Intervention* is about using methods to put right what is wrong. Dealing with personal issues, sorting them out and leaving them behind. Letting go of old patterns, problems, and reasons that hold back the individual or the group.

The *education* skills are mental skills and, like physical skills, must be practised to be improved. Mental skills follow the same learning curve as physical skills, and can be practised using the same approach and methods. Basically the coach should introduce the skill, then utilise it in the coaching sessions, so much that it becomes ingrained in the coachee's memory. That way it becomes automatic; integrated at the unconscious level and so 'forgotten', consciously. Integrated into the belief and value system of the coachee.

In sport, for example, athletes are encouraged to practice both physical and mental skills until these skills become part of the athletes belief system, part of their identity. Practice is the key to development and perfect performance, no matter what the conditions. For athletes, competitions are won by hard work and solid preparation, but they can be lost due to poor psychological skills or mental errors. Sports coaching is about developing the 'total sports person', so they have greater control of themselves in *all* situations.

Personal performance coaching is also about developing the 'total person', developing individuals, small teams and groups of people in business, to be at *cause* in life. To have greater control of themselves in *all* situations.

4 An holistic view

Human beings are an integrated system, mind and body connected, and what affects one affects the other. So, the business coaching approach is about working with that total system, that whole person. Achieving balance in life means paying attention to *all* contexts of life – to the total life of the individual being coached.

Life can be like a seesaw! If one end has something heavy on it and the other end has nothing, it will be unequally balanced. Only when the end in the air has some attention paid to it, will the seesaw begin to come towards some type of balance. Coaching is about working on, achieving and maintaining that equilibrium, that balance in life. The whole person, the total balance!

5 Getting permission

Coaching only works successfully when permission has been given, by the coachee, for the coach to work with them. That permission may be verbal or it may be at an unconscious level, perhaps in the form of a question, like, 'How would that work for me?' 'Can anyone be coached?' 'What do I need to do to be coached?' This coaching approach is about recognising when the coachee wants to change something, wants to have something fixed. The saying, 'if it ain't broke, don't fix it', rings absolutely true.

A coach is only a guide, requiring the individual's permission and then, and only then, can they start working together. It needs to be pointed out here, that 'you can take a horse to water but you can't make it drink', which means that, as coach, you can only work *with* the person, not *on* them.

6 Confidentiality

Confidentiality is another part of the approach to coaching. Once permission has been granted by the coachee, the coach is then, mentally at least, appointed. This appointment leads to a feeling of safety, which opens up the opportunity to discuss the *real* issues and problems. It's about trust in the coach. Trust that everything discussed remains totally confidential, no matter what the circumstances.

Sometimes this confidentiality may expand to complete anonymity about who is being coached within an organisation, so that no one knows that 'X' is being coached, apart from 'X' and the coach.

7 Industrial knowledge

Taking the coachee beyond the boundaries of the coach's knowledge is a real strength. As coach, it's OK to know nothing about the business inside which you are coaching. In fact, it's a very powerful factor – a real strength. Objectivity supports the coaching approach.

The coach has no need to know or have technical knowledge about the industry sector or organisation in which they are coaching. As the adage goes – a little knowledge can be a dangerous thing. Knowledge may diminish responsibility and ownership of the coachee's performance. It may also undermine the credibility of the coach.

7a The Manager as coach

On the other hand, however, managers working as coaches can be very effective within their own industry. Managing with a coaching approach is becoming popular in companies such as K.P.M.G., Woolwich Building Society, and Barclays Bank. However, it does mean an extra skill set for the manager, and quite possibly a 180° turn from 'hands on' management to 'hands off' coaching.

A shift of approach from *knowing* and *telling* to *facilitating* and *asking*, which often is diametrically opposed to the reasons that the manager was promoted to the position in the first place. People in business are promoted *because* of their knowledge and experience rather than *despite* it. Often senior management teams in organisations are usually the teams with the most technical experience in the company.

In the past, few of these team members would have been experienced to a senior level in people management. Times are changing. More and more senior management teams are being required to put people first. Hence, the move towards management by coaching. This requires managers to 'put aside' some of their knowledge, value judgements, experience and, most of all, their answers to the presenting problems. It requires a great degree of self-confidence in passing control to the coachee.

The paradox is, the more we listen the more we get listened to. Instead of telling others what to do, the good manager/coach asks questions and, as they listen to the answers, the coachee feels valued.

As manager, you grow your reputation based on this, resulting in more requests for coaching from employees who sometimes just want to be listened to; want to feel valued; want to feel taken notice of; want to grow and develop. You *are* able develop your staff and enhance their performance way beyond your and their, expectations.

Coaching Approaches

1 Face to face

Face to face coaching is probably the best known approach. This entails coach and coachee working together for a period – often of several hours – on issues, strategies and problems relevant to the coachee. With individual coaching, if run *inside* the organisation, work colleagues could have a tendency to think it's just a conversation taking place, and may be tempted to interrupt the proceedings. Worse still, they could resort to pulling the coachee out of the session for a phone call, some advice etc. The venue for face to face coaching needs to be *out* of the workplace, whenever possible.

This should be in a mutually agreeable location conducive to coaching, with flexibility to stop when appropriate and the ability, and ideally the space, to walk around outside. The environment requires comfortable seating, along with adequate heating, refreshment facilities and no disruptions or distractions from other people or 'phones.

Face to face coaching of small teams or groups of people *can* take place in-house, although all the above requirements remain.

2 Telephone coaching

Telephone coaching is another approach, and is stand-alone. More usually run on a weekly basis, for a set length of time – 30 minutes or less per call. The coach continues to develop strategies, skills and knowledge with the coachee, who is then responsible for implementing actions.

In the best instances, telephone coaching is used to supplement face to face coaching. It is an online support for a period, maybe, of months. Geographically there are no boundaries to telephone coaching. It can take place with people in the UK or abroad and can be backed up by post, fax and email communication, which makes it an attractive option or addition for any busy manager.

Some individuals prefer to have telephone coaching sessions before they start working in a morning, as this puts them at *cause* and gives them the sense of having someone there to bounce ideas off; someone who helps them to empower themselves.

3 Hands on/hands off

In the continuum of coaching styles, at one end there is the 'hands on' approach, with coach as teacher, *advising* highly experienced performers on how to achieve excellence. At the other end is the 'hands off' approach, with coach as enabler, *motivating* highly experienced performers who are aiming to achieve excellence. Effective workplace coaching requires the skills of the coach to be able to adapt and adopt different approaches along this continuum. This will be dependent upon the needs of the coachee and the *education* or *intervention* approach taken.

'Hands on' means the *coach* has control; 'hands off' gives the *coachee* control. Ideally the coachee, in both scenarios, has to accept responsibility for the results, leading to empowerment.

The Skills of the Coach

1 To empower the coachee

The skill of the coach is to empower the coachee and, as a result, make themselves redundant! The coachee is the person responsible for the results! Free the coachee to be better than you! Put them at *cause* and work with them to *stay at cause* and so get the *results* they desire in life! Coach individuals to take responsibility to own the answer, to think of themselves as a valuable resource within the organisation; within the team; within the department; within life, and to know that they have all the answers they need, within themselves.

The best of coaching teases out the unconscious answers and simultaneously practices new mental skills and processes. These then become habitual and integrated to a level where they are automatic – like driving a car. Once we have learnt to drive a car we are unconsciously competent to perform that task over and over again – without thinking.

2 To build and maintain rapport

As already stated, the term coaching is open to many and varied interpretations. In some organisations coaching is one sided, the seesaw is imbalanced, with little or no rapport between coachee and coach. Rapport is open, honest two-way communication in which first one person leads and then the other. It is a delicate dance between two people on an equal level; an equal footing. Rapport is about respect and trust. Respecting what is important to the coachee – without necessarily agreeing with it.

Maintaining rapport is the trigger to creating paradigm shifts in the coachee, through challenging their ideas, thoughts, behaviours and beliefs. A paradigm shift means a 180° change in thinking about a particular issue, person or problem.

3   To maintain your own state

This means to have control of *your* emotions, moods, and energies. To focus on solutions rather than problems and to look for outcomes, rather than blame. By maintaining your own state, you'll be able to work on getting *results* and removing *reasons*. Staying *out* of the coachee's state of mind, means you can sympathise without getting involved. You will be giving no agreement, rather, seeking outcomes, creating ways for the *coachee* to come up with alternative solutions, and thoughts, about that particular situation. Answers they hadn't previously thought of.

Preserve your own energy so that as the coach you are always in a highly resourceful state. Protect the way you use your energy by remaining in control of *your* own emotions rather than sharing the coachee's emotions, and jumping in there with them.

So if, for example, tears of sadness are shed by the coachee, the coach remains detached, external to the emotions and in control of their own mood.

4   To be non-judgemental

In many cases, the coach is required to pass no value judgement about, or to, the coachee. No judgements, no opinions, on what they think is right or wrong. During the process of empowerment it is important that the coach is neutral. Obviously, each coach will have their own set of values so, clearing *your* mind is important in order to be able to *listen to* what the coachee has to say. Having a clear mind is far more important, and powerful, than using energy to defend *your* own viewpoint. Anyway, who says your viewpoint or opinion, is correct? Only you!

The coach needs to have an empty mind before and during a coaching session. To be totally open to taking in everything the coachee gives out. This means the coach setting aside thoughts about their own life; their own issues; their own learning; their own experience and their expectations of the session.

As already stated, the coachee needs to own the answers. Coaches are required to make no assumptions, but to ask searching questions to check assumptions from which the *coachee* may be working.

A coach is able to use a series of internal questions to check whether the coachee is working from an assumption. One excellent question is: 'What does the *coachee* have to believe to be true, in order to do that – in order to say that, or – in order to think in that way?' With an internally registered answer, the coach is able to ask the coachee further questions, using their intuitive reasoning to check and re-check the assumptions the coachee is working on.

5 To provide no answers

Particularly with the intervention approach, the coach gives no answers. That is the job of the coachee! It is up to the coach to have the wisdom to recognise that every individual is different and, as such, they are unable to provide answers for anyone else.

Even identical twins think, behave and are different from each other in some way. Identical twins will sometimes interpret their shared experiences in vastly different ways. Each individual on the planet has their own blue print, their own way of thinking and being. We are all unique. The only way our personal blue print can be recorded is by finger-printing or DNA testing. No one else has the same print or DNA; no one else has the same problems; no one else has the same answers!

As a high performance coach, you need to use your understanding and coaching expertise to recognise the patterns individuals create for themselves, through their own experiences. The coachee creates these patterns in the first place and so they have the ability and resources within themselves, to break the patterns and create new ones.

6 Mind body connection

Often coaches will have a background in psychology, and how to maximise performance. As no two individuals are the same, then no two human bodies are the same, and no two human minds are the same. One of the skills of the coach is to enable the coachee to be consciously aware of the sensations in their own body. The feelings, *specific* feelings, when they are thinking something, doing something or being someone.

Just as in the sporting arena, athletes are finely tuned to the sensations of their physical body and they, with the help of their coach, know how to maximise performance by tuning into these sensations. The job of the coach is to work with each individual and help them pay attention to the feelings in their body, the reactions they have when they perform a particular task, or think a particular thought.

An example of this might be an individual who is afraid of speaking in public, and yet is required to do it over and over again. Each time they stand up to speak, they unnecessarily produce a set of sensations in the body, which may be labelled 'anxiety', 'fear' or 'panic'.

These feelings could be butterflies in the stomach, aches, pains, sweaty palms, weak knees or many other things. Time after time they produce these feelings perfectly! How does the body know how to do that each time? It doesn't, it's the mind that's driving the body. So the mind/body system can do something else instead. It can produce other sets of feelings and sensations, perhaps labelled relaxation, confidence etc., to *replace* the unwanted ones. The role of the coach is to guide the coachee through that replacement process.

7 To watch and pay attention to everything.

Coaching requires the ability to be able to pay attention to the coachee. Attention to their physical movements, gestures, breathing, eye movements, tone of voice and words, from the largest, most obvious, movements, to the smallest, most subtle, messages. Words are interesting because they count for only 7% of the *whole* message. Potentially they are the most important part of the message, but many times words are saying one thing whilst the rest of the person is communicating something else.

For instance, how many times have you had the experience, let's say with your boss, when one thing has been said and, in fact, you just *know* that something else was very definitely meant? Something in their voice, their face or their body movements and gestures, was communicating a *much* stronger message, a conflicting message. It happens all too often, both in business and in life.

It is the skill of the coach to notice these mixed messages, as they occur. To investigate the under-lying meanings, which will, to the coachee, be largely unconscious, and then to align the messages to get rid of the conflicts. Effective coaching means using intuition, your senses, to interpret and pick up the *whole* message. It means working from a position of raised awareness, in order to be effective, with each individual.

8 To actively listen

Coaching requires 80% listening and 20% talking. The more a coach listens, the more they will be taken notice of when they *do* speak. The 80/20 rule is about spending 20% of time doing things, which give 80% pay back, and results!

A coach needs to listen to the 7% of words and the voice tone accompanying those words. Listening to the coachee is a major part of the process. If the coachee feels they are being heard, they also feel valued; that they are being taken notice of; that their ideas and thoughts are important.

9 To question effectively

Questioning skills are really the flip side of listening skills. An effective coach needs to be able to ask useful questions. To be able to challenge the coachee's thought processes and to open up new, and alternative, patterns of thinking about the issues to be resolved. The main role of the coach is to ask, not tell!

Ask questions which cause the coachee to fully consider the answer from different perspectives. Ask questions to raise their awareness! From that awareness can come understanding of the 'stuck' areas. Understanding, learning and realisation about how to do it better, how to do it differently, next time. Questions are used to focus attention on the areas and issues which require resolving. Questions lead to clarity!

Well-timed questions from the coach can lead the coachee to question, internally, their own strategies. Questions gather information, which the coachee was perhaps not consciously aware of. The coach follows the answers given and uses the information to continue asking questions, helping the coachee to raise all the issues and all the patterns, that they need to deal with.

The type of questions most useful to a coach are the open questions, such as What; Where; When; Who; Which and How. *Why*, is a special case. *Why* asks for reasons and justifications from a person, for their actions. For example, 'Why did you respond like that?' The answer has to be, 'Because ———— (reason, reason, reason). *Why* leads the coach down a blind alley and only serves the coachee's purpose of defending their opinion, their actions, which further installs old patterns of thinking. Asking the question 'In what other ways could you have responded?' opens up the possibilities of new behaviours, new responses.

A coach uses questions to 'challenge' old ways of thinking, old habits, the issues the coachee wants to resolve. These challenges have to be asked in rapport, with integrity and with no value judgements and no pre-supposed answers. An example of a question that 'challenges', may be in response to a statement such as 'I always do it this way.' The challenging questions, which follow are, 'Has there ever been a time when you have done it another way?' or 'What would happen if you did . . .'X' . . .?' These questions challenge what apparently is a closed statement, and in doing so, opens up possibilities.

All too often people get stuck in a track of thinking 'inside their box'. It takes a coaching session or two to get people to think on a multi-track – or 'outside their box'. Beyond lateral thinking, the art of coaching and asking empowering questions, is a key to change, performance enhancement and development. Just as an artist has paints and brushes, so a coach has questions and the ability to pay attention. One question leads, automatically, to another.

When I'm running a coaching session I have no idea of the questions I'm going to ask, apart from the very first one – 'Why are you here?' All the other questions that follow are based on the information the coachee gives me. As coach, I'm listening to and investigating patterns.

10 To work content free

Sometimes, as a coach, it is helpful to work without specific details, and even without content. Content can distract both coach and coachee and lead to an avenue of trees or the inevitable dead end. Working content free means just that. If there is a big, painful issue to be resolved, the coachee may not want to access it again, so much so that they bury it deep inside their unconscious mind. It is the role of the coach to work with that issue without knowing what it is. Without knowing the content of the issue, the coach cannot pre-judge or pre-suppose any answers. The answers *have* to come from the coachee.

In a coaching session, I find it very useful to set one or two ground rules for operating like this, right at the beginning. One of these ground rules is, if the coachee gets into detail, content and justification of that content, I simply raise my hand with a stop sign, as an indication that I want to ask a question. When this has happened once or twice, the coachee soon gets the idea that justification, and sometimes specific content, are unnecessary.

11 Using stories to change minds

The use of stories and analogies when coaching is very, very effective. The stories need to be well constructed and well thought out having all the same issues in them, but with a different ending. A positive resolution to the emotions, the stuckness, that the coachee has been expressing. These stories may be taken from the coach's own life or the lives of others. Never, ever, be tempted to explain the moral of the story. Leave that for the coachee to sort out for themselves. That is where the power of the story lies.

Another story-telling approach is to offer counter examples to the coachee. In other words, stories which give the opposite ending; have the opposite outcome to where the coachee is right now. This counter example can be of assistance to help the coachee to think of *their* problem in a different way.

The Skills of being a Coachee

Coaching can be extremely successful for everyone as long as:

i) the coach is skilled in coaching
ii) the coachee takes equal responsibility for the outcome of the session

There are four key skills to enable the coachee to take equal responsibility. These are:

1 Taking responsibility

Total responsibility for development, change or performance enhancement, rests with the coachee. You can take a horse to water but you can't make it drink! The coachee has *control* of the learning and development which takes place. That's the main role of being coached. The coachee has to own the outcome of the session, to take responsibility for their own performance, to be at *cause*! The coachee has a choice, and that choice is about choosing to develop and change, or to stay the same. Part of the responsibility to the coaching session is making those choices! Telling the coachee they *must* take responsibility, doesn't automatically *make* them responsible.

Remember, coaching is about coaching others *how* to take responsibility. To begin with, the coachee has to make a choice to *take* responsibility or not. If the latter, coaching will have limited success. It is an intricate balance between coach and coachee.

2 Attitude

'The mind is key'. As a coachee you are required to have an open attitude and state of mind towards development and change. This will include giving yourself permission to resolve issues and to let go of things that are limiting you. Just as you gave permission to work with the *coach*, now you need to give *you* permission to work with *yourself*.

Having the right attitude is about letting go of analysis. Analysing why you do this, this way. Why you can't give up doing that, etc. It's also about letting go of the analysis of the process of coaching – the things the coach is asking you about. That is the domain of the coach. Your responsibility is to *stop* analysing.

3 Staying with the coaching process

As coachee you are required to stay with the process of coaching, and use the coach as a guide to direct your attention. I have known coachees jump ahead of the process or guess what I am going to ask next – when even I don't know what the next question is going to be at that particular moment! Coachees who jump ahead or double-guess the process, do so as a way of avoiding sensitive issues, a way of putting up a smoke screen to protect situations which, at that point, they are unwilling to confront or resolve.

A coach can spend a lot of time getting rid of smoke screens which, if the coachee has had them for a number or years, will be very, very effective. Some coachees are masters at smoke screening. Whilst it is a means of protection, the positive assumption must be that the coachee wants to let go of, and resolve, those sensitive issues. The smoke screen can become a double bind, and the coach requires time, rapport and many skills to get beneath this, to the root cause of the problem.

Behind every behaviour *is* a positive intention. So there is a positive intention to smoke screening. Human beings are always *more* than their behaviour.

4 Learning

The coaching session can provide a vast opportunity for the coachee to learn, provided they have an open mindset and a flexibility of thinking, which is open to challenges from the coach. Practice makes perfect and, if we go back to analogies from sport, great sports people practice mentally as well as physically.

They practice the skill of scoring goals; serving aces; skiing slaloms etc. That perfect mental practice, in some cases, is more important than the physical practice. A large proportion of effective sports coaching concentrates on the 'inner game', where the mind is key. That 'inner game' works equally well in business. Practising mental skills, which create new physical behaviours and beliefs, leads to success. Practising mental skills until they become automatic and 'forgotten', and are fully integrated as part of the belief system, is the way to accelerate development.

Workplace coaching

1 What if your organisation requires coaching?

The major benefits, to any organisation thinking of using a coaching approach as part of their philosophy, can be summarised very simply.

i   Higher performing individuals

- ii   Improved performance and productivity
- iii Enhanced skill development
- iv   Accelerated learning
- v   Greater rapport and more positive relationships
- vi   An environment of respect where listening is valued
- vii Reduction and release of stress

2 Making a difference

The overall benefit of coaching is that it makes a difference directly, or indirectly, by enhancing individual performance. The question is, how is that performance enhancement measured? Against what criteria? Against which standards? Who does the measuring?

I suggest that the performer, i.e. the coachee, does the measurement. Like can only be measured by like. The coachee knows where they want to get to, and they know where they started, so each step can be charted, mapped and recorded. This can then be compared to where they were, where they are now, and how far they have got to go, to reach peak performance. So measurement of results – like against like – becomes important. Without results there are only *reasons*. *Reasons* why the expected, or sought after, results are not happening.

3 Benefits to managers

The coaching manager will have an automatic understanding of each individual they coach. They will be aware of the coachee's motivation, understanding what makes them tick. With a greater awareness of how they construct their world and make sense of the experiences within it. This new found understanding leads to greater two-way respect between manager and subordinate, with enhanced rapport.

That enhanced relationship paves the way for conversations of a *different* nature, to take place. Inside and outside the coaching sessions, the manager quickly establishes a relationship based on trust, respect and open two-way communication. They are able to easily discuss potential areas of development, opportunities for future ways of working – based on responsibility of the coachee – rather than 'managing' with the old carrot and stick approach.

Far less time needs to be spent in conversations about problems. Conversations following coaching, are automatically used as a basis for continuous improvement of performance, systems, thinking patterns, relationships, etc. For managers and coachees, the overall benefit of this approach is the vast improvement in their relationship – opening up respect, dialogue and ideas – leading to self managed individuals.

4 Benefits to the coachee

4a   Coachees benefit from the raised awareness of their ability to resolve issues for themselves. They automatically take *responsibility* for being at cause in life – causing results to happen. *Responsibility* for their own emotions, and maintaining control of their own state. *Responsibility* for their own development which leads to more independence. Independence to grow and develop. They are able to recognise that they have a choice. They *choose* to accept full responsibility for their results in life!

4b   *Empowerment* is about being *at cause*; causing yourself to think in different ways; to act with new behaviours; to change negative beliefs. Beliefs need to be empowering and positive as they drive *all* behaviour – and *that* behaviour is how we are perceived by others. However, we are always *more* than our behaviours!

4c   A direct benefit of coaching some people, is about developing *identity* and self worth. This, coupled with self-belief and self esteem, make a powerful contribution to any individual. Enabling a person to enhance their positive *identity*, ensures they have a greater impact and distinct presence.

   Following one of my coaching sessions, the coachee said he felt as if he was being *noticed* by colleagues, as well as being *taken* notice of, for the first time in years! This feeling was reinforced when his manager gave him positive feed-back. His feeling of self-worth then became a self-fulfilling prophecy.

4d   Through coaching many individuals become more attuned, more *aware of others* viewpoints, and less quick to defend their *own* opinions. They are more flexible in thinking, more responsive in behaviour and have greater respect and *awareness for others*. In short, individuals who have been coached well, benefit themselves, their managers and other individuals with whom they come in contact.

4e   All these benefits lead to the ultimate benefit of enhanced performance in business, and in life. Ordinary people achieving extraordinary results!

In Summary

Why use coaching inside organisations?

Company directors and senior management	Middle managers and teams
Job stressed individuals	Learning organisations

What is coaching?
A Blueprint for Coaching
Reasons or results
Education and intervention
Getting permission
Industrial knowledge

Cause and effect
An holistic view
Confidentiality
The manager as coach

How coaching works
Coaching Approaches
Face to face
Hands on/hands off

Telephone coaching

The Skills of the Coach
To empower the coachee
To maintain your own state
To provide no answers
To watch and pay attention to everything
To question effectively
Using stories to change minds

To build and maintain rapport
To be non-judgemental
Mind body connection
To actively listen

To work content free

The Skills of being a Coachee
Taking responsibility
Staying with the coaching process

Attitude
Learning

Workplace coaching
What if your organisation requires coaching?
Benefits to managers

Making a difference

Benefits to the coachee

11 Turnover is Vanity – Profit is Sanity

After the recent recession, many businesses believe they have taken all the steps necessary to turn themselves into 'lean, mean, fighting machines', and are ideally placed to reap the rewards as world economies continue to expand.

The next world recession is possibly just around the corner following the near collapse of the far East economies but, when I talk to businesses, the apathy of many is quite worrying. Many believe that having weathered the storm of the last recession they will survive the next one.

Some will but, unfortunately, many will not.

It is well known that as many as two thirds of new businesses fail to survive beyond their first three years.

As the UK and European economies continue to expand, unemployment is reducing as small businesses start up, and as existing businesses increase their employee numbers to cope with increased demand for their supplies and services.

Despite the number of businesses that collapsed in the last recession, many survivors have not learnt the fundamental lesson of business that IN ORDER TO SURVIVE AND TO EXPAND, A BUSINESS MUST MAKE A PROFIT, AND THIS PROFIT MUST GENERATE A POSITIVE CASH FLOW.

Lack of profit results in lack of cash flow and a lack of working capital needs recapitalising or eventually the business will fail.

Profit gives you options for your future direction and strategy.

Lack of profit gives you very few options in the survival game; you end up becoming dependent on others for the survival of your business.

So what do so many business owners do when starting or expanding a business?

They concentrate on expanding sales, and 'hope' that profit comes automatically from the increased activity.

This is often the worst mistake any business person can make. I always emphasise to my clients

"TURNOVER IS VANITY – PROFIT IS SANITY – AND CASH FLOW IS REALITY".

Alternatively, it can be expressed more emphatically

"INCREASED SALES WILL FEED YOUR PRIDE – BUT ONLY INCREASED PROFIT CAN FEED YOUR FAMILY".

Consider with me a few questions:
a   Have you ever written down why you are in business and what you expect from your business?
b   When did you last discuss how to increase sales with your management?
c   When did you last discuss how to increase profit with your management?
d   What plans do you have to increase your profit?
e   What have you done today to specifically increase your bottom line and by how much?
f   Could it have been by more? Do you know?
g   Do you understand the relationship between your turnover and your profit?
h   Do you know what level of sales is required to give your business a breakeven level of profitability.
i   Do you know what level of sales is required to give your business a breakeven level of cash flow?
j   Do you know what are the key performance indicators of your business?
k   How often do you monitor them?
l   Do you understand the impact on your profits of variations in your turnover or margins?
m   What strategies does your business have for increasing its profit?
n   Have these been agreed and recorded? How often are they monitored?

You Need a Profit Plan

One of the points I emphasise to businesses is that too few managers concentrate on "profits" – and yet, is that not the reason why most businesses are in existence?

Businesses will produce business plans, marketing plans, and human resource plans, and yet fail to develop the most important plan – a profit plan – a plan *totally* dedicated to the creation and implementation of strategies focused on the increase of profit.

Most businesses merely believe that profits are generated as a by-product of the other plans and, although there is some validity in this, if they also prepared a 'profit plan', they would make themselves so much more profitable.

Focus on Profit Not Just Cost Cutting

A report by the Association of Profit Advisers studied the factors affecting the profitability of companies. This revealed that companies that focus on profit improvement, realise on average 75% more value for their owners/shareholders than companies that focus exclusively on cost cutting strategies.

It is human nature to look at ways to cut costs as a means to generate increased profit. In the short term this does work. However, it does not help to set companies up for future growth.

After the last recession, many businesses cut themselves down so lean that when they tried to expand at the end of the recession, they went out of business because they had inadequate working capital, and the banks would not support them.

Although cost control is an essential part of making profit, done incorrectly it can promote negativity and impact morale among the team on which the owners/shareholders depend to grow the business and its bottom line.

It is better to concentrate on improving what the business already does, and examine in detail what action can be taken to generate increased margins by improving service to customers/clients, by offering 'added value', and by fine tuning and improving management controls to identify and implement these strategies.

After all, "YOU CAN ONLY REDUCE YOUR COSTS TO NIL – BUT THERE IS NO LIMIT AS TO HOW FAR YOU CAN INCREASE YOUR SALES AND MARGINS".

In this chapter, I can only provide an overview of this massive subject, but I will try to evaluate what I consider to be the most essential points.

Where to Start?

1. Identify and record why you are in business.
2. Plan and set targets.
3. Distinguish your variable overheads from your fixed overheads.
4. Evaluate the relationship between your turnover and your profit.
5. Establish a "pricing for profit" policy.
6. Know and understand the sales mix of the business.
7. Supplies – establish how costs can be reduced.
8. Stock – establish your stock turnover policies.
9. Fixed assets – establish a policy for buying, renting or leasing.
10. Overheads – understand the main areas open to improvement.

Why Are You in Business?

As an owner or a manager, it is essential to be clear about your personal expectations from the business.

These need to be distinguished from the expectations of the business itself, and you need to establish the extent to which they are mutually compatible.

Why is this important?

If you as an individual are not motivated by profit or have no direct incentive for the business to improve its profitability, there are potential conflicts of interest that need to be resolved.

The same condition applies to all members of the business' management team. I question the motivation of any team who do not stand to benefit directly from increasing the company's profitability, however ethical, moral, or upright members of the community they may be.

These expectations should be recorded and should be regularly reviewed. This is a fundamental requirement of 'goal setting', and if management lose sight of the goals/objectives they have set not only for the business but also for themselves, how can they monitor their progress?

In determining expectations, you should identify and record what you believe to be the ultimate profit potential for your business. You should identify how the goals will be achieved and also the time scales within which they will be completed.

Finally, most important, you need to identify the level of profit that is required in order to achieve those goals.

Profit is Not a Dirty Word

A client once argued that my advice was incorrect, because his business was a 'charitable' business, because it did not make profits for its shareholders.

However, I was soon able to persuade him that 'profit is not a dirty word' and that if the business could make more profit, then all the good causes for which the business had been established would also benefit by this increased profitability.

Similarly, as an individual, if he has no wish to benefit from achieving profit goals, there is nothing to stop him from earning the money and distributing it to charity himself.

Planning – Set Targets

Mao Tse Tung once said "if you don't know where you are going – any road will take you there".

Before you can create a profit plan, you need to have a business plan including detailed financial profit and cash flow forecasts.

Detailed budgeting is required, and ideally should extend into at least a five year outline plan, in order to set down parameters or 'goal posts' against which the business can measure itself and its progress.

In practice, many businesses prepare budgets for owners and for bankers, but fail to prepare these budgets in sufficient detail to allow them to be of any practical use to enable the business to achieve its maximum profit potential.

You will know the old saying "what you can measure you can manage" and this remains valid today.

Put another way, if you can't measure it, it is extremely difficult to manage it.

By setting detailed budgets, showing the inter-relationship of every part of the business, managers are in a position to make management decisions as and when the decisions need to be made, rather than having to wait for historical information to be produced and analysed.

Distinguish Your Variable Overheads from Your Fixed Overheads

In *figure 1* you will recognise a summarised version of a typical profit and loss account; this business was clearly struggling and had only survived because the owner had shored it up with his own money.

The owner produced these accounts and, spotting the improved gross profit margin and the reduced net loss, felt that all he needed to do was to increase his sales to get over his problem.

IMPORT/EXPORT BUSINESS

SUMMARISED TRADING PROFIT & LOSS ACCOUNT
FOR THE YEAR ENDED 30 JUNE 1997

		1997		1996
SALES		153575		145263
COST OF SALES		135462		130297
GROSS PROFIT CONTRIBUTION	11.8%	18113	10.3%	14966
LESS: OVERHEADS				
WAGES, TRANSPORT & HANDLING COSTS		25271		20357
OTHER OVERHEADS		7502		12363
TOTAL OVERHEAD COSTS		32773		32720
NET LOSS		–14660		–17754

Figure 1

His accountant had given him the figures without making any further comment and the owner felt he needed some profit advice.

Have you spotted the problem?

Although his accounts had been drawn up correctly to comply with the Companies Act and accounting standards, they were misleading from a management point of view.

The majority of the wages, transport and handling costs were actually variable costs and, if they had been included with the cost of sales, they would have shown that in fact the business was sustaining a gross loss (see *figure 2*) and, unless prices are increased, the business would never make a profit, and there would be no point in the business continuing.

This is an excellent example of a business owner failing to distinguish between fixed overhead which, in this case, was relatively minor, and variable overhead which was significant, and varied more or less in relation to sales.

In order to be profitable, it is vital that all businesses understand this distinction.

IMPORT/EXPORT BUSINESS

SUMMARISED TRADING PROFIT & LOSS ACCOUNT
FOR THE YEAR ENDED 30 JUNE 1997

		1997		1996
SALES		153575		145263
COST OF SALES		135462		130297
"DIRECT" GROSS PROFIT CONTRIBUTION	11.8%	18113	10.3%	14966
WAGES, TRANSPORT AND HANDLING COSTS		25271		20357
GROSS PROFIT CONTRIBUTION	−4.7%	−7158	−3.7%	−5391
LESS: FIXED OVERHEADS				
WAGES, TRANSPORT & HANDLING COSTS		0		0
OTHER OVERHEADS		7502		12363
TOTAL OVERHEAD COSTS		7502		12363
NET LOSS		−14660		−17754

Figure 2

Establish the Relationship Between Your Turnover and Your Profit

In *figure 1 and figure 2*, I did not refer to 'gross profit', but rather I referred to gross profit 'contribution'.

My clients become accustomed to me insisting that where there are fixed overheads in a business there can be no gross profit – there can only be 'contribution' towards the overheads.

It is only when the contribution has exceeded the overhead, that the business has a right to refer to the 'contribution' as a 'profit'.

This is one of the most fundamental aspects that managers must recognise when changing their thinking away from thinking about the top line (sales) to the bottom line (profit).

Turnover means nothing if the cost of sales is almost as much.

What the management should be concentrating on is the 'level of contribution' that is generated by those sales.

Five Ways to Increase Your Profit

There are only five ways to increase your profit:

1. Increase the number of customers.
2. Increase your margin on sales.
3. Increase the frequency customers buy your product/service.
4. Increase the range of products you have to sell.
5. Reduce your costs, and improve your productivity.

Every manager must recognise these five ways in order to be able to adequately analyse the business and establish the relationship between the top and bottom line.

In doing so, it is important that they look at 'margins' as being 'contribution margins' which are calculated after having deducted the variable costs of making those sales, not just the direct costs incurred.

Case Study – Printing Business

I was recently advising a printing business which, although it was realising its turnover targets, was failing to generate sufficient profit.

At the time this printer was not fully computerised and was using the tried and tested system of a 'job bag', which followed the print job around the factory through its different stages of production.

Management established a budget for each job when quoting for the work. A budget was allowed for raw materials, ink and paper, an allowance was made for labour and an estimated time and cost allowed for finishing.

In order to establish the labour cost, an hourly cost was calculated based on standard hours per week.

When I analysed one month's transactions, it was evident that the 'job bag' was not being completed properly and, consequently, the sales director was unaware whether or not the quotes were realistic, based on the times it was taking to produce the jobs.

On analysing the variable costs in a month when the factory was operating at full capacity, the variable costs far exceeded the total costs taken from all the job bags for that month.

This was a fundamental problem in that the systems, although outdated, were more than adequate to identify the relevant costs involved in the production process.

However, because the system was not being implemented properly, management were not aware at the time of doing the work, that they were producing the work inefficiently and unprofitably, and, therefore, continued to quote on the basis of inaccurate assumptions.

They had not recognised the importance of recording and tracking all the variable costs in order that the customer could be billed, instead of remaining as an unrecovered overhead.

This was a problem relatively easy to rectify but provides an example of the failure of management to recognise the relationship between turnover and profit.

Establish a 'Pricing for Profit' Policy

Barry Schimel the founder of the American Institute of Profit Advisers is quoted as saying the simplest way to make profits is to charge the "right price".

Although this sounds obvious, it is amazing the number of businesses who do not follow this advice.

Let us look at the four basic ways of pricing your product or service.

1 Mark up on cost.
2 What will the customer pay?
3 What are the competition charging?
4 What do you need to charge to reduce your stock?

1 Mark Up on Cost

If we were to survey every business in the UK, I would be prepared to wager that the majority of businesses set prices based on what they believe is the direct cost and apply a 'mark up' on that cost.

The trouble with following this approach is that businesses can often achieve sales at higher prices, but fail to do so because they adopt a rigid 'mark up' policy.

Another problem with adopting this policy is that many businesses fail to recognise their real costs. For a retail business it tends to be straightforward, and often their hands are tied by the manufacturers recommended retail price guidelines.

For service and manufacturing businesses, management need to take into account the variable cost of production, as well as any additional ancillary costs, for example installation, maintenance or after sales support.

In arriving at a price based on a mark up over costs, I have seen many owners of businesses commit the cardinal sin of forgetting to include themselves as a "cost" of producing work and as such underprice their product or service. By doing this they create an unnecessary burden of having to achieve higher turnover figures to breakeven, let alone to create the profit needed as a foundation for future growth.

I believe that mark up on cost should be where possible treated as a "management measure" as a way of assessing the relationship of the sales price to the cost of sale, but it should not actually be the mechanism of creating that price in the first place.

2 What will the customer pay?

Surely the market price for a product or service is what a customer is prepared to pay for that product or service?

The price must be set at a level that will not deter them from coming back for more, but clearly adopting this strategy has nothing to do with your costs, other than the need to know that adequate margin is being achieved based on costs.

What a customer is prepared to pay depends on their perception of the value of what they are receiving from you.

Ask the Customer
Sometimes the best way of finding out is to actually ask the customer what they expect from you to establish what it is about your product or service that they like. Is it the name? Is it the reliability? Is it the peace of mind? Is it the quality? Is it the price?

More often than not, the only way of finding out is by testing the market to establish the levels of resistance. Care is needed in testing the market to avoid frightening off potential customers.

Target Price
Another way of looking at this is to set a 'target price'. If you set a price at which you think the customer will be satisfied and will come back for more,

you then have to do the calculations referred to in the last section to ensure that the price is sufficient to give you the profit you require, in addition to covering the costs of providing the product or service.

3 Competition

A major factor in arriving at your price, is the prices charged by your competitors.

A lot depends on the type of product or service that you are providing but, in many cases, although you need to be aware of what the competition is charging, there is no need to follow their pricing strategies.

Why should their price be right and your price wrong?

Again, it is vital to test the market to identify the potential levels of resistance and to be aware of what exactly a customer is seeking when buying that product or service.

4 "Reducing" Stock

Where you have stock that you need to move to generate cashflow or to create space, perhaps because the stock is slow moving or getting old, the pricing decision is not dependant on cost at all, and is purely customer driven in establishing a price attractive enough to move the stock in sufficient volume quickly enough.

In practice this is normally done by testing the market reaction at different price levels.

Much depends on your marketing strategies and budget, but marketing is a completely separate subject and one which I will not cover in this chapter.

Do Not Discount – Add Value

One of the best ways of moving excess stock is by making them part of a promotion.

Too many businesses automatically feel that to increase their turnover they need to discount their prices.

This is a guaranteed way of increasing your turnover, albeit at the expense of your profit, and it is a policy that I do not recommend as a general matter of course.

We will address the relationship between price changes and volume shortly but, if I can give you two examples of what I mean by 'added value' as a way of not only increasing your turnover, but also increasing your profit, I think you will understand what I am trying to say.

Photo Shop – Profit Increase of 30%

Think of the shop that develops photographs and sells photographic accessories.

I know of one business where profits were suffering and the owner planned to remedy the problem by starting a "25%" off promotion, to keep up with the competitor down the street having a similar promotion.

However, the owner was encouraged not to discount, but instead to offer 'added value'.

In this case, added value was 'two free enlargements with any film developed'.

Normally, the price of developing a film was £6, and the price of two enlargements was £2.75. The cost of having the enlargements done was 50p.

By carrying out a promotion of 'two free enlargements worth £2.75 with every film developed', the business was effectively giving the customer an additional £1.25 worth of value, compared to the £1.50 they would have had off the original £6 price (if the business had carried out the 25% promotion).

However, the cost to the shop was only 50p per film.

In addition, the shop assistants were trained to sell picture frames at 'special' prices to go with the enlargements.

By adopting this policy, the business not only achieved an improved margin position by not following the discounting offer but, in turn, generated additional sales that it would not have made in sales of picture frames for the enlargements.

The result of this promotion increased the profitability of the business by over 30%.

Restaurant – Increased 'Covers'

Another example is a restaurant client in a seafront resort. Along the seafront there were numerous restaurants, and holiday makers were notorious at looking at the menu prices before deciding which restaurants they would enter.

Rather than reducing their prices, I persuaded my client to offer a free dessert and coffee with every table of four or more who purchased a starter and main course.

Needless to say the cost of the dessert and coffee was insignificant in comparison to the perceived value by the customers who filled up a table of four or more, especially as the restaurant increased their dessert prices during the promotion.

This promotion not only created additional turnover, but also additional margin in that more starters were bought by holidaymakers, who would otherwise have only bought a main course and a coffee.

Relationship Between Prices and Sales volumes

Following on from the last example about not discounting, it is important that you recognise the relationship between changes in price and changes in sales volume.

Many businesses are reluctant to increase their prices because they are frightened of losing customers. Yet, a study of the example in *figure 3 and figure 4* might change their minds.

Look at *figure 3* where my restaurant client achieves a gross profit contribution margin of 55% from turnover of roughly £150,000.

However, if that restaurant was to increase its prices and margins by 10%, they would still achieve their gross profit margin of £82,500, having had their sales reduced by £23,077 (£150,000 – £126,923).

What the restaurant owner would need to decide is whether or not that level of turnover is likely to be reduced that much by putting up the prices by 10%.

RELATIONSHIP BETWEEN SALES PRICES/MARGINS AND SALES VOLUMES		
RESTAURANT		
SALES		150000
COST OF SALES	45%	67500
GROSS PROFIT CONTRIBUTION	55%	85200
IN ORDER TO ACHIEVE SAME GROSS PROFIT BUT USING 10% HIGHER PRICES/MARGINS OWNER WOULD NEED FEWER CUSTOMERS		
SALES		126923
COST OF SALES	35%	44423
GROSS PROFIT CONTRIBUTION	65%	85200

Figure 3

In *figure 4*, I illustrate how much sales can decline when increasing margins to achieve a nil change in profits and, similarly, there are figures that show how much sales would need to increase, to compensate for reduced margins in order to avoid reducing profits.

For example, a business with a 40% gross profit margin would have to increase their sales by 29% to compensate for a 10% discount, and yet how many businesses do you know that give a 10% discount without a second thought.

Understand the 'Sales Mix' of the Business

When preparing a profit plan management must understand the mix of the prod-

SALES PRICE / SALES VOLUMES MATRIX

	MARGINS	CURRENT GROSS PROFIT PERCENTAGES :-						
		20%	30%	40%	50%	60%	70%	80%
		To avoid profit reduction, Sales can decline by as much as :-						
	+5%	-20%	-14%	-10%	-9%	-8%	-7%	-6%
MARGIN	+10%	-33%	-25%	-18%	-17%	-14%	-13%	-11%
INCREASE	+15%	-43%	-33%	-25%	-23%	-20%	-18%	-16%
	+20%	-50%	-40%	-31%	-29%	-25%	-22%	-20%
	MARGINS	*To avoid profit reduction, Sales must increase by at least :-*						
	-5%	33%	20%	13%	11%	9%	8%	7%
MARGIN	-10%	100%	50%	29%	25%	20%	17%	14%
DECREASE	-15%	300%	100%	50%	43%	33%	27%	23%
	-20%	N/A	200%	80%	67%	50%	40%	33%

Figure 4

ucts/services it sells, especially when those products/services have different contribution margins.

Unfortunately, I have come across many businesses who in theory have excellent "average" contribution margins, who suffer from lack of profitability because they have not understood the whole question of the different profit margins for different ranges of products they sell.

The best way to illustrate this is to give you an example.

Outside Catering

I act for several of the leading outside caterers in London.

When I was approached by the first of these businesses, I had to analyse their businesses at length and establish with them their costs of delivering the service.

An important task was to distinguish those costs that could be charged on to the customer from those variable costs that were not.

Type of Work

The type of work they were doing ranged from small dinners at private homes and at city board rooms, through to wedding parties, corporate buffets and large sit down dinners at outside venues such as art galleries.

Establish Costs

We sat down together and worked out all the costs for providing the service for

Turnover is Vanity – Profit is Sanity

OUTSIDE CATERING BUSINESS

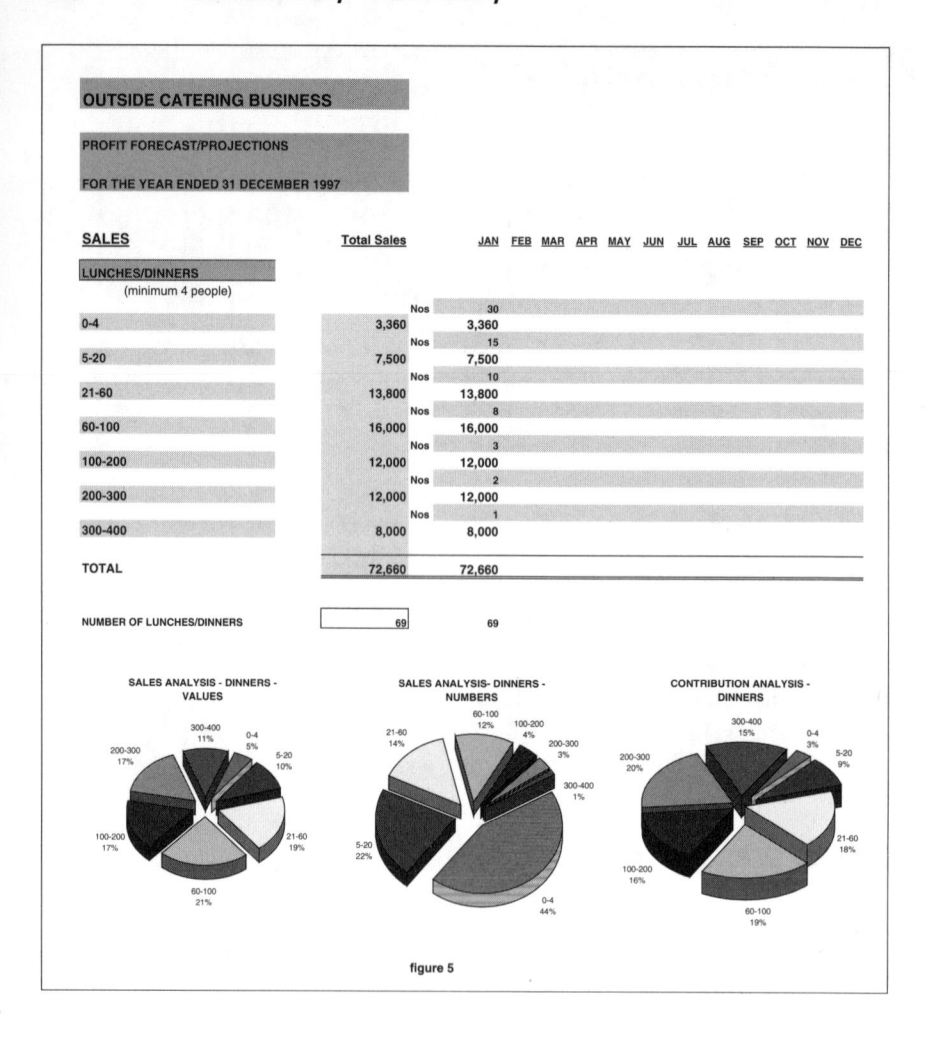

PROFIT FORECAST/PROJECTIONS

FOR THE YEAR ENDED 31 DECEMBER 1997

SALES		Total Sales		JAN	FEB	MAR	APR	MAY	JUN	JUL	AUG	SEP	OCT	NOV	DEC
LUNCHES/DINNERS															
(minimum 4 people)			Nos	30											
0-4		3,360		3,360											
			Nos	15											
5-20		7,500		7,500											
			Nos	10											
21-60		13,800		13,800											
			Nos	8											
60-100		16,000		16,000											
			Nos	3											
100-200		12,000		12,000											
			Nos	2											
200-300		12,000		12,000											
			Nos	1											
300-400		8,000		8,000											
TOTAL		**72,660**		**72,660**											
NUMBER OF LUNCHES/DINNERS		69		69											

SALES ANALYSIS - DINNERS - VALUES
- 0-4: 5%
- 5-20: 10%
- 21-60: 19%
- 60-100: 21%
- 100-200: 17%
- 200-300: 17%
- 300-400: 11%

SALES ANALYSIS - DINNERS - NUMBERS
- 0-4: 44%
- 5-20: 22%
- 21-60: 14%
- 60-100: 12%
- 100-200: 4%
- 200-300: 3%
- 300-400: 1%

CONTRIBUTION ANALYSIS - DINNERS
- 0-4: 3%
- 5-20: 9%
- 21-60: 18%
- 60-100: 19%
- 100-200: 16%
- 200-300: 20%
- 300-400: 15%

figure 5

each size function, ranging from the smallest function (a dinner for four people), through to the largest event, (a dinner for eight hundred people), working out the costs in logical tranches.

I then asked the clients to estimate (based on their previous year and based on their existing order book) what number of functions were they likely to do in the following year.

We put this information into a model that I had prepared and, with that, we were able to estimate the profit to be earned in the year ahead, given the assumptions for number and type of events.

How to Increase Profitability?

That was interesting but, what was more interesting, was when we had to decide what needed to be done to increase the profitability to the levels the business owners required, not only for quality of life, but to generate the increased cash flow needed as a foundation to expand the business in the ensuing years.

It became quite clear that the mix of work had to be changed dramatically.

Whereas dealing with celebrity clients or politicians at their homes was extremely interesting and enjoyable, the profit generated by that work, compared to the effort in doing the work, did not make sense, when compared to the profit generated by the work for corporate clients with larger numbers attending their functions.

This did not mean that the small work had to be stopped but, merely, it allowed them to adopt a strategy to increase the price considerably for this work, so that if people still wanted to have the work done at that increased price, it did at least equate more favourably with the profitability of the corporate events.

In *figure 5*, I enclose a brief extract of an actual model for an outside catering business, without revealing the detailed prices and margins.

You will notice that the smallest dinners of up to four people, represent 43.5% of the turnover in numbers only contributing 4.6% of the value, and 3.1% of the contribution, whereas the *one* function of up to four hundred people sitting down for dinner represents 11% of the turnover in value and 14.8% of the contribution.

The largest amount of contribution (20%) is earned by the *two* functions of up to three hundred people representing 16.5% of the turnover value and only 2.9% of the numbers of functions.

The point is that the effort involved in servicing small functions is disproportionately high compared to the effort involved with larger functions.

This is an extreme example, but a valid example of a real life problem, because until I had sat down and produced the model to illustrate the effect on contribution of the different sales mix, the clients had not previously appreciated the profit implications.

Generally in business, you do not normally get the extremes illustrated in this example, although I have come across many other retail businesses with extremes of margin, which are equally valid and equally as important to understand.

Look at Your Suppliers – Their Costs Affect Your Margins

Have you ever asked your suppliers if there is any way they can reduce their costs or, indeed, if there is anything you can do to help them to reduce their costs.

In order to improve your margins, it is not just a question of increasing your price, it is also a question of reducing your costs where possible, and it might well be that by talking to your supplier, a reduction in cost can be achieved much more easily than you might think.

Publisher – 3% Costs Reduction

For example, I know of a publisher who was looking at his print costs. He went to his printers and asked if there was any way he could reduce his print costs.

Apart from the usual shaving of cost as a result of competition, the publisher also achieved a further significant cost reduction, by asking the printer what price he could offer, if the publisher was prepared to pay within 14 days rather than take his usual 90 days credit.

Printers are used to having to give large amounts of credit, and the offer of being paid early was very attractive, and allowed the publisher to cut his costs by a further 3%.

Electrical Goods – 10% Costs Reduction

Another example, was a supplier of electrical goods.

They spoke to their manufacturer and asked if there was any way that they could reduce their prices.

The manufacturers had various ideas, but had never mentioned them because they had never been asked. They had merely produced electrical goods to the specification demanded.

Having been asked, they suggested minor product design changes together with changes in the way the goods were packaged, which reduced the costs of the goods by more than 10%.

There are numerous other examples I could quote but, basically, the answer is to communicate with your suppliers, and with both of you looking at the problem, it is amazing what can be achieved.

Stock – Examine Company Policy Regarding Stock Turnover

Many businesses hold too much stock, which often is the major asset on a balance sheet.

The Japanese have managed to master the art of controlling stock and the whole concept of 'just in time' stock replacement stemmed from the Japanese and their manufacturing industries, especially their car industry.

'Just in Time' has allowed industry to benefit from massive stock reductions.

It is estimated that the real cost of carrying stock is at least 2% per month of the cost of the stock and, if you look at it like that, it could be argued that holding stock is a liability not an asset.

For example, if you were aware that every £200,000 of stock you held was costing you at least £24,000 per year to keep, would you not be keen to reduce your stock levels.

The rewards for reducing your stock holding is not only improved cash flow, but also reduced finance costs, more storage space made available for production, and of course more profit.

Time Limits
Many businesses have no policy regarding stock turnover. If the stock has not been sold within a certain time scale, businesses should have a plan of action to move that stock to generate cash flow.

"Buying" Training
The cost of stock is crucial to improving margins and the profitability of a business, and yet for an aspect so vital to a business, it is surprising how little training is given to the team members responsible for the 'buying' function.

Often, the stock can be purchased on sale or return, it can be purchased on deferred payment plans, stock can be ordered and held by the manufacturer with the delivery date scheduled by the customer, and with negotiation, it is possible to agree additional pricing discounts dependant on volumes purchased and times of payment. Buyers need experience or training to achieve this.

It is not uncommon for this function to be carried out by the owner manager, because of their experience within the business but, even they, with their experience, would generate additional profit, if only they would allow themselves to be trained in the skills of buying.

Offer Incentives to Reduce Stock
Where the stock holding is too high in businesses, incentive schemes should be considered to reward managers for reducing stock and keeping stock holding down.

Fixed Assets – Decide a Policy – Buy, Rent, or Lease

Fixed assets, such as motor vehicles, and plant and machinery, absorb considerable amounts of cash flow and, it is important, that businesses have a policy as to when they rent or hire equipment, and when they buy it.

Experts who have studied this aspect of financing fixed assets, recommend that businesses should identify the amount of utilisation of the fixed assets on an annual basis expressed as a percentage of the working week.

They suggest that where the assets are used for 60% of less of the year, then businesses should consider renting the equipment rather than buying it.

Much depends on the financing cost at the time, and the future intended use, etc, etc, but I have quoted that example as an illustration of how perhaps a policy should be made, even if it is decided that much lower utilisation rates are relevant for your particular business.

There are also taxation considerations to take into account, when formulating the company policy.

One thing that is certain is, that if there is no policy, there will always be a risk that profit will be wasted as a result of indiscriminate purchasing.

Look at Your Overheads

a Staffing/Wages

I could write a whole chapter on the efficient use of employees.

In most businesses, employment costs are one of the major costs in the profit and loss account, and management needs to ensure that they are always working to achieve continually improved efficiency and productivity, whilst maintaining the morale of the work force.

A business is nothing without its employees. Having said that, they need to be trained and, sometimes, cajoled in the never ending pursuit of how to improve productivity.

Full Time or Part Time

Management needs to look at their policies on whether to employ full time staff or part time staff and, in making those decisions, they need to be conscious of the taxation and national insurance costs of employment.

Overtime

Management needs to allow for flexibility and for holiday cover, but must generally look to avoid incurring overtime costs, where possible.

Many businesses pay overtime as a matter of routine, with the employees themselves often deciding whether or not they need to work the overtime. It is equivalent to handing them a blank cheque book.

I have lost count of the number of businesses who have cancelled overtime, and then have been surprised to find that the work that used to be done in overtime, could be managed in normal time.

Management should look to provide incentives to managers and supervisors to keep the cost of overtime as low as possible.

Incentive Awards

The whole team of employees and managers in a business should have an incentive to create profit.

They should be set targets to improve profits in whichever ways are relevant to their particular working roles.

Where they are able to create profit for the owners of the business, part of that profit should be shared with those team members helping to create that additional profit.

I have previously referred to rewarding supervisors for keeping the cost of overtime to a minimum and, similarly, management should look to reward team members in a whole range of different areas where profitability could be improved as a result of their individual efforts.

There are numerous examples but, to list a few, production and warehouse managers should be rewarded for reducing and keeping stock holding down, credit controllers should be rewarded for keeping down the length of time taken by debtors to pay their bills, and staff team members generally should be rewarded for proposing profit making ideas, whether or not they are eventually acted upon.

Customer service members should be rewarded every time they receive favourable comments from customers and, the most common and most obvious incentive rewards are for the sales team to generate more sales at higher margins.

b Pay Commission on 'Contribution' Not Sales

In my opinion, one of the most common mistakes made by businesses is to pay commission on sales, rather than commission on 'contribution'. The argument against my theory is that, paying commission on sales is simple and easy to understand by the sales team

However, I credit most sales team members with more intelligence than that, and believe that, unless you set up the reward scheme to benefit profitability rather than volume, there is never any incentive for the sales team to achieve higher margins at all.

Another aspect that I increasingly come across is the complaint that the most successful sales person often earns more than the managing director. My attitude to that is that, if the sales reward scheme has been structured correctly, if the sales person is earning more than the managing director, it means that the sales person must be earning the business a fortune.

c Debtors

We have already referred to the need to reward the credit control team for reducing the age of debts in a company's debtors ledger.

This is extremely important because, when businesses go for growth, it is often accompanied by slackening of the credit control standards and, that alone, without any of the other problems of growth, can be sufficient to cause a business major difficulties, let alone to incur unnecessary interest costs.

Cost of Financing Debtors

Management should identify the monthly cost of financing every £10,000 of debts on their ledger as a way of concentrating their mind on the need to reduce debts.

Factoring

Management should have a policy for when factoring or confidential invoice discounting will be considered to generate cash flow and release working capital.

Penalise Late Payment

Management should also have a policy to reward early settlement of debt and to penalise late settlement.

So many businesses allow their customers to pay after 60 days without any penalty and, yet those customers who pay within less than 30 days, are treated no differently.

Is this not penalising the good customer? It is important to reward the quick payer and penalise the slow payer.

d   Overheads Generally

As with the purchasing of stock, staff should be trained, where possible, in how best to buy.

Often the role of ordering stationery and other incidental expenses are left to relatively junior members of staff who are totally inexperienced and unsuited to this role.

Is it no surprise then that businesses end up with unnecessary stocks of materials when in this day and age most types of delivery can be guaranteed within the next 24 hours.

Advertising

Advertising is a subject in its own right but, so often, businesses fail to have a standard policy as to the cost of advertising and sponsorship.

It is so easy to agree to take an advert to get rid of a nuisance sales person but, if the business had a policy for advertising in general, this would be unnecessary.

Conclusion

In this chapter, it has only been possible to 'scratch the surface' of the topic of profit improvement but, to return to what was stated in the introductory pages, the easiest way of improving the profitability of your business is to develop **a profit plan**.

This **profit plan** will inter-relate with the detailed business plan, detailed trading and cash flow forecasts, etc, but will be dedicated totally to the improvement of profit, setting down and recording responsibilities and time scales for different team members who are prepared to accept their responsibilities to supervise the generation of increased profit.

By concentrating their minds on profits, every time there is a meeting to discuss any aspect of the management of the business, "the person responsible for profit" attending that meeting will always be able to ask the question as to how the decisions being made will affect the "bottom line".

Change of attitude – Introduce a Profit Culture

It is important to introduce a "profit culture" within the business, and to monitor, record and control what is happening to profit, in as much detail as you monitor, record, and control what is happening to sales.

Profit Attitude

Managers need to change the way they think and I would suggest that a most appropriate conclusion to this chapter is to quote Yogi Berra, the famous American baseball player

"IF YOU ALWAYS DO WHAT YOU HAVE ALWAYS DONE – YOU ALWAYS GET WHAT YOU HAVE ALREADY GOT".

Remember

YOUR PROFIT *ATTITUDE* WILL DETERMINE YOUR PROFIT ALTITUDE.

Summary of Main Points

TURNOVER IS VANITY – PROFIT IS SANITY
- Focus on margins – not just sales
- Focus on profits – not just cost cutting
- Work to improve the value received by the customer
- Set 'goal posts' to measure your progress to profitability
- Distinguish your variable costs from your fixed costs and make sure you do not forget any variable costs when calculating your prices
- Make sure you fully understand the relationship between your profits and your sales, and the sensitivity of your profits to variations in your volumes and your margins
- The business must have clear pricing strategies to identify 'the right price' to charge in all eventualities
- Identify the desired (optimum) sales mix to achieve maximum profitability
- Work with your suppliers to identify potential cost savings
- Train the appropriate members of staff in the skills of 'buying'
- Make sure you have agreed policies for stock levels, and contingency plans for stock items that do not move within pre-agreed time scales
- Agree a policy for the purchase or hire of fixed assets
- Review overheads to establish which areas are more responsive to control
- Create a reward structure to incentivise employee team members through every aspect of profit generation. Share with them the increased profit they earn for you
- Always remember

    – INCREASED SALES FEED YOUR PRIDE

    – ONLY INCREASED PROFITS CAN FEED YOUR FAMILY

12 How to save time and money by managing organisational change effectively

There is a little-known secret to managing organisational change effectively. As you discover it, in these next few pages and understand the underlying principles, you will no doubt reflect that much of it is common sense. It is. But common sense and common practice are very different. I should know, having worked with hundreds of managers in numerous organisations during the past ten years. Much of this work has involved helping middle and senior managers increase their effectiveness during restructuring, downsizing, mergers, management buyouts and various forms of cultural change.

However, before I reveal "the secret", I need to make sure that we have a common understanding of a few terms and phrases. The first is "change" or more precisely that which is referred to as change within your organisation. I have found that when change is mentioned, it usually means "things" changing, for example, systems, procedures, ways of working, location, behaviour, company ownership etc. Usually you are able to see the change or even touch the results of it. Hence change is something that is external to your body.

Think about changes in your workplace. You will have probably noticed that individuals react in different ways and at different speeds. There are many reasons why this happens:

- Some people are more adaptable to change than others.
- Some people resist change more than others.
- Some people have more to lose than others.
- Some people have developed stronger habits than others.
- Some people deny change is happening or will happen.
- Some people don't realise the full extent of the change.
- Some people feel exposed by change.

Whatever the reasons, the fact is individuals, including you, react *internally* to the external change. Before you, or anyone in your organisation fully accepts any change, an internal process of adjustment has to happen. This internal process is called *"transition"*.

There are two important things to note here. Firstly, that change (external process) is different from transition (internal process). Secondly, that changes to things in the workplace happen at a different speed to people's acceptance of the change (the transition process). A practical example of this is when a change in working hours or shift patterns is introduced. The change happens overnight, whereas the transition can take considerably longer. I have worked in many companies where it has taken several years for employees to accept such changes.

I would like you to stop reading for a moment and think of an example in your organisation where a change has been quickly implemented and staff have taken much longer to accept it. (I will ask you to refer back to your example later, so make sure you have chosen one!).

Now let's move on to "the secret" of managing change effectively. The reason that change is often unsuccessful is related to management's perception of change and how to manage it. Many managers I encounter consider the planning, logistics, systems, procedures and the physical factors that need changing. Very few, even at the most senior level, place much emphasis on the people issues, particularly their likely reaction to change.

How many times have you attended meetings about implementing change, when the outcomes have been task-focused actions involving feasibility, logistics and planning? Managers who are good at planning and logistics often do not make the time or have the inclination to spend time considering the people issues. I have been called into companies on numerous occasions where a major organisational change has been implemented with detailed precision according to plan, yet caused a massive negative reaction in the workforce. Much of this reaction could have been easily foreseen and overcome if the managers had only been aware of "the secret".

The secret is simple – "In order for change to be effective, transition must happen".

In other words, unless individuals are helped to adapt and accept the change, the change will not have the desired impact on the business.

You can save your organisation potentially tens of thousands of hours and hundreds of thousands of pounds by successfully managing staff through the transition. In fact one of my recent clients calculated that as a result of ignoring the staffs reactions to a merger twelve months earlier, the company had wasted approximately 300,000 hours of time or the equivalent of over £2 million. When I asked him how he had arrived at these figures, he gave me the following reasoning:

> "We have 3,000 employees who on average have spent approximately two hours per week during the past year engaging in non-productive activities and

working against the changes we have implemented. 300,000 hours at £8 per hour is £2.4 million. What's more, until managers help their staff to accept change (transition) these figures will continue".

So, this chapter is not about planning, organising or managing change. It is about practical tips, tools and techniques that will have a positive impact on staff and help them to more easily and quickly accept change. This will result in you helping them to increase their productivity and effectiveness within the organisation.

I have divided the remaining pages into three sections – necessary knowledge, essential skills and intended actions. To increase your effectiveness in managing transition during periods of change, there are things you need to know and skills you need to be capable of using. However, a committed positive intention to 'make a difference' matters most. I mention this because sadly, I have met many managers who believe that knowing how and what to do is sufficient.

The following pages will give you greater insight and perhaps increased knowledge, but reading alone cannot develop your skills or motivation to apply these principles. I am aware of this limitation and so encourage you to apply the words you read to real situations and real individuals who it is possible to help. So make notes, highlight text and even write thoughts alongside the text.

The Necessary Knowledge

There are three further pieces of information additional to "the secret" that you need to know if you want to save your organisation valuable time and money. I have shared this information with hundreds of managers and refined it to the following areas:

- People's reaction to organisational change – the four underlying causes of a negative reaction.
- Adapting to and accepting change – the three stage process of most use to managers.
- Organisational factors which can help or hinder change – the five factors with the greatest impact on staff morale.

So let me explain each of these in turn and illustrate them with some practical examples.

The four underlying causes of a negative reaction to change

Over the years I have worked closely with my friend and associate Jo Stead, who is one of the leading UK researchers into the negative reactions experienced by individuals in response to organisational change. I have simplified her findings into the following underlying causes:

1 *A sense of unfairness in the way that employees have been treated.* This is most commonly based upon unwritten beliefs and assumptions made over a period of time, that the way things were done around here would always continue. This has been termed the "psychological contract" between employer and employee. Hence when change is introduced by the organisation it is deemed unfair by the individual.

   Managers often know that it will be seen as unfair by the employees when they make comments such as "I know they will be unhappy about this . . .". However, as I already mentioned to you earlier, knowing something and taking action about it are often two different matters.

   If this underlying cause exists in your organisation, you might hear comments such as "It's not fair", "We have never had to do it this way before" and "after everything that I/we have done, look what they have decided . . .".

2 *Personal uncertainty and insecurity about the future.* It is usual to find that most individuals spend time thinking about the impact of organisational change upon themselves, their current role and possible future prospects. This happens even when people are not directly affected by the change. I have known several cases when key staff including senior managers, have become unduly convinced that they are likely to lose their jobs. This can lead to people doing a variety of things in an attempt to protect their current position and results in stress.

   If this underlying cause exists, in your organisation, you might notice an unwillingness to make decisions, an increase in defensive behaviour and increased speculation and rumour.

3 *Perceived powerlessness.* The larger the organisation, the greater the tendency is for individuals to feel that changes are imposed upon them. Common phrases that might be heard include, "There is nothing that we can do", "they don't ask us for our opinions", "it's them and us, they tell us and we just have to accept it" and "Head Office have decided . . .".

   I have found that most people want to be involved, even in some small way, in change and their natural tendency is to seek to participate by giving suggestions and being heard. However, when this is perceived as futile, or changes are made outside their sphere of influence, their feelings of powerlessness may result in a lack of commitment or real interest. Examples of this are commonly seen in many organisations when new corporate logos, mission statements and competencies are introduced without consultation with the workforce.

4 *Resisting the need to adapt to change.* When things change in the workplace a need is created for individuals to adapt. If individuals do not accept the change by making the necessary transition, their external behaviour and performance will not be as effective as it could be.

This internal resistance will vary tremendously between individuals. With some, the resistance is minimal or non-existent and with others, it will last for ten years or even longer. Common phrases to listen out for include, "I don't see the point", "I'm just going to carry on", "this change is a mistake", "it's just the latest management fad" and "it won't work, it's a waste of time".

Remind yourself of the example, I asked you to select earlier, of when staff did not immediately accept the change. Consider the underlying reasons for their reaction. Which of these was the cause of the most negative reaction from individuals? (Make a note of this as I will ask you to refer back to this example again).

I am sure that you can identify these four underlying causes in other examples of organisational change you have experienced. Maybe you can even recognise the causes of some of your own reactions in the past. It is okay to admit to having them. In fact it will probably be useful to remember those examples when we move on to helping others adapt to change. Later, I will reveal the three key management tasks that will help you to address the underlying causes of negative reaction to change I have just outlined. However, before focusing on what you can do, I want you to continue developing your knowledge and understanding of transition.

Adapting To Change – A three stage process
"I wish people would just accept things".

How many times have you heard a similar phrase or sentiment? I know that I have certainly used it in the past! It would be really handy if people would immediately accept change and continue working at high levels of performance as if nothing had happened. But that is fantasy. You and I know this is extremely unlikely to happen. Yet, many organisations continue to make major changes and act as if they expect it to happen. Why does it continue? Because senior and middle managers are largely unaware of the process that individuals go through in adapting to change. Plus they have had longer themselves to understand and adapt and of course they have focused virtually all their efforts on the logistics and planning of change.

The process I am about to explain is based on a very simple three stage model by William Bridges of how individuals adapt to change.

ENDINGS ⇨ TRANSITION ⇨ BEGINNINGS

Endings. When a change happens, some things end – often forever. All change involves loss and this naturally upsets some people more than others. Imagine a large-scale organisational change or company restructuring. This might result in several of the following endings:

- Role and responsibilities (including favourite tasks).
- Contact with the people you work with.
- Personal status.
- Work environment.
- Familiar ways of doing things.
- Beliefs about what it means to work in this organisation.
- Expectations about your future career.

Before we expect others to accept the change it is vital that we understand that they have to let go and end certain things. The process of letting go does not happen instantly. Often initial feelings of shock and denial about the change are replaced by more intense feelings of anger or sadness, as there is a gradual realisation of the full implications of the change.

The line-manager has a key role to play in helping staff to deal with these endings. However, unfortunately many managers are either unaware of this or do not possess the necessary skills. I will outline these later in the skills section. For the time being it is important, to recognise that it is natural for individuals to feel this way in response to change.

The transition stage. After endings have been made, an individual's attitude towards the change is likely to be more negative than before the change took place. Once the implications of the change have been fully realised, there begins a phase of exploration and discovery.

Think of a time when you had to learn about new systems or understand revised expectations. Can you remember the experience of gradually adapting, whilst also feeling frustrated and confused at times? This transition stage involves learning, very often in the absence of role models. Let me give you an example. Last year I was helping with the restructuring of a large manufacturing company. This involved, among many things, centralising the stock control system of three factories on the same site. A new computer system was introduced integrating the purchasing with stock control. Many staff reacted against the change mainly because much of what they were familiar with had ended. Even after dealing with the endings they still experienced great frustration with the new system as they struggled to learn and adapt to new ways of working. The management had no greater technical expertise than their staff and so were unable to resolve much of the confusion. Eventually, over a period of time, the system was run efficiently and everyone began to see and appreciate its benefit.

You might be wondering what the significance of that example is. Well, there are a number of key learning points:

- Staff felt negative about the change before feeling better.
- The transition stage cannot be skipped or ignored. It has to be worked through.
- The managers, although unable to help technically, made a tremendous difference in helping their staff adapt to change. They did this by understanding

the transition process and applying relevant skills and techniques to ensure it progressed. The change (i.e. the system) was effected relatively quickly and smoothly.
- The reactions to change were predictable and managers were trained in advance to handle the people issues that result from change.

Beginnings. The change has happened and the things that were once viewed as different are now considered normal practice.

You might find the following graph useful in understanding further how individuals react to organisational change. I have adapted this from several different models and used it to help many managers over recent years.

THE TRANSITION CURVE

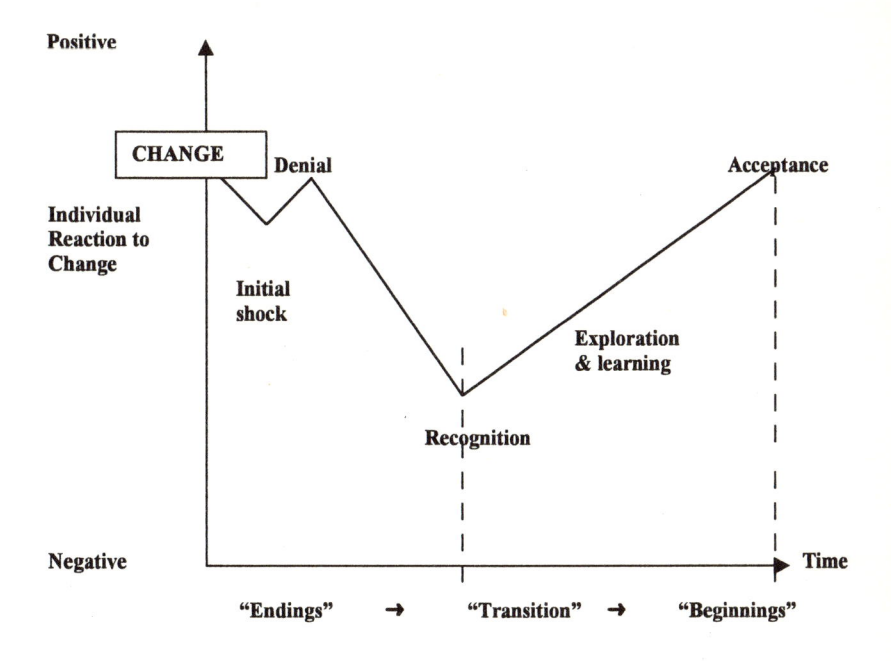

```
Positive
 ▲
 │   ┌──────┐
 │   │CHANGE│ Denial                              Acceptance
 │   └──────┘╲    ╱╲                                   ╱
Individual       ╲  ╱  ╲                              ╱
Reaction to       ╲╱    ╲                            ╱
Change                   ╲                          ╱
         Initial          ╲                        ╱
         shock             ╲                      ╱
                            ╲        Exploration ╱
                             ╲       & learning ╱
                              ╲              ╱
                               ╲           ╱
                              Recognition
Negative                        │                      │
 └──────────────────────────────┼──────────────────────┼──► Time
        "Endings"    →       "Transition"    →    "Beginnings"
```

Whilst this is a generalised model, in that it does not apply to everyone all of the time, in every change situation, it is useful to understand the following points:

- The old has to end, before the new is accepted.
- Individuals will react negatively before acceptance is reached.
- Some individuals remain in denial for longer than others.
- The strongest emotions are usually on the steepest part of the graph i.e. as individuals begin to, and then fully recognise the implications of the change.
- Exploration is a more gradual process which takes time.

- The timescale for individuals to go through the stages will differ.
- It is pointless to expect people to accept change without them first going through the transition process.

Now think back once more to your example of change. Focus on the reactions of staff in your organisation. Remember their behaviour and what they said. I imagine, you will probably be able to locate many of their reactions on the Transition Curve.

The five organisational factors which are most likely to help or hinder staff during change

Much of the information and knowledge I have shared with you so far in this chapter relates to the process of transition that starts inside a persons mind and then shows through their behaviour. Before moving on to how this information can be practically applied, I would like to briefly explain the five major organisational factors which influence an individuals reaction to change.

Communication

Imagine for a moment, that the following diagram is a gigantic hot cross-bun, as large as it could possibly be, and you are standing in the middle of it. As you look around you can see and are affected by activities in each of the four quadrants. All around you, information is whizzing by as you stand in the centre of the communication crossroads. You notice that the more helpful information about change appears to come from certain quadrants, whereas rumour, speculation and mixed messages tend to come from other quadrants.

Clarity of Future Direction

When change happens in organisations, research has shown the importance of having a future direction that is clearly communicated and enables the workforce to:

- be involved in moving forward
- feel inspired by the vision and mission
- receive positive, optimistic and consistent messages
- understand that the best aspects of the past are still being retained.

This last point is important to remember, as all too often I experience organisations who sell the benefits of change by focusing solely on the future. In their vain

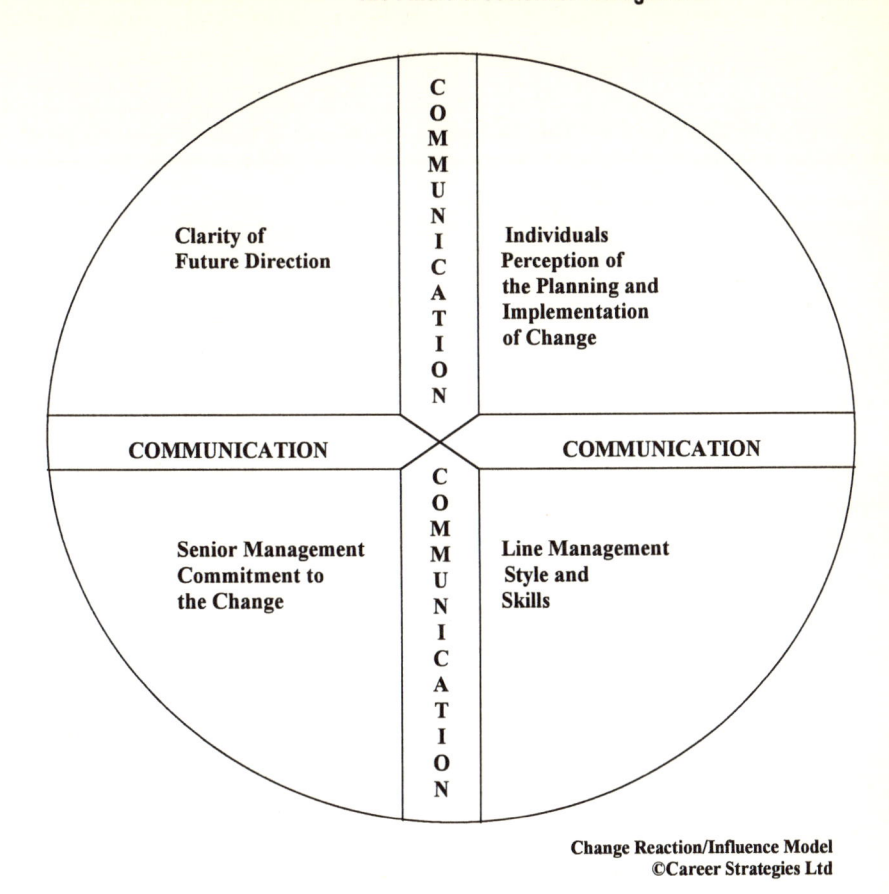

```
                    C
                    O
                    M
                    M
                    U
                    N
    Clarity of      I    Individuals
    Future Direction C   Perception of
                    A    the Planning and
                    T    Implementation
                    I    of Change
                    O
                    N

COMMUNICATION          COMMUNICATION

                    C
                    O
                    M
                    M
    Senior Management U  Line Management
    Commitment to   N    Style and
    the Change      I    Skills
                    C
                    A
                    T
                    I
                    O
                    N
```

Change Reaction/Influence Model
©Career Strategies Ltd

attempts to get people to accept change quickly, they often completely overlook the fact that individuals need to make *endings* first. This can create greater insecurity and uncertainty in the minds of individuals who are not yet ready to accept the messages. Instead, I have found it more effective to balance the benefits of change with deliberate reassurance about familiar ways and practices that will continue to happen in the future.

Senior Management Commitment to the Change

The Senior Management team need to be seen as strong, inspirational and unified in acting in accordance with the mission and goals. At times of major change, their commitment will be examined in detail by staff to spot any inconsistencies and weaknesses. Failure to act as role models and change champions will undoubtedly affect staff morale.

Perception of the Planning and Implementation of Change

Whilst individuals are obviously affected by the planning and implementation of change, their perception of it's effectiveness is likely to differ widely from those involved in the planning. I have worked with several organisations where the planning was meticulous, detailed and well thought through. Yet because it was done by a small group of people perceived as remote and inaccessible, staff were unaware of how good the plan was. In fact the only thing that these organisations hadn't planned for was how to manage the staff reaction! Remember "the secret" – in order for change to be effective, transition must happen.

Line Management Style and Skills

The fourth quadrant relates to the style and skills of line-managers in managing change and specifically to their interaction with staff. Arguably, this is the most influential factor as the day to day actions of a line-manager will either help or hinder staff with the process of transition. The following section focuses on many of the key skills and will enable you to assess your own ability and those of other managers in your organisation.

One final thought before leaving the "hot cross-bun" diagram. It is possible to use this model when planning change to identify:

- Where is communication likely to be more and less effective?
- Which quadrant is most likely to help or hinder effective change?
- Which areas of organisational weakness need to be addressed?

Certainly when I have used it to facilitate senior management thinking about staff morale during organisational change, it has been relatively easy to identify the above-mentioned points.

Having read the previous pages, I believe you now have the necessary background information to make a difference. Based on my experience you are probably in the top 1% of UK managers in terms of knowledge about change and the reactions it causes. Now we need to move on to consider effective ways of applying this knowledge.

Essential Skills

I'm sure you recognise by now that the process of individual transition cannot be avoided. It can, however, be speeded up and this is a key role for line managers during organisational change. If you can help your team to move more quickly through the endings and transition stages to acceptance, you will reap the benefits of the change through increased individual productivity and improved team performance. To ensure this happens, your actions need to address the underlying causes of individuals negative reaction to change.

Now at this stage there is good news and there is bad news to share with you. The bad news is that one of the four underlying causes cannot be resolved in the short-term. The sense of unfairness in the way that employees have been treated causes a negative reaction to change. This sense of unfairness, or break in the psychological contract, cannot be repaired quickly, as it requires line and senior managers to consistently act fairly over a longer time frame. Even then, trust may be difficult to restore.

However, the good news is that the remaining three underlying causes can be addressed by your day to day line-management actions. There are three key tasks, which a colleague of mine, Kathryn Roberts concisely describes as "The Three I's".

- Information and explanation
- Involvement
- Individual attention

1 Information and explanation

Personal uncertainty and insecurity about the future naturally causes individuals to seek further information and have questions answered. If the uncertainty and insecurity still remains, then this results in the desire for even more information and so on. I honestly believe that I have never worked with an organisation experiencing change, where everyone is totally satisfied with the amount or type of information they receive.

A useful starting point is to help individuals understand and accept the need to change. To do this the following five questions need to be answered either on a one to one basis or as a group, for example in a team meeting.

- What specific events brought about the changes in our organisation?
- Why was there a need to change?
- Who was involved in the decision making process?
- What other options were considered and why were they rejected?
- What is the change intended to achieve?

Before asking these questions of your staff, be sure that you have given some thought to your answers and checked them out for consistency with other managers. I mention this in all seriousness because I am continually surprised at the wide variation in answers given to me by managers in the same organisation.

Even if your staff are not asking these questions for you to hear, the chances are that they are asking themselves or each other. You might even have asked them yourself. Often during change, information intended to assist staff can have the opposite affect when communicated poorly. The following notice-board bulletin was brought to my attention last year. I have changed the names to protect the innocent, but otherwise it is reproduced exactly.

> **Attention**
> **Staff Change**
> As from today, Tom Jenkins has replaced Steve Howarth as Quality Assurance Manager and will now report directly to Peter Mackintosh.
>
> 9th December

If you worked in this recently merged organisation, particularly if you knew Steve Howarth, what thoughts might go through your mind? Probably very similar questions to those previously mentioned.

- What has caused this change?
- Why has Tom replaced Steve?
- Who made the decision?
- What is happening to Steve?
- What difference will it make?

It might cause you to question the planning and implementation of change, as so little information is included and the short notice given. For most, if not all, of the 480 employees it raised more questions and created greater uncertainty then intended. I certainly witnessed a large amount of talk and speculation about the notice for the next four days. Now, let us estimate the possible time and cost implications of this example.

If each of the 480 employees was negatively affected by this notice (speculating, gossiping or worrying to themselves) for 30 minutes, it totals 240 hours. This is the equivalent of one person working for six weeks or in financial terms one and a half months salary. All caused by a memo that probably took less than two minutes to write! If only the writer had spent ten minutes and answered the five key questions, a considerable amount of time and the equivalent of £2-3,000 could have been saved.

I mentioned this to the Personnel Director who admitted responsibility and asked for help. In less than fifteen minutes I gained the answers to the five questions and helped him to write this alternative.

The skill in writing information about change is to consider it from the readers viewpoint. What will their reaction be? What questions will it cause them to ask? What further information will they require? How can you demonstrate that the change has been planned and implemented effectively?

> **UPDATE INFORMATION ON QUALITY SYSTEMS**
> **from Peter Mackintosh (Divisional Director)**
> Following the merger with Engineer Co. Plc, there has been a need to standardise our quality procedures to ensure consistency, both internally and to our customers.
>
> Over the past 3 weeks, Steve Howarth and Tom Jenkins have led a review of both existing quality systems and involved the 12 department heads from both sites. 17 of the 22 procedures have been identified as closely compatible and require little or no modification. The remaining 5 procedures relate mainly to document transfer and storage, where both sites have previously identified that improvements needed to be made.
>
> Rather than adopt either of the existing site procedures, I have decided to invest time and resource in ensuring we have an effective and efficient way of handling this critical area of our business. Steve Howarth, in his new role of Systems Manager, will continue to provide assistance to Tom Jenkins who will manage this project for the next 3 months and report direct to myself. Please give Tom your full assistance.
>
> Thank you

Now think about the example of change in your organisation. How effectively was the information communicated? Were the five questions satisfactorily explained? What could have been improved? Estimate the potential time and cost savings that could have been made.

A question I commonly get asked by managers is, what to communicate about the change when there is no new information available to them? This is usually in the context of restructuring, buyouts, mergers and acquisitions, but could equally apply to any change that has long been talked about. Often managers feel it is best not to say anything if there is no new information and the situation is still unclear. This, however, does nothing to help the individual who is feeling insecure and uncertain about the future. I have found it is more helpful if you can firstly acknowledge that some things are still unclear. Secondly, give a date or milestone by when you expect more information to be available. There is always a reason why information is currently unavailable. For example, a decision needs to be made at next months meeting or certain processes and procedures might need to be carried out before further information is available.

Hence, it is still possible to give explanations about the process which will eventually lead to questions being answered. Whilst this does not remove the uncertainty, for many it provides some relief in knowing that their manager is in a similar position to themselves, has no further information, but is aware of key dates and milestones.

Another point worth mentioning to you is about the need to repeat information and explanations several times. An individual might be in the denial stage of the transition curve and perhaps acting as if the change is not happening. If this is the case, you might need to repeat the same information several times using different communication methods before it is understood. Hopefully you will never use the excuse "but I've told them that already". I have seen examples of people being given the same information about change at least six or seven times with no apparent reaction or acknowledgement. Yet the next time the information is given they treat it as if they have just received it for the first time!

2 Involvement

Obviously, individuals cannot be involved in every aspect relating to change. However, if there is a total lack of involvement in the change then the perception of being powerless will increase. As a skilful manager, it is always possible to involve staff in some aspect of the change, however small that might be.

One of the easiest ways of ensuring staff involvement during change is to have participative meetings on a regular basis. Examine the way you conduct meetings and consider how involved others are. How many of the agenda items are suggested by your staff? To what extent do you allow them to contribute during meetings? How much encouragement and responsibility do you give individuals to take actions and develop ideas following a meeting?

Remember the three-stage model of endings, transition and acceptance. You can accelerate this process of adapting to change by facilitating greater involvement in the following ways:

- Identify *endings* as a team and discussing the implications of each ending. You could use several of the example endings I mentioned earlier to prompt their thoughts. Be attentive to how individuals react during this discussion, as some are likely to become more aware than others of what will be lost. You might need to follow up the meeting with one to one discussions to help some individuals manage their endings. I recognise that you might not feel comfortable with this task. Many managers avoid doing it and hence some of their staff never fully let go of the past. In the long term this avoidance costs time and money.
- Help individuals to identify those factors that are the "givens" of a situation (i.e. pre-determined decisions about the change which are outside your control and hence cannot be influenced) and differentiate them from the things that can be influenced.
- Brainstorm ways of moving forward and overcoming obstacles.

- Delegate responsibility for exploring and investigating alternative ways of doing things in the future.
- Encourage staff to report back their findings and seek the opinions of the rest of the team.

In helping staff move through the transition phase a group coaching process can be useful. One of the most practical to use is the GROW structure (Goals, Reality, Options and Will). Listed below are the various stages and some example questions for each stage.

Goal
- What is the objective?
- What are we working towards?
- What do we want to achieve?

(note: the goal might be an existing operational objective or relate to resolving a current problem or concern).

Reality
- What is the current situation?
- What are we doing?
- Who else is involved?
- What are the implications?
- What problems have we experienced?
- What ways of overcoming them have been attempted?
- How do we feel?

Options
- What are the known options?
- What are other possibilities?

(note: this stage could involve brainstorming)

Will
- Which are the best options?
- What will we do and by when?
- Who will do what?
- How committed are we?

Probably the most simple and quickest way to increase an individuals involvement is to ask their opinion about an aspect of the change affecting them. It only takes a couple of minutes, yet can make a massive difference to someone feeling powerless. This leads us on to the third key management task of giving individual attention.

3 Individual Attention

If you manage more than one person, you will have recognised that individuals react to change differently. You will also now be more aware of why this happens. However, in order to fully understand the reasons why staff resist the need to adapt to change you have to give individual attention to each person. Naturally people worry about different things for different reasons and will therefore take a different amount of time to move through the transition curve and accept change.

A key skill is to identify who in your team is most affected by the change. Whilst past behaviour is usually a good indicator of future behaviour, a different change will mean different *endings* and hence possibly a different reaction. A starting point is to consider what will end for each person as a result of the change. Also consider from their perspective what they feel might be lost in the future. For some people these endings will be welcomed and seen as opportunities, but for many others, they will result in things being missed.

I was recently working with Michael, a Divisional Director in a large U.K. service organisation undergoing massive restructuring. His role remained largely unaffected and his work continued much as before. However, he was deeply affected by the change because something important for him had ended. His career goal was no longer applicable. For the past six years Michael had set his sights on a certain position on the main board of directors. That position had now disappeared. Fortunately, his manager realised this ending and the importance of giving individual attention. In many other organisations, this would have gone unnoticed and the individual would have taken much longer to make the transition.

It may not be appropriate to *manage endings* in a group meeting, particularly if you have already identified that some individuals within the team will experience substantially more or greater losses than others. This is when it is important to talk with staff on an individual basis. I have identified below some key points to bear in mind when doing this.

- Clearly explain the reason for the meeting. Notice the difference between saying "can I see you in my office?" (possibly intimidating and causing fear of reprisal) and "I would like to have a chat with you about the recent changes to see what I can do to help you".
- It can be useful to mention in advance that you intend to have short meetings with each person. Again, be careful about clearly explaining the purpose of these meetings.
- Notice how each individual reacts when you meet with them. Their body language, tone of voice and eye contact will all give you clues about what is happening inside the person and how they are reacting to the change.
- Avoid selling the future and the benefits of change.
- Focus on their concerns.
- Plan in advance of the meeting. What issues and concerns might you anticipate?

The Pillars of Successful Management

- Agree any actions for either you or them.
- Agree a follow-up review. This will help the individual to feel that you are committed to helping them on more than a one-off occasion.

I was recently challenged by Brian, an experienced manufacturing manager, about the emphasis I was placing on the people issues. His point was that he had a factory to run, equipment to commission and operating changes to make. He talked at length about all the tangible hard aspects of change – planning, feasibility studies, actions, timescales, and implementation reports – without once mentioning the staff, except to say they had low morale. He wanted to know what he could do to improve their morale without spending much time doing it! I established that Brian had eight staff directly reporting to him, and a further ninety staff below them. I asked him if he could spare each of his direct reports just ten minutes of his time this month? He stated he could easily do this, but asked what he should do with this ten-minute slot. I told him to spend the time identifying how each individual was reacting to the change and then helping them move forward to help their staff. Then to keep doing it on a monthly basis.

After several months Brian told me that he had developed a system of spending ten minutes per month with each of his staff and they in turn spent ten minutes with each of their factory staff. He was beginning to notice the difference it was making and proudly stated that with one member of staff he had even spent twenty minutes!

When talking to staff in organisations across all industry sectors, that are successfully managing change, I ask the question, "What has made the greatest difference?" One of the most common answers relates to the behaviour of effective line-managers. It makes a tremendous difference when a manager takes the time to understand not just what an individual thinks, but also how they feel and are reacting to the change. Think about yourself experiencing change in the past. Remember a time when you have received individual attention and someone has spent time helping you. If this has never happened, imagine it. It makes a difference.

Now focus on your organisation and members of your staff. How are they reacting to change at the moment? Look back at the Transition Curve diagram and identify at which stage of the process they might be. Listed below are several approaches and strategies helpful in encouraging individuals to move towards the next stage.

Initial shock – Encourage them to talk about their understanding of the change and the information they have received about it.
- Clarify what has been understood.
- Identify and provide any missing information.
- If necessary, give them space to think things through.

Denial	– Provide information.
– Repeat information in different ways.
– Talk about changes and implications (endings).
– Confront them (non-aggressively) with reality and the need for change.
– Encourage them to ask questions.
– Bring them into contact with others who have moved forward.
Recognition	– Let them have their say and express feelings
– Acknowledge their feelings without accepting blame.
– Re-emphasise and explain the reasons for change.
– Help them to identify and manage endings.
– Start to promote positives (without being too pushy)
– Allow them time, but ensure the work continues.
Exploration	– Reassure that others are unsure and unclear about certain things.
– Establish what is unclear and clarify.
– Be patient with requests for information and possible confusion.
– Find ways of involving them and allowing a sense of control over some aspect of work.
Acceptance	– Don't stop. Keep on using the three I's – Information and explanation, Involvement and Individual attention.

Intended Actions

I mentioned at the start of this chapter that there is a great difference between knowing how to help staff through transition and actually doing it. The purpose of these last couple of pages is to give you a few points to consider about yourself and possibly to raise with other managers in your organisation.

Let's start with some simple calculations of how much time and cost your organisation could potentially save by managing change effectively.

(a) How many employees are likely to be affected by change in your organisation?
(b) On average how much non-productive time is spent per week by each employee reacting against change or on worrying, gossip/rumour mongering activities?
(c) How many weeks has this been going on for?

(d) How many weeks will it continue to go on for unless action is taken?

Calculation one: a x b x c = the number of lost hours so far.
Calculation two: a x b x d = the number of additional hours which will be potentially lost.
Calculation three: multiply the numbers of hours by the average employee hourly rate to calculate the monetary costs.

All of these calculations are based upon the labour cost of production and do not take into account a potentially higher profit loss during this time period. A simpler way of looking at things is to ask yourself, if you could help staff to adapt and accept change within three months, rather than six months, would the effort be worthwhile?

Start by understanding the effects of change on yourself

Most individuals are influenced day to day by the people they see and communicate most frequently with. For many this will include their line manager. If you are reacting against the change or struggling to accept it, then that message will be passed onto your staff. This will happen, whether or not you are conscious of it, by the information you communicate, your tone of voice and body language. Hence, you can be of more help to others if you first help yourself.

Use the previous pages to help you consider the effects of change on yourself.

- Establish if any of the four underlying causes of a negative reaction to change apply.
- List the endings that the change has caused, or might cause you in the future.
- Locate your reaction to change on the Transition Curve.
- Analyse which of the five organisational factors hinder you more during change.
- Identify those things already determined and outside of your control (the givens).

Consider the three I's:

- What further information and explanation do you need?
- How involved do you feel?
- How much individual attention do you receive from your manager?

This last question is increasingly important the more senior you are in your organisation. I have noticed that many senior managers and directors receive little individual attention from above. If this is the case, then external coaching and support might be an appropriate option.

Raise awareness and involve others

Consider your answers to the following questions and then decide your intended actions.
- How aware are other managers likely to be of "the secret" of managing change effectively.
- How skilful are other managers in helping individuals move through the transition process?
- What can you do to raise their awareness and ensure their skills are developed?
- Who else do you need to involve?

Key questions to ask at management meetings where change is being discussed or planned include:

- How will we involve staff?
- How will we help staff to adjust?
- How consistent is our management communication about the change?
- What will we do to help staff move through transition?

Putting the three I's into regular and frequent practice makes good management sense, whether or not change is happening. I believe that the knowledge and skills covered in this chapter are common sense. I also know that during change common sense and common practice are often two separate issues.

Put the secret into practice

There is little more for me to say other than go and do it. During the next few weeks, months and years you are likely to hear and talk about *change* many times. Hopefully that word will be a reminder of the *transition* that has to happen in order for change to be effective. Once reminded, commit yourself to take action to ensure it does happen.

Go MAD (make a difference) about change in your organisation and reap the rewards of time and cost savings.

Summary

The Necessary Knowledge
- The difference between change (external) and transition (internal adjustment process).
- The secret – for change to be effective, transition has to happen.
- The 4 underlying causes of a negative reaction to change.

- Sense of unfairness in the treatment of individuals.
    - Personal uncertainty and insecurity about the future.
    - Perceived powerlessness.
    - Resistance to the need to adapt to change.
- The 3 stages of adapting to change
  (Endings Transition Beginnings)
- The 5 organisational factors which have greatest impact on staff morale.
    - Clarity of future direction.
    - Senior management commitment to the change.
    - Individual perception of the planning and implementation of change.
    - Line management style and skills.
    - Communication.

The Essential Skills and Tasks
- Address the underlying causes with the key management tasks (The Three I's)
    - Information and explanation
    - Involvement
    - Individual attention
- Help others accept the need for change by answering the 5 key questions.
    - What specific events brought about the change in our organisation?
    - Why was there a need to change?
    - Who was involved in the decision making process?
    - What other options were considered and why were they rejected?
    - What are the changes intended to achieve?
- Review the effectiveness of your written communication.
- Help staff to identify endings.

Intended Actions
- Calculate the potential cost savings your organisation can make by successfully applying the secret of managing change.
- Understand the effects of change on yourself. Identify your own endings. Be a role model.
- Put the three I's into frequent practice with your staff.
- Raise awareness of the people issues and transition at management meetings and with senior management.
- Remember that common sense is not common practice. It is easier to know than to do.
- Commit yourself to making a difference.

Authors

Elizabeth Morris
Buckholdt Associates
Buckholdt House
The Street
Frampton on Severn
Gloucestershire
GL2 7ED
01452 741106

Stanley J Smith
Century 2000 Services Ltd
90 High Street
Evesham
Worcestershire
WR11 4EU
01386 765533

Michael Lewis
Management International
63–69 Eltham Road
London
SE12 8UF
0181 318 4327

Jan Phillips
Phillips Consulting
St Andrews House
141 West Nile Street
Glasgow
G1 2RN
0141 353 0977

Ken Marshall
Marshall Vere Associates
Sherwood House
38 Mulberry Drive
Bicester
Oxford
OX6 9FY
01869 325962

Richard Owers
The Sales Training Consultancy Ltd
07050 115239

Michael B Harrison
Leongate Limited
PO Box 24
Tewkesbury
Gloucestershire
GL20 7EL
01684 772464

David Mackey
Winning Formula
3 Greenacres
Primacy Road
Bangor
Northern Ireland
BT19 7AP
01247 271793

Gillian Horton
Chartist Cottage
Nottingham Road South
Heronsgate
Rickmansworth
WD3 5DP
01923 286120

Sheila Holt
You and I
20 Windy Arbour
Kenilworth
Warwickshire
CV8 2AS
01926 513165

Michael Ogilvie
Ashdown Hurrey Consulting
Ashdown House
2 Eversfield Road
Eastbourne
East Sussex
BN21 2AS
01323 411222

Andy Gilbert
Career Strategies Limited
The Old Stables
25A Anstey Lane
Thurcaston
Leicester
LE7 7JB
0116 235 9014